It was a romantic life, maybe to be looked back upon as the glory days of youth. If it was poverty, it was poverty only on paper. Poverty is a mathematical equation, an expression of how much one can buy. What about how much we can *steal*? Doesn't *that* count for anything?!

And poverty in pocket means richness of experience. We had spent uneventful periods of our lives paying rent and long practiced the dull habit of paying for things. But those years of school, work, and middle-class lethargy are a blur. Being "born again" for us wasn't finding "God," but shedding convenience. Then life began, and since then we remember each dumpster, abandoned house, and foot-chase by retail security. At night, after running around, plotting and scheming, our checklist items all crossed out, we paused to think—"What to do *tomorrow*?" and the answer was always "As we please . . ."

Unemployment . . . when one's role in life shifts from passive observer to active participant. When "every day is April Fools' and every night Halloween." When we stopped shopping inside stores and began shopping in back. When we stopped going to the mall to buy things and started going to collect derelict baby strollers for the 75¢ refund. When we looked at the big, crazy urban chaos and suburban sprawl, and it all began to look suspiciously close to a big playground.

Late night mob action advances on the thrift store donation bin, long bike rides through the industrial ghetto, shopping cart races, and competitions to see just how many times we could make the "Police Blotter" column of the local paper. We left behind the other kids, their path—working, drinking, and being grown-up—and rejected all that made them grumpy, uncreative, and lifeless. We dumpstered, squatted, and shoplifted our lives back. Everything fell into place when we decided our lives were to be lived. Life serves the risk taker . . .

Some of us read all day, others chanted and held signs, some were full-time defendants. Every day, and every plan and plot were a reaffirmation that our lives were our own. Notebooks of conspiracies, crimes, schemes, and maps to abandoned buildings . . . When everything was possible, but there wasn't enough time for everything. And even though we never completed *The Complete Manual for Urban Survival*, made the *front* page, aired the dumpster diving public access show, stole every "No Skateboarding" sign, or patched things up with the bread delivery guy from whose truck we stole fresh bagels every morning, well then we were content knowing it was possible.

They said not working would never work. I mean, you have to *eat* right? We ate . . . we ate what they threw away, whatever we could fit in a basket and walk out with. Ironic that as perceived "struggling" and "starving" kids, we maybe gave away more than we ate. What does a vegan do with fifty packages of Chips Ahoy anyway? And why did Walgreens throw them all away? We began to think maybe they were on *our* side. Until the manager flew out the back door, shaking his fist, demanding to know why we were in the dumpster. We explained our positions as "free-lance excess reduction engineers engaging in the reallocation of surplus." He told us to get a job. We reflected on past dives in that very dumpster—the functioning CD player, nutritional supplements, photo department discards with scandalous pictures of former high school classmates . . . A job? "Well if you didn't make unemployment so easy . . ."

Our philosophies evolved—from general dislike of work, to the feeling of exploitation, then seeing the American way of life for what it is and turning our backs to it.

Our skillz evolved—from starving, to subsisting on table scraps at the food court, to humbly scraping by on discarded American excess, to an extensive dumpster diving/shoplifting course. And when we felt like the craftiest kids in suburbia, a new all-you-can-eat salad bar would open and we would laugh at suburbia's endlessly accommodating nature. "What's next? Dumpstering money at the bank?" Somehow, at that time, in that place, it seemed possible. But the easily liquidated video games from Blockbuster were just as good, and we found plenty of those . . .

"You're not free . . ." they would say on their way to work, "you're homeless and you're poor." Money means freedom? It was an interesting theory. One we pondered on long plane rides overseas and cross-country boxcar trips. Homeless? If rent legitimizes a residence, we were homeless—because in our house, we didn't pay any . . .

They said, "You can't live this way forever." Some of us agreed, and secretly planned to leave youth behind one day. Others thought—"We're good *now*, in ten years we'll be pros, in twenty we'll conquer the world!" Some hoped not. They wished people wouldn't throw so much away—food, books, whole *buildings*. That one day the means of production would be returned to the people so we wouldn't need *their* food, or *their* old houses. They made the mess, may as well dance in it. Some of us shrugged and said, "Why not?" Others found the implication odd that they could live *their* way forever—working and drinking and watching TV—and why they would want to.

Could it last forever? We wondered, and while we played and plotted against the *Man*, none of us wanted to acknowledge the impending obsolescence of our lifestyle, signs they wouldn't let us get away with our fun forever. The loose door on our favorite apartment building hot tub—fixed. Video and police night surveillance of the thrift store. Dumpsters being replaced by trash compactors. Our favorite supermarket removing their microwave, and along with it our simple pleasures that fueled the fight—oatmeal, tea, and the only method we knew of to freshen a stale bagel. Then the same supermarket stopped leaving out the keys to the motorized handicapped shopping carts and we had to begin *walking* home . . .

Some of us went off to school, or went gangsta. Others crossed the line into a bourgeois void. Some of us are still here, taking the holy war national and even global. Back in the old hood one can still find scars in the landscape from a time when some of us lived dangerously. Signs of ancient battles when we armed ourselves with ambition, passion, stale bagels, and fought back—the salt water residue around the dollar slots of every Coke machine in town, blotted out graffiti, and the crowbar marks in the door of the poor old lady whose decayed home turned out *not* to be abandoned . . .

Something happened when we quit our jobs, quit paying rent, quit paying for *anything*. And I think back to the early days—when, like clouds parting to reveal the sun, we discovered what we were told had been lies, that it *could* be done, and that it would mean the time of our lives.

Those first moments . . . A new house, a new life . . . Artists, vandals, philosophers . . . Up on our favorite rooftop, with a view of the city, passing dumpstered granola and thinking—

"Maybe we're on to something . . ."

additional copies of this book
can be obtained for $5 + postage from:

CrimethInc. Far East
PO Box 13998
Salem OR 97309
USA

or get current information at:
www.crimethinc.com

by
anonymous

I'm going nameless for this one. There's a bumper sticker that reads: "I'm not vegan beause I love animals, I'm vegan because I hate plants." I don't think it's funny either, but here's what I'm saying: I'm not going nameless because I love roller skaing in L.A., I'm going nameless because I hate you asking like it matters. Names are things for the scorecards of police and historians. Better to stay off the radar of both. For those unsatisfied, write the address in the back, wait for my reply, then run the prints. Actually, I've never been arrested. I'm out of ideas. One more thing: Please stop asking if I had other people write some of the stories. The Obviously False Rumor Corp. issued a recall on that one a long time ago. Duh!

\- The Author

five

THE WRONG TRAIN
FREE BOATS, RETIREMENT LEISURE, STARVATION, ETC.

It was a cruel trick—putting a naïve and aspiring hobo on the wrong train, telling him he was going to Minneapolis and sending him to Missoula. The wrong train, unplanned adventure . . . perfect. I always secretly looked forward to nothing going as planned. That way, I wasn't limited by my imagination. That way anything can, and always did, happen. Being stranded in Missoula would make my summer dangerous again. If everything "worked out," if I pulled off my plans without deviation, I would be on that train towards Minneapolis to visit friends and follow my favorite band around the Midwest. Maybe not a bad plan, maybe a *great* plan. Best to travel with a plan and hope for chaos. Either way I win.

The wrong train on the wrong day.
The storm broke like a smack upside the head, and I scurried to seek refuge—climbing between boxcars, dashing over tracks, racing through this ghetto . . . The long run to the University of Montana library was worth it . . . for about five minutes until it closed. I tried blending into the wallpaper, but they threw me out into the heaviest rainstorm I had ever seen. As an amateur hobo, I think it was what they call "paying your dues." But it's always to be trusted that one who leaves home alone with little money and a sketchy plan will be looked after. Any person who takes this leap of faith can be guaranteed the time of their life . . .
So when I found the back door to a computer lab in the student center *unlocked*, I wasn't really surprised, I just wondered how I would fit a hard drive in my backpack and if the pawn shop would ask for ID. Still wet, but warm and happy, hidden away in the computer lab— I could just listen to my walkman and play on the computers all night! So I "surfed the net" taking notes and making new plans. The band my friend was on tour with was playing Chicago, a Cold Crush Brothers reunion in NYC . . . When the janitor walked in at 1 a.m., I ig-

nored him, but he interrupted my research. "Excuse me, do you, uh, *work here*, or . . . ?" Despite a lifetime of "getting caught" experience behind me, my best acting, the power of suggestion, social engineering . . . nothing could preserve my position. "How did you *get in*?!"

I really liked Missoula, the downtown core and college neighborhood was free from chain store homogenization with a little record store, coffee shop, and vegetarian restaurant. There was definitely a history to that town, and I wanted to read about it, but I couldn't find the library. So I wrote a letter in the coffee shop, explored the riverfront, and thought maybe if I had a personal crisis and needed to escape, maybe I would move to Missoula. But I had a train to catch . . .

Grasping for human connection in a state where every car was a truck, and every truck had a gun rack, I found something close on aisle 8 of Safeway. Two friendly kids, with unreserved admiration for a third who looks at freight trains and jumps on them. They followed me to the train yard to see me off. We talked about life in Missoula, and they spoke of a street character who would grant anyone who could answer his riddle *one wish!* That sounded like a pretty good deal. We sat on the loading dock of a warehouse alongside the train yard. After hyping them up about freight-hopping, and kicking my stories, there was pressure for *action*. They clearly wanted a show, a dramatic drive into a quickly moving boxcar as they cheered me on. But hopping trains—I had learned—was a lot of waiting, hiding in bushes, kicking rocks . . . So the kids were quickly bored, and we parted. But if I was ever really down and out, I thought, I was going to find that riddle guy . . .

Waiting for trains is almost as much fun as riding them. Like watching another crazy rainstorm from the loading dock of that warehouse, or four barefoot kids putting on a ghetto fireworks show, and just eating bagels for hours. But I had eaten a lot of bagels, and I was beginning to wonder if the train yard was abandoned, or a diversionary front, or the hallucinatory mirage of a city kid in Montana. I cornered a brakeman who told of a massive derailment in Idaho, and that Northern line train traffic was shutdown until at least 1 a.m. Golly, a big train disaster . . . maybe, I thought, it was the train to Minneapolis I should have been on, maybe that lying hobo saved my life. It was moments like this that made an atheist believe in god. I still didn't believe in god, but evidence was mounting to suggest the presence of a *Hobo God*—an eternally filthy and drunk celestial guardian who saved punks from train crashes, left doors unlocked at critical moments, and made rational people throw everything imaginable into dumpsters.

By 6 a.m. I had listened to every tape I had, eaten many bagels, and felt threatened a few times by crazy old hoboes prowling and pacing the yard, but, no trains. Exhausted, dehydrated . . . Then another storm broke! The wind angled the rain in my direction. Life was plainly trying to provoke a fight, but I was having too much fun to notice, and as the rain poured, I was still totally convinced this was the most exciting life had ever been.

The sun had risen, and I left the dock for the trendy coffeehouse. The paper that morning confirmed the yard worker's story—big derailment, traffic halted until an undetermined time, no casualties . . . But no train pulls out of a yard in the Northwest without a hobo hiding in the shadows of an empty boxcar. I gave a moment of silence . . .

On the I-90 on-ramp, I recalled past rides . . . The masturbating truck driver, the girl in L.A. I still haven't gotten over, and the shady gangsta from Long Beach—"Do you know *Snoop Dogg*?" I asked. "Mmm . . . I seen 'im around." I don't know, I thought that was awesome. As hitchhikers, we play the role of actor, ego stroker, counselor, etc. There are the small town secrets, scandalous confessions, tears even. The rides where I am outside myself thinking life couldn't get any crazier, or more real, or more *dangerous*. My ride out of Missoula wasn't dangerous, but he told a good story. He was a middle-aged, working-class man who had recently divorced his wife, freaked out, and hitchhiked around the country for three months, ending in a climactic ride with a woman who just *gave him her car!* Though, that didn't seem too incredible. When traveling, crazy things like that happen in desperate moments. It was often awkward the way many lonely drivers latched onto me. I had been given money, lodging, a knife, two bibles, and lots of good advice before. Certainly if I hitchhiked long enough, I too would be given a car, or written into a will, or something.

In Bozeman that night, the townsfolk were in the streets celebrating, all happy about something. Ooops, it was the Fourth of July, I had totally forgotten. Lucky me, dropped off in the home of Montana's largest fireworks show. I was feeling festive. I wasn't a patriot, but I had feelings bearing a guilty likeness to "loving my country." I loved the free coffee and liberal return policies, the intrigue, danger, the crazy small towns, not really ever having to work . . .

In the West, there is always a Safeway nearby, and in the West, no one need go hungry or pay. I stole very animal-free, very un-American food for the celebration. The streets surrounding the fairgrounds were a sea of flag-waving, hooting, and tailgate barbecues. For a good view of the show I crawled onto the giant arched roof of a church across the street from the fairgrounds. This was patriot country—a rodeo, high school marching band, and fireworks. "Patriotism . . ." I looked at the fireworks, tasted the unpaid-for food, and savored the open-ended craziness of it all. Yes, "patriotism," I can almost see it now . . .

Looking for a train yard the next morning, I found a single lane of tracks and a wall of uninspired hobo graffiti under the overpass. The hoboes definitely needed an ambitious artist to inject life into the stale graffiti scene. I made an effort, and hoped the next hobo that passed under that bridge would take as much from the Unbroken lyrics I scrawled as I have.

Now where are those trains . . .

Trains, hitchhiking, Montana, Miami . . . either way, I was free! I rode to Livingston with an employee of Montana Rail Link, a railroad company. He drove me to the Livingston train yard, and then *into* the Livingston train yard! The guard waved us in, the yard workers saluted . . . My new friend was a man of great influence. He pointed out the train I wanted and promised to put out the word around the yard that I was "OK." So, I had free, unobstructed run of the train yard. For a hobo, it was a moment of rare privilege. And surely he thought he was doing me a favor. But take away the risk of hopping trains, the danger, and so goes the fun. Free run of a train yard, great. There would be no sneaking, running, or hiding from the bull. No cat-and-mouse thrill. The tense moments I relish, glued to the interior boxcar wall, the sound of crunching gravel closing in—it's the bull, and he's coming for *you*. My new friend thought he was doing me a favor. What a jerk.

He hated hoboes, but I wasn't "like them," he said. Not yet maybe, but whatever it takes to get there—I'll do it!

I felt better at the mini-mart across the street—where I could drink tea, write letters, and feel a little less welcome beneath the "No Loitering" sign. And I shared the loiterer's bond with the bored teenage youth of Livingston. Together, we traded cookies and traded hitchhiking stories. The nicest kid of the bunch had recently moved to Livingston, and wished he was back where he had come from: Astoria, Oregon. Livingston or Astoria . . . I wasn't sure myself. They love hitchhikers in Oregon, but my potential fan-demographic in Montana had yet to surface. Hitchhiking out of Astoria, the woman from Burger Barn saw me in the rain, all sad with my soggy sign, and brought me coffee. Before hitchhiking out of Livingston, I would be shamed for an oddly shaped parcel by the postal clerk, who would then lose my package. In Astoria, I slept under an abandoned trailer. In Livingston, I slept *in* an abandoned trailer. Livingston had cheaper used cars, Astoria more abandoned houses. I knew no one within 500 miles of Astoria, but after three hours in Livingston I had connections with the local railroad workers and knew half of Livingston's "Class of 2001." Livingston or Astoria . . . My choice was clear: both. And everything in between . . .

"Where are you from?" the sketchy driver asked.

"Um . . ." It's sort of a little game that is played while hitchhiking: telling a different, completely fabricated story to each driver—all to flex acting skills, practice creative storytelling, and avoid being tracked down by an obsessed driver. And this driver was clearly bonkers.

"Um . . . Idaho!" I said.

His look was possessed, his stare fixed. "Idaho . . . yeah . . ." he mumbled raspingly, the words passing through barely parted lips. "Idaho . . . our storm is brewing in Idaho. . ."

The *storm*? Hmm . . . The labor movement? Nazis? The vegan revolution?!?!

"What is your destination?" His voice was hoarse, nearly inaudible.

"Florida," I said.

"Florida . . . yeah . . ." Gulp. There was fire in his eyes. "Our tide is rising in Florida . . ."

On the side of I-90, dazed, I tried to make sense of it all. So . . . the aliens had landed, and in fact were among us. No doubt, I agreed with that. But the balance . . . After a massive meeting of militia representatives the previous month, it was decided that it was time to turn up the heat. "They're talking next fall," he warned, and only those with stored food and rural property would survive the revolution. But I felt those precautions for the downfall of society were overrated. In the impending Darwinian scene he painted, dumpster diving, I was sure, would be the most functional survival skill. Trains provided a means of travel untraceable by Big Brother, and a fully-stocked arsenal of unlicensed weapons would never yield the results of an angry have-not with a crowbar at midnight. By economic collapse or armed militia revolution, I couldn't wait for society to crumble. The social elite of today just might be on their knees begging me and my friends for shoplifting tips after the next Great Depression. But there sure will be a lot of poseurs riding the rails . . .

A young gazanksta girl gave me a ride to Laurel, and left me with a warning—"Stay out of Billings," she said. Her friends were waging a gang war, and she didn't want me caught in the crossfire. The way I was dressed, she said, I was dead, guaranteed. I looked "Southside," and if seen, the Northside rivals might pull a "drive-by." Looking myself down, being mistaken for a Southside Billings gangster seemed unlikely, I was confused. So, the Montana gangstas listen to *Chain of Strength*?!

My next ride slid a little too close to me as I went to get out and said, "Promise me you'll stay in Billings tonight." He was an insurance salesman—and an overprotective insurance salesman. "If you get stuck in the reservation tonight . . ." he said, handing me his card, "give me a call." Going beyond Billings, he told me, would put me in the Bighorn County Indian Reservation, with the savages, which would mean certain death. "They start drinking and take out their anger on white people." (Social commentary: drinking alcohol, uncontrolled stupidity . . . suspiciously like the behavior of *most white people*! Ninety-five percent of the punk scene, eighty percent of "progressive activists," etc. etc.) All across the North and later in South Dakota I would hear this racism, of the raving mad red man drinking and getting riled up, burning tourists' cars and randomly attacking people with bottles. No one I talked to was sympathetic to the Native American condition—majority rates of alcoholism, general hopelessness—I heard only contempt. Well, I had a lengthy list of life goals to accomplish before I was ready for martyrdom, but I had to make the choice between death by bullet in Billings or beer bottle in Bighorn.

Late into the night I read in the 24-hour truck stop near the I-90/I-94 junction, and slept on the grass outside. The next morning—after a sloppy shoplifting attempt at IGA resulting in banishment for *life*—I walked back to the on-ramp, hungry but anxious. There was so much to look forward to—the Corn Palace, the world's largest truck stop, vast expanses of nothing, small town hospitality, high school parties in abandoned buildings, retribution for 500 years of genocide . . . who could say?

On the ramp, waiting for a ride, a couple approached on foot. They seemed nice, but distant, hard to pin down. The woman was pregnant and carried only a small backpack. Their situation looked maybe a little desperate, and I offered them my spot on the ramp. No, no, they said. They were *walking*. They had walked, I learned, along interstates the entire distance from Southern California. Occasionally cars would stop and offer rides, but mostly they had walked, humbly, for thousands of miles. Everything they spoke of was related in vague terms—I suspected a religious pilgrimage. Maybe it was their faraway gaze, maybe it was their tattered homemade sandals. They made no direct reference to god, only indistinct allusions—"We're looked after" and "We are never of want, everything is provided." Ooops! God forgot to provide you with *shoes*! Ha ha ha. We wished each other well, and they left, walking, up the ramp onto the mighty I-90. I had met such people before, guided by the "voice of God." Certainly a voice telling people to do *something* adventurous and subversive like traveling and living simply was positive, even if it was the voice of god. I respected that voice more than the one that whispered in the ears of my friends—the "middle-class work ethic voice," or the "voice of spontaneity after obliteration by blender and small explosive devices."

One ride later, that afternoon, after four hours on one spot I was certain I *would* die on the Indian reservation—of heat, boredom, isolation . . . It was the loneliest ramp in the West, and when cars did pass, they only slowed, pointed, and laughed. So I found a ride back west, to Hardin, where there was sure to be more traffic. Hardin was great, having a hotel with waterslides, and at the IGA I dumpstered a whole bag of cherry pies! Meanwhile, shoppers were inside the store *paying* for food. What were they thinking?! I sat on the on-ramp and ate an entire cherry pie, while shocked passersby recoiled in disgust. There was still a whole bag of pies left, and I left them organized in a neat stack for the next hitchhiker . . .

My next ride, a jovial and obnoxious Latino man, spoke proudly of his truck while pounding his fist on the dashboard, and shouted his distrust of women—both popular themes of conversation with drivers in rural America. His rough 'n' tough old truck sputtered and hissed as we entered Sheridan, Wyoming, and finally broke down on the edge of town. He groaned and rested his head on the steering wheel. I had my eye on the Safeway across the street. You can't trust women *or* trucks I guess . . .

"Never hitchhike at night," they say. But I wasn't going to stay there, not in Sheridan. If the Indians in Montana didn't kill you, the Wyoming cowboys would. That was another thing they said. And Sheridan, I was told, was cowboy capital USA. And the crystal-meth capital—that's Casper, 150 miles south. Sheridan was the Old West town archetype; and I saw the saloons, cowboy hats, wooden shutters and thumbs in belt loops. Maybe it was genuine culture frozen in time and isolated in space, but today it seemed a bad parody of itself. I walked down Main Street, though in Sheridan it felt more like *sauntering* down Main Street. Maybe it was the sun, or the sugar; but I was drawn into the Old West atmosphere and I created for myself a delusional role of a shadowy stranger, a roughish nomad in a town not big enough for the "both of us" . . . Women peered from behind curtains, men sat on windowsills stroking shotguns as I passed. A mysterious high plains drifter, an outsider certain to commit an inexcusable offense and be run out of town by an angry mob, driven from one town to the next, one step ahead of my past. An outlaw, thieving loot, and with a final tip of my hat to the ladies, fading into the wind . . .

Yes, there was a very thick air of patriotism. Sheridan prided itself on being the last vestige of the American West, and of course throwing edible food in a dumpster was as inseparable an American cultural practice as roping cattle. As a dumpster diver, pulling fruit from Safeway's trash, I was a proud practitioner of "rugged individualism."

"I'm a cowboy, in a steel horse I dive."

Everything was working out great. Crosswalks were always green, my maps always folded up properly on the first attempt, and they say crime doesn't pay—and sure, my karma was a mess—but I had more money than I'd left home with. "There will be quiet before the storm"—something disastrous had to happen, right? Well maybe, but not that night. My ride out of Wyoming was a ride with the rockinist girl in the high plains. The two hundred miles to Spearfish, South Dakota were through some of the most desolate and quiet regions in the country. We talked about our youths, our ambitions, she versed me on Native American culture and I broke down for her a few theories I had been working on. She picked them apart, showed me the holes, and cut them down. Golly, she was smart. And I felt comfortable with her, so I wasn't embarrassed when she told me I had cherry pie on my face. It was a three-hour ride, and when we pulled into Spearfish I told her she could just drop me off in one of those cornfields, or maybe there was a ladder to the roof of Wal-Mart, or . . . or her couch? That would be fine too, I said. Not as thrilling or tough as an abandoned barn, but . . .

We read each other passages from books we were reading, she played me the Grateful Dead and I played her Turning Point. I schooled her in vegan cooking and we ate and laughed and it was all very crazy—eating cookies with a girl in South Dakota.

When I woke the next morning I folded my blanket, left her a big letter on my pillow, and went to go steal food somewhere . . .

At some point on the spectrum of comically easy shoplifting targets—between the chain book stores at the mall, and every other store in my hometown—are the Wal-Marts of South Dakota. Oh my god. The absence of any anti-theft precautions was almost insulting. No alarms or phony security guards, and sometimes at 3 a.m.—no employees! Well you have to run around to find them anyway . . . So in the rural Midwest, in the small towns and backroads, I feared there may not be consistent opportunity for receipt scams. And though I really only spent two or three dollars a day, jobs in my field wouldn't always be as easy as they were in South Dakota. So I decided to employ a scorched-earth policy on South Dakota and forget about working for a while. Wal-Mart was a store a socially conscious criminal could feel good about stealing from—even if it was only vitamins. My plan was three-fold: liberate and sell easily liquidated CDs; exploit Wal-Mart's soft cash refund policy (no receipt/less than 20 dollars=OK) by returning smaller, expensive items (vitamins, etc.); and do the receipt scam. Looking at me, it should have been obvious to everyone I wasn't a *paying* customer. I couldn't have been more conspicuous unless I wore a shirt stating "Born To Shoplift," but I had left that shirt at home. After waiting a few minutes I returned the vitamins and got my $19 cash. I was set for a week, at least. The huge, creepy, South Dakota Wal-Marts—where "suggested retail price," really, is only a suggestion.

A Rapid City firefighter drove me to Sturgis. A town of 30,000 which swells to 200,000 each year for the

"Sturgis Biker Rally," the largest gathering of bikers in the world! He worked security for the event and listed the celebrities who turn up each year: Jay Leno, Dennis Rodman . . . and one year, he told me, at the height of their fame, Poison showed up on their Harleys and played a surprise set! Hitchhikers hear the best stories!

I couldn't remember where my obsession with small towns began, but for months I had done research on and dreamed of a hundred random Midwest small towns and the adventures I would have—eating cookies in cornfields and chatting with locals at the Ole Greasy Spoon. New York, D.C., Atlanta—I'd heard enough of *those* travel stories. And if I had a friend in New York, I suppose I would like to visit there too. But there was a theme I wanted to explore—that of a big city stranger in a small farming community, and an adventure-seeking youth's drive to explore uncharted punk territory . . . Without ever having visited most of the larger cities, I already felt familiar with them through the endless hype. But no one, search as I may, could tell me about the dumpster scene in Lemmon, South Dakota; or the Mexican restaurant in Galena, Illinois that leaves corn chips by the back door. So there, in Sturgis, it almost felt risky and spontaneous when I thought I just might part with I-90 and take the smaller two-lane highways to Minneapolis, through the more forgotten and lawless regions of the great plains. And I felt that exploring the isolated small towns would be an opportunity to finally take notes and addresses of the empty and abandoned structures in America's dying farming communities, to line up a few potential rural squats to hide out in when it all goes down. I'd been putting that off for a long time . . .

It was my gateway to rural country—the mouth of State Highway 79—and I was a little nervous. Huge supermarkets were as life-giving to me as the blood through my veins, and without such conveniences off I-90, well, this may be the part in the story where the boy becomes a man. No all-night truck stops to read in, hotels to swim in, or record stores, or any of my favorite fun places. On the shoulder of Highway 79, with my thumb, my thoughts always returned to the supermarket issue, and that I draw the line on adventure at paying for food. No way. But I left the highway culture behind for vast cornfields, grain elevators, and huge, creepy, gray buildings set far in the distance—where if you listened closely, one heard the dying shrieks of slaughtered pigs . . .

My first ride was a sympathy offering, because no one would pick up a hitchhiker outside the largest halfway house/drug rehab center in the state, right? It was a path I had chosen randomly—north on State Highway 79 and east on Highway 12, both lightly travelled two-lane highways into a great void, total emptiness from every perspective. It was empty space on the road atlas, whiteness on the train maps, absent from the Beastie Boys tour-date list, and on the Thrasher Magazine Skate Park Guide—nothing.

I paced Main Street in Newall and wished everyone would just quit staring at me. Newall was a sad model of decaying small town America. I had read of the emigration trend towards urban centers, the slowing flux of young people into positions in community and industry needed to sustain an economy as they fled to the cities. After exploring Newall, I had guilty feelings that my small town interest was somewhat exploitative, like South Dakota was a dead world and I was probing the corpse, laughing. To a city kid South Dakota was a novelty—the wood and nails Newall jail, the one room library, and the big old house for rent: $200 a month. It was a sad scene of isolation and desperation. Nonetheless, someday I would likely end up living in South Dakota. When reading my favorite magazine—*Rural Property Bulletin (Your Guide to Cheap Rural Land)*, I saw the ads—"South Dakota - $99 an acre!" they read. Certainly one day, all old, angry, and clench-fisted, when most of America was a paved over strip mall, and no band ever *did* take me on tour with them, I would return a few boxes of cereal and laundry detergent at Safeway and buy a $99 acre. I would grumble and growl, read too much, and give out razor blades on Halloween. In my disconnected and hopeless state I would adopt lifestyle choices contrary to my nature such as going to the town bar or joining a militia, and to compensate for my guilt at having sold out completely, I would swerve to hit hitchhikers and throw rocks at trains. It was all too depressing. But $99 sure is a great deal anyway . . .

In Mud Butte, I was a thousand miles from home, or another vegan, or any place I would ever be ever again. No people, just a post office, an occasional passing car, and me—rolling around on the shoulder. All I recall about the ride away from that place were my parting words—"Thanks, you saved my life!"

In Faith I watched a softball game, slept in a field, and in the morning got a ride through vast expanses of wheat fields and grain elevators to Lemmon. I toured the world's largest petrified forest and noted Lemmon as a choice town for criminals—where one could commit brazen crimes, cross the street, and taunt the police from North Dakota!

"Tell you what," the old man said as we entered Mobridge, "let me buy you a burger."

"Oh, well thanks . . ." I said, ". . . but I'm a vegetarian."

His countenance shifted to indignation. "Vegetarian huh?" he mumbled, "You just keep that to yourself . . ."

My surroundings in Mobridge—and the prior two days—were alien, confusing, and completely messed up. I wasn't sure if it was still America, and I had to check the grocer's dumpster just to be sure. There was always the consistent and confounding thread running through each town and region in America: edible trash. And Mobridge's trash was of exceptional quality. I dumpstered countless boxes of ghetto brand Cap'n Crunch and went to hang out by the train tracks and check out the forgotten-and-boarded-up warehouse district. Along the tracks I hopped the fence to an abandoned car junkyard. From the roof of a car I watched the sun set behind the abandoned buildings and felt the beginning of a light drizzle. The mist turned to rain, and I wondered where a vagabond might sleep in Mobridge. I looked at the boarded-up house, under the warehouse loading dock . . . and while the rain fell even harder, I tried desperately to rip the sun roof off that car. I was getting nowhere and I thought maybe I would go find a big rock somewhere and bust in desperate-drug-fiend style. But, oops! I was soaking wet before I checked the car door. Reclined in the seat and laying motionless in my sleeping bag listening to the rain beat on the roof; I thought of staying in Mobridge, living in the car, hanging out by the tracks and eating ghetto Cap'n Crunch for a few days. It almost sounded like a worthy plan. I had at least enough cereal for a week stashed behind the grocer's dumpster . . . Well, maybe *next* visit. I had a country to explore . . .

"Hello, do you have any throwaways?" I was outside of Mobridge at a mini-mart on Highway 12 around 8 a.m. and the bread truck man was making deliveries. It was an old trick, legal but effective. The driver scowled, "Sorry you're going to have to *pay* like everyone else!" Ha! Oh yeah?

After another ride I was in Aberdeen—South Dakota's third largest town. Maybe Aberdeen did have a "glory days," or even the rich history I had read about, but had at this point sold out to the paved and neon ghettoization of America by the chain stores . . . which served my immediate interests: stealing CDs, scamming money from Wal-Mart, and eating. Aberdeen was a town where I was sure I had been before—endless streets of obnoxious lights, broken concrete, and choking exhaust. Aberdeen became the ghetto standard, and from that time—whenever lost, lonely, failing or desperate, I would think—"At least it's not Aberdeen. . . "

People often ask—after "Where do you get your money?" and "Why don't you *get a job?!*"—"How do you stay clean?" I open my wallet and show off my extensive collection of *hotel key cards!* Swimming in hotel pools is a great leisure activity, and a fun way to stay clean. The Aberdeen Best Western didn't have the expected hotel amenities like banquet leftovers in the ballroom, or the free and convenient "continental breakfast buffet" in the lobby, so I was feeling a little cheated. But every hotel has a pool, and a spa, and careless maids who leave cards exposed on top of their unguarded carts. The card I took wasn't working on the pool door, so I showed my card to the maid and shrugged. She let me in, and it felt great to kick-it in the spa and stare at the ceiling. Then a group of girls—in town for a horse show or something—turned on the jets and climbed in. It was like a *gangsta rap* video!

Life's most beautiful and inspiring moments occur at 3 a.m., just prowling, looking for nothing but always finding something. Like when the guys at the construction site back home left the keys in the steamroller, or when the paint store left their back door unlocked. I was definitely inspired to stay up all night, but the maddening swarms of mosquitos had me confined to the 24-hour Food 4 Less. I tried sleeping, walking, *rapping*, everything; but the mosquitos were inescapable. So using a well thought out "broken car" story I was able to stay up in the Food 4 Less café—all night!

In the morning the mosquitos had retreated and the sun was rising. I'd had all night to think about life, stare out the window, and get all introspective. Morning customers drifted in with bagels and coffee, crowding my space and mackin' my style. I thought for a moment, and decided that when people want to be alone and think about their place in the world, just be emotional and enjoy solitary moments of regret and reflection, they walk along train tracks. After ten hours, I was on a casual first name basis with the entire cashier and janitorial staff of the supermarket, and they gathered to see me off— "Good luck with your car!"

The tracks took me to a small train yard a few miles west near downtown. My plan was to crawl into a random car, fall asleep; and if I awoke in Fargo, or where I'd come from, or off the edge of the Earth, well at least it would be away from Aberdeen.

Usually younger kids only visit train yards to throw rocks at me and my friends the hoboes, so when I awoke alongside the tracks with a kid on a bike hovering over me—I was scared. But he asked me a few questions, and turned out to be *down* with the hoboes! Where was I from? How did I come to be in Aberdeen? And why was I sleeping in a train yard? I explained my situation, told him Aberdeen was the most ghetto town ever, that I was going to *kill* the cashiers at Wal-Mart for not taking back the headphones I had stolen, and be on the next train out—guaranteed! When he heard I planned to hop a freight, my status ascended to Godhead. My friend was a train *fanatic* who lived in a house along the tracks, spent all day riding his bike around the train yard studying trains, and waited for the one day a hobo passed through his lonely town. He knew all the important information—what trains were going where, and an excellent abandoned caboose with an elevated view of the yard. So we hung out in the caboose all day while Lil 'Bo versed me on the location of every Midwest railroad transfer point, and the history of South Dakota railroads. One day, he said, he too would hop a train out of Aberdeen and on to better things. Lil 'Bo was a shining star in the vast wasteland of uninspired 90's youth. So I get excited thinking of Lil 'Bo out hopping trains, carrying the tramp torch . . . Certainly he was a radiant example of what Youth of Today referred to as "positive youth." So if you ever see a short silhouette in a distant boxcar as it rolls across the prairie—it's Lil 'Bo, and he's trying to make it home for dinner!

There were no trains going out that night, the yard workers snarled at us, and Lil 'Bo had a curfew to obey; so I made other plans. I walked the two or three miles back along the tracks to the mall and pushed my way through a crowd exiting the movie theater and into a back door.

There. No mosquitos or cars or ghetto, and I could almost write a letter by the light of the screen. My very innocent eyes were averting a love scene, and my glance fell upon the curtain below the screen. The film ended, the theater emptied, and I crawled beneath the screen and went to sleep.

The I-12/I-29 junction was a crossroads with several options, and I sat outside a truck stop with my walkman to think it over. Continuing east on 12 would be the most efficient path to where I thought maybe I was going at some point. South was Sioux Falls, where in the evenings the crazy mean slaughterhouse workers get drunk and drag people like me to the banks of the Missouri for a high plains beating. Or maybe I would visit that little town named after the best book I'd read recently—Ivanhoe, Iowa. I folded up my Midwest map and took out the full U.S. one. Then I gave up on thinking about it and listened to my walkman.

Ooops! I was, like, a thousand miles from home! It seemed habits such as traveling thousands of miles to see one person, or see a single show, had diminished my appreciation for distance. So, when outside that truck stop, a young couple made an unsolicited offer for a ride to North Dakota, a detour of hundreds of miles, it didn't seem odd that I might *go* to North Dakota. Wherever that was . . .

During the ride I read the paper in the back seat and sifted through my memory to make one connection to North Dakota, any point of reference—a band, or a famous criminal, or piece of history . . . I had struggled with South Dakota, but come up with a Tom Petty song and Laura Ingalls Wilder. Montana had hosted the Unabomber. But no person or Hardcore band of consequence ever rose from the cornfields of North Dakota, I was almost certain.

"We're going to the casino, do you gamble?" the woman asked. Gamble? Not for money. I gambled with my life, friendships, my legal status and my future. All that I valued . . . not money. I may need it someday when technology renders shoplifting obsolete.

Moments after arriving it was clear my new friends were two well-connected people of high standing in the casino scene, i.e. big casino scensters. The I.D. checker nodded, the guards waved, they received handshakes from everyone, and I couldn't be sure, but I think the doorman smiled, *made a gun with his fingers and shot at my friends!* High plains coolness!

Someone had left a casino-money card in a video poker machine with 2 dollars credit, and I supposed it would be permissible to meet my ethical judgement halfway and gamble with *other* people's money. But after reading over the rules, pacing around, looking over shoulders, sitting down and hitting random buttons, I had only confused myself and the computer. Gambling was silly.

Elsewhere around the casino, security carded people randomly, and occasionally escorted a sneaky teen to the door. I felt safe with my big-shot friends. Surely the guards were whispering to each other—"He's ok. He's with, you know, *them* . . ." But what if they *did* card me? Would I make the cut? What's the legal age for being a passionless, uninspired gambling zombie anyway?

It was late, too late to hitchhike. They understood this, and invited me to stay at their home in Whapeton. We stopped at a bar. Not my first—my second actually—but it still felt like a real big event. They even ordered me a beer! Yuck! It was 1 a.m. or 3 a.m., and I'd covered a lot of ground that day, so I fell asleep at the bar. When I awoke, someone had *drank my beer!* Sort of like the old joke every straight-edge kid hears—"Straight, huh? Well . . . (burp) more for me!"

That night was my first exposure to the life I was supposed to be living at my age. I don't know, I didn't get it. "You'll get a job, hate your life, and you'll want to drink too!" they always say. To my left, two men were having a touchingly honest discussion about a woman by the door, or parts of her. Behind me, several others labored at a commitment to total manliness by way of female conquest. Gambling, beer, *meat* . . . I'm never growing up! Ever!

The next morning they drew me a little map to the freeway and brought me a surprise meal from McDonalds.

"Vegetarian, huh? Well, more for us!" Ha ha ha . . .

Take it! Take it all! Big Macs, beer, and the 40-hour work week! Bye!

She picked me up at the mouth of highway 210 on the Minnesota border and launched into her story—"Blah, blah, poverty. Blah, blah, homelessness . . ." We had a lot in common. "Blah, blah, unemployment . . ." All very liberating circumstances, possibly the optimum conditions for a full, rich life. Then she told me of her dying daughter and exploded into tears. I was helpless to do anything but shake my head at the tragedy of it all. Entering Fergus Falls, Minnesota I spotted a Wal-Mart. "Uh, you can let me out here . . ."

It was a storybook life—hitchhiking the West, subsisting on misdemeanor theft. All credit and love is, of course, due to the Wal-Mart corporation for their long hours, generous refund policy, and conservative use of today's anti-theft technology! And romantic in more thematic ways—the enchanting tale of youth discovering America and the exploration of rural culture. The most revealing glimpses of which came not in the miniature towns, but the rides in-between. Old farmers barreling down the two-lane highway to bring in the hay before the rain hits—the rain they *know* is coming, because they can read the sky, or because Old Man Huxley is saying rain, and the old-timers are never wrong . . . Talking with the lifetime residents of remote prairie towns who had never left their county and did not get out often—"Did you pass through *Rapid City*? Isn't it crazy? Isn't it *wild?!*" A region of the country where asking someone what they did for a living was to ask what species they exploited—"I got me some hogs . . ." Where somehow it wasn't so surprising to lift the dumpster lid behind a small town grocery and find the entire front half of a cow, fur and frozen expression of death and everything. And each day, walking down Main Street, feeling the weight of suspicious stares . . . Old hobo books are often tinged with sentiments of migration, exploration, and vagabondage as a civic duty—"Every red-blooded American should hop a freight once in her life." You know, "Go West young man . . ."

The landscape started to become a little more rolly, the conversation a little more stimulating, and Minneapolis was just ahead. My best Minneapolis friend wouldn't be in town for another week, and phone numbers to other friends had been left at home. So I thought maybe I'd hang out on rooftops in the suburbs for a few days. I got a ride into the Minneapolis suburb of Brooklyn Park, and wasted no time reacquainting myself with the chaos and drama of the more paved regions of this country. Activity centered around a whirlwind receipt-scam campaign striking brutal blows of underclass justice against the corporate retail community. Stimulating enterprise included all forms of unproductive and irresponsible behavior disregarding the establishment of any groundwork on which to build a stable future for myself. A smiling transient, eating bagels—all day! The proudest moments: pacing the aisles of greater Minneapolis' colossal supermarkets—maybe the largest in the world—at 1 a.m., eating bagels and drinking tea in the Cub Foods café, plotting and scheming on the roof of Dunkin' Donuts, watching the Beastie Boys record release frenzy at the stroke of midnight, shaking my fist at a Catholic priest when ordered out from under the church awning and into a crazy Midwest rainstorm, pleasant conversation with a sweet girl at the donut shop, and haggling with the buyer at the used CD place over fair payment for the new Master P CD—"Look man, it's a *double CD set* . . ."

Maybe it was luck, or the consumers in Brooklyn Park throwing away a lot of high ticket receipts, or something, but somehow after those two days I had earned enough to retire for the summer, and in another week—maybe for life. Wait a minute . . . I had retired *four years ago*! Well, even if digging through trash and returning lots of expensive vitamins never really felt like work, it would be great not to see another Walgreens for a couple months anyway.

It was a surplus of what is known as "discretionary income," and my new place among the ranks of the middle class inspired me to take a bus into Minneapolis and visit Extreme Noise Records—where I spent obscene amounts of money on vinyl. Outside the store I sat on the sidewalk and held my records up to the sun. My condition and behavior were a disconcerting detachment from romantic poverty, from a not too distant time when I took blank tapes down to the listening station of my favorite record store and covertly dubbed records onto cassette . . . How soon one forgets one's roots.

Assuck and Reversal of Man were playing, and I found several of the people I had been looking for at the show. My friends—without phones, and often without homes—can be difficult to locate, and I appreciate that about them. Rockwell was a big scenester from the straight-edge old school, and has the lyric sheet "thank you" lists to prove it. Still vegan, still drug-free. We had met the previous summer, and I had marveled at his record collection and free-rent arrangement. We caught up outside the show. He had just returned from Europe. So had I, I said. The past winter he had hopped trains around the country. Oh really . . . ? And had received a ticket the previous week for dumpster diving. Stop it, I thought, you're only telling me what I want to hear. The late 80's Hardcore scene had borne some of the biggest drunks and most successful capitalists of the 90's. But, I gave him the test, and he was solid! I detected no career-mindedness or middle-class aspirations. Nope, he was all tramp! Rent-free youth, true 'til death!

"I'm sick of this place . . ." he said, scanning the crowd. "Let's go to Chicago." Did we *know* anyone in Chicago? Who cares! We're tramps!

24 hours later we were huddled in the shrubbery on the edge of the Fridley train yard, known as one of the "hottest" in the West. The train cops were everywhere, but, as thieves in the night, we spotted our train and within minutes were on a hotshot to Chicago.

We threw rocks, rolled through the small towns, and dove off on the edge of Chicago . . .

The El train, bootleg rap tape vendors, and after listening to *Paul's Boutique* for ages, I got to jump my first turnstile! It was all so exciting!

Off the train and on the streets. And in Chicago, it really was "the streets"—sketchy zombies, long shadows, adult bookstores—and it wasn't South Dakota anymore, where if you're tired, you just crawl into a cornfield and sleep. Our references included extensive lists of every vegetarian restaurant and record store in Chicago, and phone numbers of two people not home. We walked to a vegetarian restaurant to sit and assess the situation. Rockwell ordered a plate of something. I eyed the menu suspiciously. Really I hadn't eaten that day, but I wasn't going to sell out to save my life, hungry as I was. So, they give you food, and a napkin, and ask you to *pay*? It sounded pretty sketchy . . .

Chicago was hot and the streets were mean. Well, if there was anything I excelled at, certainly it was vagrancy. Faced with no resting place in downtown Chicago, hmmm . . . I looked at it as a little transient test. It didn't seem the standard "roof of strip mall" stand-by plan would be applicable in the surrounding skyscraper sprawl. We could maybe hide under the table in that restaurant all night, or if the peep show booths were in fact 25 ¢ for five minutes like the sign said, well then camping out there was still less than Best Western. We settled on the roof of an apartment building garage. Rats can't climb walls, can they? What about crack zombies? *Oprah Winfrey?!* You see, we were very new at this . . .

In the morning we followed up on our second lead— Rockwell's friend who worked at the natural-food supermarket chain Whole Foods. A woman told us Rockwell's friend was on vacation until Friday. So it was a dead end, but a *great* dead end—where we could graze on bulk foods and free bread samples, soak up the highbrow atmosphere, read *Vegetarian Times*, and sit in the sun all day in blatant violation of Chicago's anti-loitering laws! Whole Foods' bulk foods selection was first class. At a certain point, after several hours of grazing on carob chips and dates, perilously in view of shoppers and employees who may or may not be on our side, we had to adapt ourselves tactically to avoid detection, employing covert techniques such as the "off-balance reach of support" and the more brazen "hit and run." They were one step ahead of us, however, and had included in the store's design a perch *above* the bulk foods, where a lookout was quickly posted to our dismay! This unsporting maneuver inspired me, in a final act of symbolic resistance on behalf of hungry hoboes everywhere, to steal an armload of food before making our escape!

The unspoken purpose of the trip—besides loitering—was record shopping. There was simply no end to the hours spent in record stores pouring over 99¢ LP and 10¢ 45 bins. Rockwell was a rabid collector of 80's pop music, while I sought early 80's hip-hop and modern Hardcore records. Entire days were spent zig-zagging across Chicago following up leads on record stores and flipping through dusty bins in dimly lit shops, all the while coping bravely with our incessant guilt over spending money acquired dishonestly. The number of great record stores in Chicago was overwhelming. One record store was so vast we spent six hours going through records, at which point the shopkeeper sensed we were "down," and took us through a back door and down a staircase into a vinyl dungeon—a music cellar filled with endless stacks of unsorted records. Maybe somewhere in that basement I could find that record, the one I'd been looking for the past month, of that song, the theme song of my summer, the one that reminded me of that girl. Maybe in one of those stacks was that record . . .

One of my earlier rides that trip had been with a sly and beautiful girl, another in my medium-sized list of hitch-hiking crushes. "Tell me a story," she said. I told her the curious and totally made-up story of the time I threw a water balloon through my parents' bedroom window, shattering it, to later find the water balloon unbroken on their bed! She was the kind of girl you wanted to impress. I looked through her tapes—all Madonna! "You like Madonna too?" she asked. I did. "I think I'm going to like you," she said. We listened to *Like a Virgin*, the entire album, all the way to her destination. The tape ended as her exit approached. There was a long moment of uncomfortable silence . . . "Let's listen to it again," she said, and drove on—40 miles past her town! The very best song of the album—"Angel"—became the anthem of my trip, something to sing to myself late at night in ditches on the side of two-lane highways and get all emotional over. And to this day, when I hear that song, I think of that very sweet, very angelic girl . . .

Finding a top 40 hit that sold millions shouldn't have been any trouble, but somehow each time I asked for it, the record store people either didn't have it, or busted out laughing. Well, I found the 12" single in that cellar, and it only cost me a dollar.

Each day, after shopping *all* day, we would find a park and show off our finds to each other. I think Rockwell was impressed with my gatefold double LP dramatic recreation of the Chicago 8/7 Conspiracy Trial. And I was maybe a little jealous of his "Over the Edge" soundtrack to the punkest film *ever*—a true story of frustrated suburban kids who take over their high school, blow up cars, set fires, and take their teachers hostage! Too often overlooked in discussions on punk film. At some point, after admiring our purchases, talk would turn to the very serious issue of just how much money we had spent. Our behavior was an uncontrollable and guilty exercise of unwise spending habits —it was sheer reckless fiscal irresponsibility!

The "Revelation Records Tour" was in town. Rockwell opposed any mention of going, and I was only casually interested in the festive nature of it all—the hoarse-throated dinosaurs of Hardcore and sporty new-jacks getting all "positive" after being "let down" and "stabbed in the back" and everything. He grumbled and I growled, then he caved and we were on our bus . . .

Ooops! We arrived very late. An error definitely to be blamed on our little regard for an artificial man-made system of time. Long-term unemployment: We suffer the consequences . . . So when we arrived we had almost missed the entire show . . . almost. Our timing was in fact perfect, though I didn't appreciate it until later. We slipped past the doorman and onto the floor of the Fireside Bowl. Inside it was 110 degrees and completely packed with white-bread kids. Hardcore figurehead Ray Cappo was on stage. The only words I heard were—"This is our last song. We wrote this 12 years ago. It's for everyone who's straight-edge. It's called '*TAKE A STAND'!!!!*"

The place exploded. It was 2 1/2 minutes. And it was the best show I had ever been to.

The kids poured onto the street. We sat outside Fireside and Rockwell pointed out every Hardcore big-shot scenester. "That's Dan O'Mahoney." Mmhmmm. "That's Tony Victory." Right, ok. "He did (such & such) label." "He was in (blah blah band)." Rockwell remarked he thought Ray Cappo was wearing leather shoes. No way, I said. When Youth of Today pleaded "Meat eating, flesh eating, think about it!" I listened. They weren't leather, not a chance, I said. Only analysis at the straight-edge crime lab could make me consider otherwise. Although, I don't know . . . I mean they *all* sell out, right? "Ray of Today" may betray the cows, but he'll never betray "the *kids!*" Go!

Sitting on the sidewalk—watching the well-groomed and domesticated kids—I was thinking that Hardcore needs more bums. Like I wanted to bust out the "Will Work for Food" sign, or just fall asleep on some cardboard outside the show or something. Maybe Rockwell and I weren't asserting our "bum" status loudly enough, I thought. But then, after the crowd had mostly faded, the Fireside Bowl bouncer walked past several straggling clean-cut straight-edge kids, right up to us, and told us to leave! We didn't even have to break out the spare-change cup!

Rockwell swore he had friends in Chicago, though after three nights of sleeping on rooftops with the cockroaches, I wasn't sure. But after the show, he connected with Einstein who came down right away and picked us up in a big cargo van. Einstein was a wacky, middle-aged eccentric making me instantly nervous with his wildly animated demeanor, flailing arms, and afro like Abbie Hoffman. Einstein was a lifetime Chicagoan, and as we drove around Chicago he pointed out points of interest and seemed well versed in Chicago history. My knowledge of Chicago history was limited to readings on the exploits of the Yippies at the '68 Democratic Convention, several books on the Chicago mafia, and Upton Sinclair's turn of the century depiction of the Chicago stockyards in *The Jungle*. Last fall, sick and stranded in a small coastal town, with two weeks to wait for my ride, I had holed up in the little library and read several of the "classics." *The Jungle* made a big impression . . .

In the late 19th century, the major meat companies of the day consolidated their operations in Chicago's Southside, creating "the Jungle," an entire square mile of slaughterhouses. "What do you know about the Jungle?" I asked. "I'll show you!" he said, swinging a u-turn. We were going to the Jungle!

. . . or what remained. The Jungle—as depicted in the book— no longer stands, and was condemned in the early 1970's due to community pressure and as a business decision by the meat companies. The wholesale murder corporations moved their operations to the countryside near the farms to cut down on the cost of transporting cows by train. (There was an old hobo trick— when it's so cold you might die, ride with the cows!)

I was a little worried about visiting a place that had inspired so many nightmares, but thought of it as a history lesson. Though really it wasn't history at all—the same bloodshed was going down at that moment in big shadowy fortresses off in the countryside. We arrived at the entrance. The Jungle, which no longer stands in its entirety, has been given "historical landmark" status, and many monuments have been preserved—like the huge arch at the entrance with a giant looming cow head sculpture. The murder of billions as proud history . . . shameless . . . We drove slowly through the neighborhood, now mostly an industrial manufacturing district. We did, however, find a few slaughterhouses still in operation, with the sickening stench of death and rows of cattle trucks lined up outside. We heard the roaring machinery, the clanging of metal, and saw the cows sticking their noses through holes in the trailers for their last breaths of air. Earth Crisis/ Vegan Reich lyrics seem a little more relevant looking into the eyes of a cow outside a slaughterhouse. We drove on in a morose silence . . .

The largest and scariest of the slaughterhouses was a massive fortified complex surrounded by razor wire and guarded by armed security. Einstein pulled up and called to the guard—

"Excuse me sir! What goes on in this building?" he asked.

"Food manufacturing," said the guard hesitantly.

"What food is produced here?"

The guard became visibly nervous, wouldn't answer, and told us to leave! Guards, razor wire, guns . . . A setup suspiciously similar to a Nazi concentration camp. What are they hiding . . . *murder?!*

Einstein lived on the edge of Chicago. The next day Rockwell rested, and I hit the strip mall scene to replenish my funds. On my way out I told Rockwell I would return by 5 o'clock. I paced the gritty fast food and drug store strip, picked up dinner, found a few good receipts, etc. . . . At 5:30 I was walking back to Einstein's when a car screeched up behind me. Doom . . . I thought it must be the Safeway manager, coming to reclaim his pasta sauce! Gulp! It was Einstein and Rockwell. When I hadn't returned at 5, they were concerned I'd been caught and came to look for me. "We thought you had been arrested!" And I thought—when you're a half-hour late, and your friends think you're in jail, it's probably a sign you steal too much.

My list of celebrity sightings was shamefully short. I was always loitering around the big hotels back home, but somehow had never bumped into anyone with worldwide fame. Must be that I hadn't watched TV in years, and walked out of most every movie in less than fifteen minutes, so who *were* the celebrities of the day? *My* icons were those responsible for the recent rash of retail burglaries where the criminals just smashed their car through the front door and loaded up! And the pro squatter found stealthily *living* in the basement of an office building for five years!

Rockwell spoke often of a vegetarian restaurant called The Chicago Diner—"We must go to the Chicago Diner." After record shopping one evening, we caught a couple trains and walked a couple miles to the Chicago Diner—a small hole in the wall with several small tables, a few booths along the wall, and no hippie nonsense. Rockwell read the menu while I looked at records. He asked the waiter for a recommendation— "Well . . . *Roger* over there . . ." the waiter tilted his head towards the booth next to us, ". . . is having the tofu chili." This didn't register with either of us. Rockwell ordered the chili and I scanned the surrounding floor for crumbs. Rockwell was brought his chili. Then the waitress looked at me—all sad, hungry, and stubborn—went to the kitchen, and brought me back a plate of cornbread! This was, of course, a criminal gratuity providing no incentive for a shiftless, unemployed, social leech to better himself and rise above dependence on the labor of others, totally detrimental to the economy and society as a whole, but, food is food! I was hungry. Moments later the couple in the next booth stood up to leave and passed our table. It was a young woman with . . . *Roger Ebert*! The celebrity film critic was clearly giving a "thumbs up" to the vegan revolution!

Everything was perfect, we were doing exactly what we wanted—buying records and exploring new places. Best to leave before the flaws in our plan surfaced—before we spent all our money on records, became sick on Whole Foods vegan chocolate, or broke a leg jumping turnstiles. And besides, Rockwell had a plan . . .

There is a place in Wisconsin where each year blackened spirits by the thousands converge and commit barbarous acts of blasphemy . . . *The Milwaukee Metalfest!* 100 bands! Three days! Fifty dollars! Miles of hair! They'll sell you the whole seat, but you'll only need *the edge!*

It was the love of Satan and cigarettes taken obscenely far. In the metal underworld it was the grandest of events, attendance the ultimate expression of a hatred for god. People from around the world gathered at the Eagle's Ballroom to fling hair and check out the most evil of the metal underground. It was thousands of dyed-black-haired burly men gripping beer bottles—and if you tried to tell them Emperor were not the gods of metal, they just might hit you with that bottle!

Traveling a hundred miles to Milwaukee . . . Rockwell had the driving love of metal. I hadn't ever heard metal that wasn't straight-edge, but I did have the driving love of "a story to tell," and an attraction to the absurdity of a huge, drunken, satanic invocation set to music. Metal was all new to me, and Rockwell was there to walk me through what so far had me confused. He explained metal scene politics, the European black metal inter-band rivalry with band members *killing* members of other bands, burning churches, and generally living their lyrics. We were definitely getting in. Rockwell and I agreed $50 for tickets was unthinkable. We could pay for at least two vagrancy tickets or a hundred meals with that. No way. Rockwell's plan was the crude but effective *panhandling*. To play on the metal brotherhood, you know, "spare some change for a ticket?" Getting into the show was at least as—or more—important to me, but I had a policy about panhandling . . . Really, I hadn't ever panhandled, I saw it as apathetic and unthreatening to redistribute wealth among the bottom 5% of the population when those in the top 1% own a store across the street. You can ask for what you need from a comrade in poverty, or *take* it from the bourgeois . . . Try it! They usually don't notice . . . And panhandling made the very overt statement that without work one must beg, scrape by, and struggle to survive. Bwhahahaha . . .

Rockwell was making money slowly, but the bands were coming and going, and impatience inspired him to dedicate himself to a shmoozing campaign with the girl at the gate. Finally—either through Rock's sheer charisma, or just wishing to be left alone—she waved him in! My social skills were lacking, I didn't know how to talk to girls. But I *was* skilled in the general art of "getting away with it" . . .

Subcultures other than metal were represented—burned-out old punks, a group of straight-edge kids who kept our bags in their trunk, a tribe of gutter punks with *Slayer* shirts who rode in by freight train for the love of metal, and me—in the best people-watching spot in the country at that moment. I sat on the grass by the gate, totally caught up in watching the people in line—the huge Norwegian black metal dudes and the crazy living dead in makeup and full vampire gear . . .

I attempted hopping the fence in an obscure corner, but a lady in the adjacent apartment building began yelling and blew my cover! Climbing the fence anywhere seemed impossible, though I learned that, give those gutter punks a few beers and no fence will keep them from their metal! Getting into the Metalfest . . . it was a ponderous challenge. One shared by a hundred others milling around outside the gate with me, all of us broke or unwilling to pay. Some were reserved, idle, walking in circles, scratching their heads; but dozens more were militant and un-compromising, having traveled across the country or the world to Milwaukee, and their desperate efforts to get in were a great show in themselves—aggressive begging, mob action advances over the fence, crude attempts to pass old ticket stubs, and those huge Norwegian black metal dudes— broke and sobbing—with outstretched arms and upraised palms. Heartbreaking . . .

Those metal bands ordered a lot of pizza backstage, and, like, every 20 minutes a delivery guy would pull up with a trunkfull of orders, spending ten minutes running in and out with armloads of pizza. As pizza-man, he en-joyed unobstructed freedom of passage, and I could sense the more ticketless and desperate among us making abrupt career plans. He was a hard worker. I thought I would, you know, give him a break, ease his load a bit—"Let me give you a hand," I said. He loaded me up with a dozen pizzas. "Follow me" . . .

Once inside, I immediately made a note to definitely buy a Domino's Pizza uniform at Goodwill, dumpster or steal one of those insulated pizza carriers, and just travel around the country next year sneaking into Beastie Boys concerts.

This is where words fail. Inside the Eagle's Ballroom it was, like . . . well it was just *lots and lots of metal*, you know? 3 stages, 3 floors, 3 bands playing concurrently, and in the base-ment—a metal mall! Immediately I felt a sense of family in that building—everyone was drunk, but no one was fight-ing. Rockwell and I soon found each other. Hard to do in a crowd of 2,000, but made easier because he was the tallest, and I the only one wearing white. I complimented him on his (dangerous) manipulative skills, and he applauded my penetrating Machiavellian vision revealing the criminal ap-plications of pizza in a state obsessed with dairy products.

We agreed that when people dance, people lose things, and between bands we swept the floor with a flashlight and cleaned up the debris— Rockwell found a hat, and I picked up a CD by a death metal band from Iowa.

Two days of continuous metal in a hundred shades of black, and after the first 25 bands the growls all began to blur together. Was Emperor the all-female death metal band, or the act in viking costumes surrounded by frozen cow heads on sticks? It was an alien world, and I was happy to connect with a familiar and sober old friend—Lucy, the friendliest girl in L.A. She made me so happy, remembering my name after 18 months, and while we talked I tried hard to remember hers. Lucy offset the snarling machismo, I was glad to find her. She too was traveling the country for the summer, and like me, was casually drawn to Metalfest by the novelty. Thousands of miles from home . . . for this? It was the randomness of youth.

After one more day and 40 more bands, Metalfest was over, and it was all very sad . . .

Lucy dropped me and Rockwell off in a field beside a church on the edge of town and waved goodbye.

In the morning, a church pastor woke us up, and with the will of god behind him, said—"Leave!" I rolled over, Rockwell stirred a little, groaned, and went back to sleep. The pastor returned, asking why we were in Milwaukee, and I told him—"The Metalfest!" What goes on there? What was I doing with my life? Did I *believe*?!?! He invited us to a sermon. From a musical celebration of Satan to a Christian sermon . . . it seemed perfect . . .

Instead we snuck into a movie next door. Rockwell waited by the back door and I entered through the front, brushing past the teenage ticket taker and giving her a hard, intimidating stare . . . I think I *scared* that poor girl! I couldn't enjoy the free movie thinking about that . . .

Madison? It sounded like a plan. I was suspicious of plans. But Rockwell promised a big university library, record stores, and a street next to campus where he swore no cars were allowed. Books, records, my pedestrianship . . . Maybe the three things I value most. If I wasn't reading or rocking out, I was probably walking, or watching others walk. It sounded pleasant. Maybe we could think of Madison rather as a suggestion, or move in the *general direction* of Madison; and if we were invited to a frat party in La Crosse, or offered a ride to Tampa with Bloodfeast, then that would be ok too. We fixed our hair a little and put out our thumbs. It was just after Metalfest, and the Bloodfeast tour van probably passed us, but didn't stop. A rusty cargo van did.

It was *Anal Blast*.

"Get in dudes! Beer in the cooler, vodka in the back!"

It was a long ride.

State Street in Madison is the hip student pedestrian strip extending from the University of Wisconsin to the state capitol building. A charming unpretentious avenue lined with shady trees, benches, punks with dogs who need "18 cents," and restaurant patios with tables full of abandoned half-eaten meals! Rockwell ran inside to ask a restaurant cook if his rice was vegan while I guarded the food. Strangers in a strange town, and Madison had a hot meal waiting!

We took over a corner on State Street to wait for the random encounters that occur in a foreign town when you sit in one place long enough. As a remedy for loneliness, a lost gaze and big backpack are guaranteed every time. Two college girls invited us to play pool. Rockwell talked with them all evening. I trailed silently along, deflecting questions like—"What's wrong?" and "Do you talk?" I talk . . . sometimes. Not with self-important and phony college girls.

The next afternoon their pretentious airs grew too much and I fled. An escape strategically timed just *after* eating their food. I wanted to explore Madison, not watch TV. I wanted a view from the 3rd floor library window, or from inside a dumpster, not through a haze of incense in a house with beads where doors should be. And I wanted the voice of the street. Certainly not the "yaaaaa . . ." lazy tone indicative of trendy marijuana use by drugged-out zombies. Rockwell found me later that day. My timing was perfect, he said. "Just after you left, they pulled out the pipe." He fled as well. I laughed.

We lived on one bench for the next week. It was one particular bench on the west end of State Street across from the UW campus. Right there on the main artery of campus pedestrian traffic. Each morning we crawled off the roof of the bagel shop directly above, and sat on that bench all day. It slowly happened over several days that passing students and State Street regulars noticed that we were very committed to that bench, and in fact were not going anywhere. Friendly and curious people stopped to talk, asked us our story, and introduced us to their friends, who became our friends. We were the bums on display! Soon it seemed that as one person left, another would sit down, and after several days it seemed we knew everyone on State Street. We knew the delivery man for the pizza place across the street, who each day promised to leave cheeseless pizza by the dumpster at closing. We knew the crazy old mumbling street philosopher who sat with us each day. "Blah, blah, blah." Talking talking talking, often while we talked to other people. And our straight-edge friend with the straight-edge tattoos he'll regret one day . . .

While we sat, and talked, some would ask—"Why Madison?" Rockwell would say—"To break some hearts." They would ask, "Why this bench?" We couldn't answer that question. It would take hours and involve maps and charts. Why *that* bench? Because it was twenty feet below the roof we slept on, and fifty feet west of the bagel dumpster we ate from. And just when scurvy was about to set in from an all-bagel diet, we were two blocks from the grocery store with bananas—$0.19 a lb. Our bench was across the street from the University of Wisconsin, with the showers in the tennis building, the campus library, and the lake front gazebos—Madison's best morning reading spot. Two blocks north of the punk record store, and two feet from the trash can outside Walgreens—the one full of receipts used for low risk scams to buy those records. And two doors down from the bagel shop, where each morning I pulled a cup from the trash and drank "free" flavored coffee. Until something went horribly wrong . . . "You're going to have to start *paying* for that!" Ooops. It was a nice bench.

One day our straight-edge friend brought us two bikes as gifts. I think it was his polite way of suggesting we explore Madison outside the bench. Leaving State Street? It was a suspicious idea. Probably a trick. Rockwell wouldn't think of it. The bikes sat on the bike rack next to our bench. For a day I eyed them as suspect, a threat to our idle comfort. In a moment of weakness I grabbed a bike and rode all the way to Best Western for a swim, and then to Whole Foods Market. I did it again the next day. Then I would return to hear from Rockwell of those who passed by in my absence, and I sulked in regret over missed conversation with Matt the Atari 2600 collector over our shared 80's video game fancy, or Becky the vegan cook. Life outside State Street . . . it was a foolish idea. Life wasn't "out there," but all around us, on State Street, on that bench.

I returned from Whole Foods on our last night in Madison, and from a distance could see that someone was sitting on our bench. So I was going to, you know, *kill* that person. But it was Becky. She had been waiting for one of us, all alone, with a plate of cookies on her lap. "I baked these for you and Rockwell."

Yummmm . . .

* * *

There were more towns, crazier rides. No "better cookies," but the coconut haystacks in St. Louis came close. Rockwell went on to be banned from whole regions of the country, and I soon fell in love under a waterfall. Before returning home, I thought of that train—of the old hobo and his bad advice. What I did soon *after* that advice only shocks me now. Really, I can't believe I was so naïve . . .

Please, don't make my same mistake again—don't do it.
Don't *ever* call it "the wrong train."

There is no *"wrong train."*

I couldn't believe my luck: an epic road trip, rough plans and no money, three kids and a car—*cancelled* at the last minute. Anyone else would sigh and return home, but anyone else didn't just have their abandoned house boarded up by the city, their mattress and improvised lighting system locked behind "No Trespassing" signs and yellow tape. Which is what led to this plan. But when Penny backed out, demanding closure to a broken relationship before going anywhere *near* Miami, or anything eastbound, I was left standing before a two-week void. A casual glance from the wrong angle could mark it as a disappointment, fizzled hope. But I'd been here before, and looked skyward with dreamy eyes for what came next. You know, whatever I wanted.

Amazing . . . So well disguised, these clean slates of hope, traveling under assumed names and masked as doom each time. "Cancelled Plans"—that one was easy to spot. "Return and we'll call the police" at a half-dozen points back home during my 18th year drove me to that first crazy and profound hitchhiking tour. "We're through" once led, within days, to an obscure Kinko's in a random town, and heartfelt conversation with a sweeter girl, snowballing into grandiose plans of rusty trains and Florida beaches. And "I quit," well . . . there's not one smile since that can't be traced to that one.

Penny would drive one thousand miles north to say a few words, drop me off at any point along the way, and pick me up in two weeks. I was almost certain I had read this zine before, or heard this story, or at least danced to this song. One kid, two weeks, strange town . . . I had one day to choose a locale, she said. Immediately I crept into Barnes & Noble, compiled a small stack of travel books, and walked out. I gazed with star-filled eyes at the shiny photos of white sand and whiter people, then at my maps, then rubbed my chin. There was the college town I had exploited for years: comfy, but since last visit—rushing a dying mouse in a glue-trap to the emergency vet at 3 a.m.—under a sad cloud. The coastal town: if the girls at the Mexican restaurant would take me home again—worth considering. Or maybe that *other* coastal town: certainly I could spend two weeks doing what I did last visit—live in a tent behind a trailer of alcoholics, dance in the little mall with that girl, and sneak behind the gift shop for the big inflatable trampoline. Not the latest trendy "progressive" community: where each visit I stumbled to the door moments *after* the greatest band in the world had played. Heartbreaking . . . and if I approached the club as Catharsis struck the last chord one more time, I would die, or sell out, or something.

Stitch chose to forgo any hope of a good story—two weeks at his parents' house. Long ago I turned my back to the warm, inviting chokehold of "Parents' House" comfort. A house I pledged to never use as a substitute for creativity—laundry only. I had rejected a furnished bedroom at "Parents' House," dragging futons to three abandoned ones mere blocks away. So you see, I was very committed to this position.

Surrounded by books and maps, on the floor, I sat staring into the two-week chasm that had opened before me . . . With barely more in my pocket than three dimes from a failed saltwater raid on the Coke machine at Best Western, I was graced with a return to "the struggle"—the self-imposed desperation of sleeping in ditches, exploiting public space in alarming ways, asking the Round Table girls to look the other way while you raid the salad bar, getting on your *hands and knees* below a drive-through window for the obligatory nickels and dimes . . . Solitary abnegation that on paper begs a quiet tear of sympathy, but in 3-D: the time of your life.

A plan took root—identify traditional middle-class criteria for vacation choices, eat a bagel, then do the opposite. Hurl myself into the most desolate small town with the worst weather, no supermarkets, and festivity you have to fight for. Five minutes on my bag outside a gas station and it usually came. I took fuzzy comfort in this. One town, two weeks, three dimes and four books. These episodes of near-death and mockery of the senses were thematically timeless, the essence of literature and *art itself,* and when I took my first kick to the door of an abandoned farmhouse, I would remember . . .

Ooops. My 24 hours were up. I had the theme, but not the physical coordinates. Penny told me to get in the car. I collected my books, and my maps, and reconstructed my travel research office in the backseat. There were two types of small towns—those people escaped *to,* and those people escaped *from.* Ashland and Salem. Cannon Beach and Minot. Arcata and Pine Bluff. I chose the former—to be a struggling artist amongst struggling artists, and not pig farmers. Probably strangers would screech up, insult me, and drive away just as often, but the insults would be more refined, philosophical even. And instead of throwing beer bottles, maybe I'd be hit with, like, sandals and wet clay. A warm thought, enough to narrow down the list. Lines were drawn, harsh judgements made, and entire states denied my tourist dollars with one pen stroke. My vision was coming into focus. At home, at my supermarket chair by the espresso counter, I often endured head-in-hands despair in my quandry over the correct choice for that day's adventure. No small decision, perhaps none greater. Two weeks was, like, the weight of the world—fourteen of them! I was sort of traumatized over this. At the exact point my list had been beaten down to two, I threw the question to Penny and went limp. Which one?!?!

"The one you haven't been to."

Pure poetry. And the dumbest question I'd ever asked.

One thousand miles later I stood in the rain, at the ferry terminal. In 30 minutes the last ferry for the night would leave for the obscure and foggy little island, where herbalists in sweaters weaved baskets. And where—surrounded by water on all sides—I couldn't betray the theme if I wanted to. Consistent with my "struggling artist" role, I had almost no money. Poverty, I felt, would really legitimize my art. So when the boat docked, I circumvented the ticket booth, blended in with the bikers and boarded on the car deck. Like a warm handshake from a new friend . . .

Stepping off the ferry, I could almost hear the property values plummet. Rain fell, and I stood in it. From the waterfront park, I scanned the little downtown. Looking it up and down, it would be nice to have been neutral in judgement, but the town was about to give me a free vacation independent of its opinion on the matter, so you could say I was already in love. No slave to practicality, I had chosen this little town. The one where artists go to get away, so far out they usually can't find their way back. Here, I would live a stripped-down and raw two weeks, without amenities, and if my plan came through—without *food*. Yes, art. And when the artists doing Yoga in the park gasped as I stumbled from the bushes at 5 a.m., wet and scary, they might not recognize it as art, but they should. I wanted a little credit. Rooftop sonnets and moldy bagel blues. A novel is born each night in an unlocked U-Haul. Yes, I would show them art . . .

It was after midnight. My options were to walk the dark streets with lowered eyes in the misty rain, or . . . wait, that was it. My path was direct in an almost possessed fashion—along the waterfront, winding through the floating web of the harbor in the rain, past the seedy old bearded guys drinking on the dock, to the abandoned boat at the edge of the world. A modest, half-sunk, floating house. It rested on the harbor at the furthest point from land, and beyond its rotted hull—only forbidding waves and doom-filled clouds. Shining my light in the window, I could see the old boat had a story. And after looking over both shoulders, I would sneak myself in as the next chapter . . .

Waking up, the musty blankets felt glamorous, the disregarded property law a sinister pleasure, and exact reasons why I wouldn't just stay forever weren't yet clear. I could see out my window what the darkness and rain had obscured the night before—a misty old boat town. Thick evergreens enveloped the wooden staircases and rows of old boats, old boat guys played guitars in the fog, and everywhere rough sailors and young artists in knit caps stretched and drank coffee and read books on benches in the haze. There were the cool old wooden shops on the waterfront, the little park, and a general sense of ungovernable community. If there were laws here, certainly I agreed with 9/10 by way of general respect—and the rest, well, I still wasn't going to pay for food. On the decks of boats and waterfront seats, everywhere I looked, proud people were plainly seen *doing nothing*. Eagerness for my own self-serving role in the spectacle flared. "Doing nothing"—I knew from on-the-job experience—equated to doing quite a lot, but lacking the paycheck stubs to prove it. Traumatic at tax time, but from my new favorite spot on the end of the pier—sort of poignant . . .

With a bed, comforters, and little radio, this had to be some sort of record—in a strange town, bumping into furnished abandoned shelter inside of ten minutes. Though, having hurled myself into uncertain circumstances before—to be expected. Like gravity and the one person in the front of every bus talking to the driver—one of life's true absolutes. A new town and a nervous smile: You've thrown yourself there, the town is of course flattered, and throws you a rope. We all knew this, rested on it, afraid to name it fearing to do so would kill it, or dissuade it from kicking down unlocked doors and bagels. Hippies call this faith "surrendering to the universe." I like to think the towns know we're desperate, and they're *afraid!*

Everything was falling into place. A boat, and now, 50¢ coffee. From the deck of the coffeehouse, I could wave to my little boat bobbing in the waves. Maybe so much festivity had never been fit into one room and one patio. The coffeehouse biosphere: maybe you never have to leave. And with some—I couldn't verify they actually did. This was "the island," and I was partaking in an almost sociological study of it from my corner table. Like, asking for coffee, and that's it, only confuses people. You don't place an order, you shout it, high-five everyone en route to table, then sit down and paint a picture or something. Everyone knows everyone, unless you're blonde, *not* wearing a sweater, and——yes—at the corner table, tracing carved table-graffiti with your finger. Self-serve refills may or may not be free, but if a tree falls in the forest and no one hears it . . .

You slept together once, but is it love? Looking across the harbor at her rolling with the waves, I thought that just might be the case. Forgotten and neglected, I would return Old Musty Boat to grace. And she would lift my dignity and pride to that of a humble man with an angelic beauty, of the stubbornly unemployed with an entirely rent-free home. Somewhere between the two-story suburban palace no longer my own, and my one-wall-and-a-roof gem on the roof of that university library. There's a lot of shelter in this country, and sometimes the owners forget it's there! Then we show up, break in, sleep there, put up a few posters, etc. etc. . . . It's sort of complicated.

50¢ coffee, the big city paper, real artists, and boat guys. I drank the 50¢ coffee, read the big city paper, and wondered if I was a real artist or a boat guy. Swallowed by fog on the deck of the sole hangout in town, I pioneered my role among this crowd of regulars, the woven handbags and sketch pads. "Kid in art/boat town" . . . had more soul than "Kid in big city," lacked the beer-bottle-from-a-moving-car charm of "Kid-in-small-Midwest-town," with a slower-moving plot than "Kid-stranded-in-dangerous-ghetto," but demanded a more resourceful craftiness than

"Kid-in-tropical-resort-town." And when drops of liquid gold aren't falling on exceptional public transportation, I know this isn't "Kid-at-home." This was all fresh and exciting, and like the other plotlines—I was obsessed. Such unhealthy admiration was akin to its human counterpart, where infatuation burns so red, you can be *insulted* by the person yet remain true . . . The absence of visibly free food was a stinging slap. But the coffee was rich and the mornings profound. No hard feelings. The others had abused me in their own cute ways—rain, poison ivy, 5 a.m. sprinklers, um, 1 a.m. sprinklers . . . but this . . . "Living-in-abandoned-boat-in-small-town" . . . this was all new. Wait. Oregon coast—summer '96. Nevermind. Well I didn't have to endure a Jehovah's Witness's passenger seat to get here anyway . . .

Busting out of the coffeehouse—real dramatically—I was tough, wired, and set to cross a few lines for my food. Basic sustenance in this place was a rich challenge. Drama building up to a certain near-death triumph of that single bagel at the bottom of a dumpster—in precise accordance with my plan to come as a struggling artist, struggle, and almost die. I found the sole grocery in town—taking their food was ruled out at a glance. Within my abilities—and those of small children and the quadriplegic—but I failed to sufficiently demonize an institution the size of a living room, where the owner worked the register. Like burglarizing Mr. Hooper's on Sesame Street. Sick and wrong. 16 hours into starvation, I stumbled upon an apple tree behind the church! Rosy and sweet—sweeter than left-over fruit cocktail from trays outside hotel rooms. Who would have guessed?! Sitting down below the tree, I ate apple after apple, then realized—wait, this was "Hobo eating apple under tree"! I was *living* the Norman Rockwell painting! Not as fun as "Living the rap song," but close . . . Turn the page on another shocking moment of the hobo looking up, looking around, and being *inside* a cliché scene of idyllic Americana. Sunsets from boxcars and the donut shop counter—they wouldn't be clichés if they weren't so *great*, you know?

After the apple tree, my "food tour" quickly lost the youthful positivity of Youth of Today's "Break Down the Walls" tour. I spotted a bagel shop—and if it was a starvation induced mirage, I'd chosen my pastry delusions sharply. Face it—without the bagel, we're dead. After tearing open every bag, sifting through it all with desperate attention, I finished with messy hands and general confusion. I mean, the dumpster seemed to be saying "No Bagels"! An unheard-of break from known laws, and I feared physics itself was next to go. Returning the following morning, I found the gate to the dumpster locked, and in fact fully barricaded with patio furniture! Clearly the fearful response of a business owner never before graced by those who break into their garbage and liberate the edibles. I'd *scared* them! I was an island first, and if past experience was any indication, exaggerated details of my story would soon appear in the "Police Blotter" column of the paper. This "danger" fear of garbage eaters is the hype of ignorance. Leave us no food however, and we shed the confines of reason—witnessed by several back room rats at Trader Joe's the day the dumpster was empty, forcing us into the storeroom to recover desperateley needed soy milk! There's always a "Plan B," and we're not always proud of it . . .

Sunny hope brought me to the grocer's dumpster. Whatever richness lay within would surely be welcome after the 18-hour "all apple diet." In an anxious moment, I lifted the lid to find a thousand slimy lettuce leaves, and . . . apples. Whoever set up these moments of black hobo humor was writhing on the floor somewhere, dying of laughter while I died of hunger. Not knowing if one can subsist on apples alone, in two weeks I was certain I could deliver the answer. The next morning at 7 a.m., stumbling through a little dumpster tour, and *failing*, I came full-circle to the rear of the grocer's. It seemed too good to be true, a hobo hallucination perhaps: Behind a delivery truck, four crates of bread and pastries—unattended. Vegan loading dock raiders enjoy the added charm of having to read ingredients at the crime scene. After a rushed job, luck turned to insult. Three loaves of bread . . . and one apple pie. Laughter roared from above. Yes, it was god. Mr. Funnyman had put me in Salt Lake City the night tornadoes destroyed downtown, placed the gum in my dumpstered *Titanic* video that destroyed Mom's VCR, and he was here, slapping his knee while killing me with apples. Without "His" support, how can we win? With free apple pies, *how can we lose?!*

Back at my boat, I was sifting through boxes and emptying drawers, piecing together the story I knew was there. Raking through debris, I held up the ripped t-shirts, checked dates on receipts, performed carbon-dating, etc. and after turning over a few drawers, I thought I had found it—one "Notice to Appear," on drug charges, three months old. "Owner in Prison" offered a level of comfort just below "Owner Deceased" and "Owner Faraway with Alzheimer's." Another hood-rat up in the joint. Great. I felt the warm outlaw affinity of kindred spirits, even if it was drugs. While he slammed dominoes with the others, I was reading by candlelight, listening to his radio.

Nothing is forever, and if the owner was released, or escaped, there was my backup discovered the night before—up Main Street, past the bed and breakfast, and a left at the landing strip. One forgotten house. Looking for food, or love, or maybe just a story, I instead found an abandoned cabin—hiding in the woods, neglected and sad. Her owners sat in another prison, or maybe the same one, or who could say? This was part of the excitement. A landlocked counterpart to ole cozy boat, her debris told a different story—"High School Drinking Spot." More of a warning than a story, marking it as no place for a sober pirate. Straight-edge as a "personal choice"—a sentiment suiting the other kids, but after years of attempted break-ins at my repossessed shelter by kids with six-packs, sobriety was more like a little war. At 16, drug-free activism came in visiting the "smoking corner" at lunch, shouting insults, and running. At 24, I rub my palms in darkness, plotting strategic placement of leghold traps and landmines . . .

My solid routine had taken form in 24 hours. I was a little proud of it. Awaking to the lawless wake of the morning ferry, I soon grew impatient waiting for it to depart—so I could ride the waves again! My feet dangling, I chewed slowly my two slices of bread on the edge of the pier. Maybe the edge of the *Earth*, though I never proved it. 50¢ coffee across the street solidified what we all knew: loitering is awesome. A near-microcosm of anarchist community, the coffeehouse harbored a creative crowd of dozens, coming together in cooperation for the common goal of breakfast, no cops, and the obligatory deviant who ruins it for everyone—taking refills without paying. Though, I never confirmed they were not in fact free, and was afraid to ask. In the 8 a.m. bob-and-weave food frenzy, we never collided, and—all diving for the same paper when its owner left—we never fought. So what *did* we do? Some read, or drew. I leaned an ear toward nearby conversations and looked over shoulders. For one hour or five, I read a book or the paper, then caved to the seductive fog and gazed into the ocean. What filled the following hours is utterly untranslatable. Call it my small town fancy. Losing myself in the side streets, rubbing my chin outside the cool old houses, and patting unleashed dogs on the head. My analytic strolls always took me to the rear of the grocer's, and back to the understanding I was, um, almost dead! I perused the dumpster for food, the pavement for scraps, and the lot for the mythic "forklift with key." Outside the post office stood the triangular community bulletin board—the soul and story of a town in nine square feet. If you've spotted a wild mink inside of two years, the wildlife club wants to hear from *you!* Thoughts of cheap used cars and two-figure monthly office space brought me to the library, and my own seat in the corner. Six hours in a book, with half-time lunch of bread and apples. The truth of my time in that chair, I don't know, it was impossible to dodge—that moment under the tree? Happening again. I was "Bum in library chair"! The rustic old guys who played chess all day by the dictionaries—that was *me!* When you become the guys who scared you as a child, it probably means something. And I have no idea what. At closing, I would run to the little hotel and jump in the wooden spa. This always climaxed in an uncomfortable moment when *actual guests* crowded in—asking too many questions demanding elaborate lies of just who I was and where I lived. Two questions which—when answered by me honestly six months of the year—shocked and upset most white people. A quiet, contemplative walk delivered me to the bagel dumpster—a big, stupid, empty metal thing I cursed and thought was stupid. Walking became shuffling, and when heads turned, I dove into my boat. Blink and you missed it—I had a secret to keep. My crude efforts to barricade the door led to something more funny than fortified—less intended as a blockade than something to make loud crashing sounds when the owner returned. I read by candlelight, falling asleep to the fuzzy sound of a sad song . . . and when the morning ferry docked—I'd get to do it all again!

There were the ad-lib breaks from the story, when my "Kid-stranded-on-island" plot demanded a subplot. Trying to sneak into the little cinema—futile but fun. Nowhere is it written the emotional peaks and valleys experienced in an afternoon at the post office, reading other people's mail. Returning from the library to spot an interpretative dance performance at the community theater, slipping past the ticket taker, and taking my seat. I don't know what happened—two hours passed, the curtains closed, the crowd rose, and a man stormed up, shaking his finger at me for "disrespecting the theater"! He probably paid.

Over coffee each morning, I intensely pondered entirely new, almost legal ways of passing sixteen waking hours in four square blocks. I would the peruse the "Community Calendar" column of the paper, reread my travel guide for missed passages, browse the phone book, look out at the water, scratch my head, then just invent bad jokes. Like my daydream scenario of, say, an artist sitting down at my table, and with the pretentious tone of sculptors and dramatists, asking—"Hey man—what's *your* art?" I would stand, refill my cup without paying, and sit down—"Performance Artist." I thought that was funny. Hobo humor—without it, kids begin confusing precious towns of limitless possibility with boring voids. Tragic . . .

Almost as tragic as the library kicking me out at 6 p.m. each evening, leaving me to feel my way around in the dark, and eat bread. If I were to understand Marx correctly, society *owed* me a place to go! In 3-D application of political theory, I began—each evening at 5:45—to take a stack of books, walk towards the restroom, then sort of "get lost" all the way to the community room, hide the books in the cupboard, and prop open the back door. After my spa, the librarians were gone and I would just hang out inside the community room for hours! There was a little microwave to heat the bagels I never had, and a 20-person table to sit at the head of and feel real important. Some nights I even slept there. I could boil water for tea, read old novels, and go through the cupboards. And if the cops showed up—Marx was on shelf 5, they could read it themselves . . .

My morning ritual I held as precious—"Coffee please." One week into that and the girl would just smile and say —"The usual?" The usual . . . I didn't think people really said that.

Two bread slices, two apples, thrice daily. Beyond that —only empty dumpsters and my empty wallet. I had rapidly exhausted most points on the "Free Food" spectrum—dumpster food, tree food, unguarded loading dock food . . . No salad bars or bulk food bins in town, no youth infiltrators driving delivery trucks. "The kids" seemed to lack representation in the entire industry of food production, distribution, service and retail. Ruling out the old standby—"Can I have this . . . *for free?!*" Then my bread went moldy—while I slept! I reconsidered my boycott of the little grocers, maybe even the visionary "Payphone Coin Return Slot Guy." I bet they eat more than apples. From other food groups even. I saw, at this point, only a few obscure loopholes to the unimaginable. Extend my route to the apartment building dumpster. Eat moldy bread. Pluck and dine on crops in surrounding farmland. Board ferry for a roundtrip ride—free leaving town—and raid cafeteria for dozens of little cereal boxes. Those things are great. I stood curious about the crazy directions my hunger would take me: unexplored side streets, forced conversation with strangers, the anxiously anticipated "Will work for food" sign—and also apprehensive about unspeakable tragedies: eating grass, paying, etc. etc.

There is a little hobo maxim that when matters turn so hopeless, the clouds so dark the only exit seems death or parents' house, the tide will turn *at the exact point it becomes funny.* Half your barely sustainable food supply going moldy—I thought that was pretty funny. In their consistency, I feel these rules of poverty are matched only by gravity. True to the maxim—hobbling through the streets and taking an inspired "left"—I almost bumped into a giant supermarket! I don't know how I had missed it. I was certain it hadn't been there the day before, but owed my life to the construction of it overnight. The bins of produce outside would feed whole boxcars of hungry hoboes. But I wished to reacquaint myself with missed corners of the food pyramid. I have a right. If it wasn't an apple, it probably went in my basket. And if its purchase soon after could be verified with a sale's receipt—it probably wasn't mine! Broke kids creep out the backdoor. Back at my boat, I laid out my food, smiled real big—then the crumbs flew. And that night—a feast in the library. The collective work-free movement raised a quiet fist of support to my victory that evening. A night remembered as the triumph closing a dark period when hunger had lost its charm. We never thought it could happen . . .

I loved my boat. Ole musty sad eyes rocked steady— faded but proud. This was a feeling I knew—the bond between a runaway slave and her illicit, rent-free place of rest. The abandoned buildings, rooftops, storage sheds, that treehouse in Fort Collins . . . A union sealed tight with that "not allowed to be there" allure. Like together you're both in on a real big secret. The couches are forgotten, the names of my hosts fade, but that abandoned pizza parlor in Santa Rosa is the richest of memories— the moldy mattress, self-installed lock, a couple hundred giant rats . . . "Squalor," they say, but when properly contextualized—glory and grandeur. Creating something from nothing—and the freedom that follows has side effects generally characterized as "bad for business." It's the love of the almost-oppressed towards our secret places of refuge, the connection of the almost-desperate with the shadows in which we hide, the sneaky admiration of the almost-fugitives towards our co-conspirators. In an underground existence, the inside joke of doing it right under their nose can bring you to sit up and stroke the walls . . . The rent-free youth all know the feeling—it's not "your" property, but it's your secret, and by the flicker of candlelight, you've never felt so at home . . .

I owned neither calendar nor watch, only a date on the paper at my table manifested the actual extent to what I'd almost thought was books in the fog *forever.* We had a cross-country road trip planned, to the *other* coast; where maybe I would find another boat, whose owner had a *longer* sentence, or just fell over the side.

I snuggled with ole cozy boat one last night . . .

I stared at her ceiling, thinking of my two weeks in her belly—costing only "a chance taken." Perhaps one day they *will* start asking me to pay for this stuff. But until then . . .

I'm on vacation!

FOUR

MEMOIRS OF A DUMPSTER DIVER
EXPOSING INDUSTRIAL WASTE AND EATING IT
DUMPSTER LOVE
PICKING UP WHAT YOU WANT AND RUNNING FOR IT
LOSS PREVENTION EXPOSED
GAINFUL UNEMPLOYMENT

It seemed an absurd idea—that everything necessary to live could be found in a dumpster. But for a long time, I had been hearing things . . . hearing things on the street, and reading things in zines—of self-sufficiency through dumpster diving, and a renegade faction of society living and prospering on what we throw away. And I began to look at our wasteful habits. Dumpster wealth no longer seemed an absurdity, but a naïve oversight which had taken me years to awaken to. Yes, in the late 20th century it made perfect sense. We value nothing. We make things—like trash bags—just to be thrown away. Life is disposable—we take a life at each meal and call it food. So it would logically follow that food, clothing, anything and everything would be discarded as well. But one hundred bags of granola? That's puzzling . . .

It would be fun to speak of a profound instant of awakening when I cast away my past life and surrendered to the dumpster, but the process took years. Slowly I stopped paying for skateboard parts. The crazy loony-toons at the skate shop threw away everything I needed. Those were the years of materialistic dumpster pursuits, before I began reading books and thinking about a different life. It seemed the most common apartment building find was televisions. Now I believe a dumpster is exactly where a TV belongs, but in the early days I collected them. I no longer paid for bikes, record needles, or *Thrasher Magazine*. I started buying more records and less of everything else. The supermarket had a dumpster as big as my house, full of fruits and vegetables. So I stopped paying for food. But that supermarket was so easy to steal from I never paid for food anyway.

It hardly seemed a fruitful endeavor—like, why would they just *throw* valuable things away? I was skeptical . . . until I began lifting lids. The ten working VCRs at Blockbuster Video convinced me. To a dumpster diver, everyday is Christmas! And Christmas is boring. All the stores are closed, it's the same trash from the 24th.

Dumpster diving could save the world, I believe that strongly. Reducing consumption and living on what others throw away was the last recourse for a dying planet. Maybe the environment's destruction could be reversed through dumpster diving— removing the giant plastic lid of secrecy from our wasteful practices, bringing America to face its trash and answer for itself. Somehow maybe I *could* expose the criminal waste that lay behind every business—in the dumpster. Mainstreaming dumpster diving seemed improbable, and in my suburb—impossible. All I could do was speak out. But I was left to stand alone, and for years to dig through trash—alone.

Preaching salvation through trash, I was up against a lifetime of upper-middle-class conditioning. "You'll get sick and die eating that food," they said. The living-dead of the "work force" giving health advice. By what logic was food deadly the moment it entered a trash bag, or passed through the back door? Food that had been on the shelf hours prior. It was a naïve faith in the purity of store-bought food, and a staunch sureness of trash as poison. Almost funny. Well, I couldn't be sure where they learned their garbage superstition, but they paid for it each day from 9-5. It was sad, deep-rooted conditioning. Conditioning of benefit to the corporations only, at the expense of millions of broken backs and wasted lives of those who work to eat. All so well trained . . .

But the conditioning affected everyone, even amongst our own ranks—the bums! Sigh . . . In the city, I couldn't even give away Fig Newtons to the homeless and indigent— nobody would accept trash. Maybe I was the loony one. I mean, I could listen to abrasive anti-god music, display disturbing antisocial behavior, eat only plants, and somehow I was still tolerated. Until dumpster diving became my favorite hobby, then . . . exiled from middle-class society. Which was fine. I didn't need them, I needed their trash.

I wondered what crafty and subtle methods would convince my friends that trash could set them free. Certainly they would have to be tricked. Sometimes, out with friends, I would route our path past some of the suburbs' more fruitful dumpsters. "Look . . ." I would say, as we passed the thrift store dumpster, "Record players, books, furniture. . ." Most were not convinced. "Get out of there, let's go, you're embarrassing . . ." In denial of visual evidence—clearly there was a sinister behind-the-scenes bourgeois influence at work. Nonbelievers had to be dealt with militantly—like my parents. I would offer them food without revealing its source. Or sneakily cook them entire dumpster meals, in violation of the "no dumpstered food in the kitchen" rule. They would eat with cheer, praising my culinary skills, unknowingly defeating their own arguments as they ate "garbage" . . . and loved it. It was my secret tool, to use as leverage in any future debate on the merits of dumpster diving. "Hey mom, remember that fried eggplant dish last week . . . ?"

My more progressive friends were mildly curious. They would see my dumpstered stereo or furniture, or extensive collection of Atari games, raise an eyebrow, and say—"Someone threw *that* away?" Some were open to it, and asked to come along on a dumpster excursion, but remained skeptical. Then, when they didn't find a Super Nintendo or VCR on the first trip—gave up, retired, said, "I told you so." If they were looking strictly for material wealth, I said don't bother, or made sure they wouldn't find it. They were the people I was happy to see slave away in the rat race. The politics of dumpster diving were lost on them completely. They wanted "free stuff," middle-class amenities. Of course sustenance, not material wealth, was the true motive . . .

Although, in practice, I was hardly an ascetic. There were the tempting dumpsters I would pass each day, the dumpsters so rich in treasure they would luminesce with a gilded glow. I had a fine pair of shoes, but how could I pass up the dozens of free shoes to be found in the skateshop dumpster? A shoe collection, yes, I should have been ashamed. And when preaching a righteous life of simplicity, I hoped no one would notice my dumpstered Star Wars toy collection.

Words are ignored—better to lead by example. Out with my friends, we might stop at a supermarket. They would enter through the front, and I would go around back, meeting them at the car with a bag of bread or a crate of produce. They would stare with an anticipatory smile as I ate, waiting for me to turn blue and die. Or point to an apple with a minor cosmetic imperfection, proof that dumpstered food was inferior, smugly convinced my entire argument for subsistence through waste had been discredited.

I grew weary, quit preaching. But someone would always ask where I got this or that—my speakers, or, like, my 100 boxes of valentines cards, and I would tell them the truth. Except when my parents asked about their Christmas presents—then I lied.

And it would always bring pleasure to see a friend slowly come around. They might cautiously take a sip of my dumpstered carrot juice, or eat one post-dated potato chip. I would beam, so proud of them, because I too was deathly afraid of dumpstered food at one time. It took so long to strip away the layers of conditioning like so many banana peels, so long to overcome the fear, and much longer to overcome the shame . . . And I think to when I would sneak discarded bagels to eat alone in dark corners . . .

In my town, preaching the basic necessities of life to be found in the trash was met with disinterest. I should have seen that, in suburbia, the basics of life were already provided. On my way home from the video store dumpster with a bag of videos, or video games discarded for no obvious reason, I would run into a friend, and they would ask, "What's in the bag?" and I would tell them. I should have known when you let the kids in on your secret, when the suburban kids learn video games, stereos, and CDs lay beneath the dumpster lid, the kids just might put on gloves and start digging! And they did, for all the wrong reasons . . .

It was tragic. I lifted dumpster lids in my neighborhood to see the dumpsters had clearly been picked through. In the city I would have smiled, happy to see the lower class becoming militant, repossessing food that belonged to them. But this was the suburbs, the homeless in my town were run out as they crossed the city line. No, it was the kids, whoever they were . . . and they transgressed every law of dumpster diving—"leave the area surrounding the dumpster cleaner than you found it," etc. I would find torn bags and trash strewn around my favorite dumpsters. Bad for community relations. Store managers and shopkeepers grew frustrated, padlocking our spots of choice. What had I created?!

I set out to reclaim the dumpsters from those killing the scene. The word was put out in the hood—stop or be stopped.

The kids, whoever they were, fell off or sold out in a few weeks, and I was left to clean up the mess. With padlocked dumpsters, sabotage, really, is the only solution. Dumpster liberation can be won through the "Universal Dumpster Key," or the other method: superglue. Using the Universal Key was sketchy because . . . well, because walking the streets with four-foot bolt cutters always looks sketchy. So I was left to roam the streets at night, under the cloak of darkness, jamming dumpster padlocks with glue. The shopkeepers would cut off the lock, and replace it. After a few midnight visits and jammed locks they would quit replacing them, surrender, and the dumpster would be returned to the people. It was Robin Hood vandalism.

So the suckers were weeded out of the scene, and the loyal few remained. We organized, formed the *Royal Family Dumpster Crew*. We screened t-shirts—"Dumpster Diving is Not a Crime." Our first ambitious project was the "Dump-umentary," a video document of the local dumpster scene. We began filming, honorably enough, with a B&W 8mm-camera dumpstered at the local thrift store.

We toured the area's finest dumpsters and recorded some impressive dives. We traded the food we collected for interviews with the two or three homeless dumpster diving pros we met along the way, and solicited on-camera editorials from random suburbanites about their feelings on "the dumpster diving trend sweeping the youth of America." They would express shock and disgust, and we would give them a loaf of stale bread.

Odd, it seemed, that dumpster diving was viewed as a habit of poverty, used as a last recourse of the desperate to provide just enough to scrape by. If people were starving or just scraping by on trash, they weren't dumpster diving in my town. As a dumpster diver—with so much food, and the race to eat it all before spoilage—I've gained weight. It was, in fact, easier to get carried away with excessive materialistic pursuits as a dumpster diver than as a paying consumer. VCRs, video games, any number of unnecessary distractions waited to be rescued, and our rescue missions yielded all that and more. We weren't rich—we didn't even have any money—but as long as no one saw our bank accounts, we had everyone fooled.

But from one extreme to the other—gluttony to abnegation—we shed the clutter and felt voluntary simplicity was a better path. And when we found a new home—rent free—we could break free from all that held us back: our jobs. So along with the bagels and love letters, the books and credit card receipts, we found liberation . . . stained with coffee grounds.

There were the little nuances of dumpster diving learned through experience: Never dive the pet store dumpster. In any apartment complex at the end of the month, people lose their minds, or something, and throw everything away. The best things are never within arm's reach, you have to *get in*. Food expiration dates are a diver's best friend. If there isn't a local law against dumpster diving (there never is), the police will invent one. Explaining dumpster diving to anyone is impossible, you have to live it. Your neighbor has the appearance of a puritanical family man—he's not, I've read his mail. They say that girl is a model of white-bread saintliness—she's not, I found spring break pictures of her behind the photomat. People have confidence that to throw something in the wastebasket is to erase it from existence. It makes for good reading. If you like the store, you'll love their dumpster. The apartment dumpsters surrounding the University of Oregon at semester's end—*MOTHER OF GOD!!!*

There were the fun little ongoing wars with management at certain stores, the battles that made us feel we were on a righteous crusade instead of just digging through trash—the "hot" dumpsters where it was guaranteed we had only seconds to dig before being thrown out. Like that drug store manager—we were sure he had radar. And the thrift store manager, who, over time, was able to insult us by name. Sometimes I think our fears of violent crime and life without TV are surpassed only by our fear of the poor. Which would explain the most common reaction to a stranger in their trash: fleeing in horror. Many of these store managers wanted us desperately to leave their dumpster alone. They feared us, and they feared a confrontation with us—the savages. The most hilarious form of response were dumpster signs—like the bookstore who wrote "Trash pickers will be arrested," on the dumpster lid. We responded with our own message, and they wrote back! This, over weeks, expanded into a philosophical debate on dumpster diving, in black ink, on the dumpster lid. The supermarket left us a sign as well—"This food is poisoned." What type of poison works best on dumpster divers anyway? Bleach? Rat poison? "Poisoned . . ." They wanted us dead. You never feel like a threat until the enemy decides you're too dangerous to *live*. It was sort of flattering. Clearly they didn't understand our psychology. A more effective deterrent would read "Free food here." We wanted free food, but we wanted to fight for it. The best dumpster sign was at the used record store—who apparently grew so tired of us cutting their locks, that they declared a truce. In a rare act of diplomacy between retail management and the underclass, a sign was erected—"Attention dumpster divers," it read, "the dumpster will now be left unlocked every Tuesday during business hours." The terms of the compromise were, of course, completely unacceptable. Sooo . . . that would mean we could only pull bags of records and tapes from their dumpster and sell it all back to them on *Tuesdays*?

If at times it all seemed like a big "us vs. them" war, we were reminded that we did have allies sympathetic to the cause. Diving for bagels was always messy, until our friend the bagel man started bagging the bagels, just for us, and leaving them behind the dumpster. Those who grumble about the suburbs don't know the suburbs—suburbia has borne some of our kindest sympathizers, our most ardent supporters. There were the kids who lived behind the drug store, who looked up to us, and would hop the fence and say hi when they saw us digging. And the random inexplicable incidents when people saw us diving, and— somehow assuming we were needy—gave us money. They would tell us to buy ourselves some food. Paying for food was a crazy idea, we wouldn't think of it. All money went for music— food for the soul. Our *best* friends were the behind-the-scenes benefactors—those throwing it all away. Perhaps the Corporate Man was on *our* side, maybe the wasteful practices of the corporate machine were for *us*. It would explain our most common question, the one where we would hold something up to the light, examine it from all angles, and ask—why would they throw *this* away?

Did I mention the moments of shame? The skeletons in a dumpster diver's closet, deviant acts in violation of proper dumpster conduct. Disregarding the dictum "Trash for sustenance not profit." Like dumpstering several 7-foot posters of Jimi Hendrix and Madonna, and a feeble attempt to sell them in an abandoned storefront. The rain pouring, mumbling, "Posters, two dollars,"—and retreating, humiliated. It was a corrupt exploitation of dumpster diving. Or dumpstering 30 boxes of Aplets and Cotlets candy, and a botched attempt to sell it all—taking over a table at the entrance to a local mall with a crude little sign—"Support Northside baseball." A man bought two boxes, then returned demanding to know why the boxes were slashed with a box-cutter. Walgreens slashed the boxes for exactly this reason—to prevent resale. I didn't tell the man that, I just refunded his two dollars and skated off in defeat. A lesson learned—"sustenance not profit." Ignore that and you'll fail every time.

That's actually not at all true, selling dumpster wares is great supplemental income. Never mind what I said before.

· There is the odd paradox—the casualness with which they will throw something into the dumpster, and the lengths they go to to protect it once it's there. How an innocent and harmless act—dumpster diving—will be confronted by greedy shopkeepers, store managers, and employees with scathing words, rage, and violence. Memory fails to produce a single anecdote, just hundreds of insults, shoves, screams, threats, and police calls that all blur together. These dumpster confrontations are 2/3 the fun, often absurdly hilarious. I think of the countless debates with store managers—me in the dumpster, them shaking their fist from the back door. Get a job? You're calling the police? The only people who went to greater extremes in the name of trash than us were those who threw it all away. Threats, insults, taking license plate numbers and dumping trash on my head. The dozens of times I have asked why they would rather see waste go to a landfill than the mouth of a hungry person. Hearing empty arguments and bitter insults, getting frustrated and saying they should be ashamed of their greed—you filthy bourgeois demons. And it never feels right to just walk away from a confrontation without fighting back, without some form of dumpster diver revenge. Not vengeance in a macho sense, but too often social deviants "yessir" the man and are pushed around without resistance. So when they snarl, I snarl back. I'm not here to make friends. But winning a verbal battle is unimportant—when I walk away to visit the next dumpster, or read a book, or do as I please, I look back at the man straightening his tie and returning to work. That's victory!

There was the clear trend towards the obsolescence of dumpster diving, disquieting reminders that one day we might all have to get jobs and start paying for things. One by one, slowly, the dumpsters were becoming trash compactors—giant, impenetrable, trash eating machines; rendered inoperable only through high explosives. The installation of a trash compactor was a final defeat after an often well fought battle, comparable to *Bugs Bunny vs. Elmer Fudd* cartoons, where each pulls out a weapon bigger than the other until Bugs has, like, a *tank* . . . Well we didn't have a tank, but as their dumpster padlocks grew larger, so did our bolt cutters. And when it was all over, there were only two possible outcomes—victory or trash compactor. We did, you see, take a more militant approach to dumpster diving . . .

We looked forward to the defeats. We embraced a challenge. The thrilling escapes and dangerous failures always made the best stories. They say most criminals secretly want to be caught. I don't think our dumpster related crime was a "cry for help," we just wanted to be punk and make a narrow escape now and then. The games at the local arcade awarded tickets, which could be redeemed for prizes. Five tickets for gum, 50 for baseball cards, 5,000 for a Super Nintendo, etc. The setup—viewed through dumpster-colored glasses—raised the question, "Where do the tickets go?" And the dumpster was, of course, filled with tickets. We snatched several bags and dragged them around the corner. We had at least enough tickets for five Super

Nintendos. It seemed too easy. But it *always* seems too easy. The manager flew around the corner moments later, shaking his finger, "Don't even *think* about redeeming those!" We dragged the garbage bags home and counted out 5,000 tickets. And in the brazenness of youth, returned the next day in crude disguise for our Super Nintendo. Maybe our photos were posted in the break room, maybe the kid had been given our descriptions, maybe they knew that *no one* accumulates 5,000 tickets. When I handed the girl at the prize counter my neatly boxed and rubber-banded 5,000 dumpstered tickets, she just looked at me and said, "Where did you *really* get these . . . *where!?*" Yes, there were the dives that were too good to be true. Why would the chain record store throw away a small bag of unwrapped CDs? I hadn't heard Jimmy Buffet, but I was sure I would like the new Snapcase CD better. Taking advantage of their soft return policy, I took my loot inside to the cashier— "Hi, I wanted to exchange these, I lost my receipt . . ." etc. etc. The cashier just looked at my CDs, "Hey . . ."—and looked at me— "I threw these out yesterday!"

I wondered who the barbarians were, the contemptible. Those operating the machine, enslaving the people, and bleeding the Earth dry. Producing things only to throw them away, digging a hole only to fill it up again. Or those who saw the absurdity of it all, and chose to humbly wait in the shadows of that machine and pick up the crumbs.

Last year the dumpster divers made national news when the Malt-O-Meal company reported that midnight bandits had removed *thousands* of bags of cereal from the dumpsters of their factory! The war had begun! Time to put a gun to the head of corporate America—give us your trash!

Factories, duh. Of course . . . it all seemed so obvious now. For years we had limited ourselves to the retail circuit . . . totally amateurish. The suburbs had great trash, no doubt, but if the health food store threw away a few cases of soymilk a week, what about the soymilk *factory*? How much did *they* throw away?! It was very upsetting to think of trash being thrown in dumpsters we had somehow overlooked in our own neighborhood. So, in an act of solidarity with the Malt-O-Meal pioneers, we decided to take their bold and innovative approach to dumpster diving on the road! This was a trip I could get excited about . . .

We visited the local health food store with notepads. Penny took the cereal aisle. Stitch took the cooler. I took the baked goods and snacks. We pulled food off shelves, examined labels, took down addresses, and noticed an obvious pattern—the best vegan foods are made in California! And it was our theory that, consequently, the best foods would be *thrown away* in California. Um, wait . . . we'd been proving that for years! Well road trips are always fun anyway . . .

Looking at our food factory address list, the Bay Area specifically appeared to be the epicenter of health food companies. We decided to make our first dive the Naked Juice Company in Santa Rosa, makers of fresh squeezed juice. So obsessive was my Naked Juice habit, I once found myself face-to-face with a company "high-up" at a product promotion—and for 20 minutes assaulted her with questions on Naked Juice! I stood mesmerized over "inside" facts on the carrot juice process, like how the machine was the size of one whole supermarket aisle, and noted a thinly veiled intercompany jealousy—"Odwalla's a great company, but . . ." And in one of my proudest moments, *the* Naked Juice lady looks me in the eye and says—"You know a lot about juice!" She gave me a sample, we shook hands, then I picked up a quart of carrot juice and stole it! The Naked Juice factory was buried deep in the seedy industrial ghetto. We crept up—real sneakily—down the long driveway, through the barbed-wire fence, totally excited about what might be a carload of Naked Juice. I had watched the Naked Juice vendor stocking the cooler at Safeway for years, hauling crates of post-dated juice to his truck, destined for the dumpster, and well, it just didn't seem fair. To obtain what we needed, some of us paid, some of us stole, and some of us went without, but most of what we all needed always ended up in the dumpster . . . Deep behind property lines, we found the dumpsters, licked our lips, and looked in, but . . . all fruit peels! Where's the juice? The life of perishable food followed a predictable timeline, the end of which was usually the trash. So you see, this was totally puzzling. Across the lot, a woman noticed us standing by the dumpsters, our hands full of carrot tops, sobbing.

"Can I help you?" she said.
I gave the standard produce dumpster stand-by line—
"Oh, we're just looking for rabbit feed."
"Rabbit feet??!!"
"No, no, *feed*, for rabbits."
"Feed them orange peels!"
"You'd be surprised how picky rabbits are."
Etc. etc. It was a pleasant exchange.

We left for Barbara's, makers of Puffins and other tasty snacks. We hoped to find our favorite cereal—Barbara's Raisin Bran, which we discovered last spring when Trader Joe's left a 24-box case on their loading dock! Since then we've been brand loyal. The Barbara's factory is located a conveniently short walk from the Sonoma County Poultry Processor's slaughterhouse in Petaluma, so, if you had no luck at Barbara's, you could walk up the street and dumpster chicken heads. Yuck. We parked and prowled and found the dumpsters—all empty! And in fact spotlessly clean inside, leaving us to wonder if the dumpster was a dummy to throw us off the track—sort of like that Whole Foods dumpster marked "Cardboard Only," but full of food!

We went around front to demand some answers. The door was open, the lights on, all the signs of an operational business, but, no *people*! From the lobby, we stuck our heads in the production room with all the crazy big cereal making machines. It was all very eerie, like what one experiences in a 24-hour supermarket at 3 a.m. We could, like, just walk over, hit the switch on the raisin bran machine and *shoot cereal into our mouths*! There seemed no reason we couldn't spend all night calling our friends from the offices upstairs, loading up the car with food, and rearranging the furniture. We ran upstairs to explore and surprised a straggling worker. No, wait, I think we *scared* the man! We had him cornered. Stitch stammered and asked something about a tour. "Uh, you want a tour?" What we *wanted* was that fax machine over there. He told us to come back tomorrow. We probably had a few minutes before the police arrived, so we walked down the stairs and took our time admiring the framed portraits of the Barbara's owners, directors, executives . . . the smug-looking CEO, the president, vice president, the . . . wait a minute . . . no *Barbara*! She didn't exist! It was a shocking moment exposing deception and deceit in the health food industry. In non-violent protest, we pulled a case in the lobby displaying their product line away from the wall, slid open the back, and ran out to the car with armloads of food!

The Fantastic Foods factory had us excited. Fantastic Foods makes widely distributed healthy foods—Nature's Burger, Cha-Cha Chili, Falafel, Tofu Scramble, etc. We pulled up, saw the huge factory, the billowing smoke stacks, the massive warehouse, the row of Fantastic Foods semi-trucks, and sighed. I thought about how I'd walk out of Whole Foods with Puffins, or any one of my favorite foods from big health food companies. Then how I'd sit outside, like, by the payphones, eat my food, and read the package. And how all the companies put a little picture of a rugged but glowing old man in a flannel shirt or something, with a very personal letter explaining his crusade to save the Earth, and *your* health, and that 1% of the profits go to save the rainforest. Then the authentic-looking signature at the bottom, always concluding with some warm and homely parting words like, "From our kitchen to yours . . ." Sigh . . . We looked at that huge complex and, well, it was heartbreaking. And a total slap in the face to find no dumpsters, only a row of trash compactors—the bane of dumpster divers. Like I said—heartbreaking . . .

To explain how much Rice Dream vegan ice cream products mean to each of us, how far we went to avoid paying for it, and how excited we were to be headed to the Imagine Foods factory would be futile, hopelessly limiting using the written word, and probably best expressed through improvisational dance. We were giddy, giggling children on Christmas morning. It would require perfect timing to retrieve still frozen Rice Dream from the dumpster. But we were prepared, in true transient form, to *wait* by the dumpster, for hours or forever, until they threw away a batch. I've always respected and enjoyed the company of the grumpy, old, scruffy homeless guys that hung out by the supermarket dumpsters just drinking hairspray and spitting on people all day. The address in Palo Alto looked suspiciously like an office building, and was in fact only the Imagine Foods corporate offices. The building was locked, and we couldn't even schmooze with the secretary or go inside, or anything . . .

We are still to this day looking for the Rice Dream factory, and still taking wild and unnecessary risks at retail centers to get our fix. But it's heartwarming to think that maybe, somewhere, vagrants like us *do* know where the factory is—and just hang out by the dumpster, plastic spoons in hand, waiting for the throwaways and eating rice-based frozen desserts—all day!

Clif Bars are small, individually wrapped bars. Like candy, but made with oats and no sugar. We all ate Clif Bars nearly everyday at home, sometimes *all* day. It's fun to visit the health food section at Safeway and reach far back in the shelf for a *sealed case* of Clif Bars, left-hand the whole thing, and not have to think about food for a couple of days. It's hard to fully respect Clif Bar Inc. when their product is so shamelessly marketed towards sporty middle-class white people as an "energy boost" of "complex carbohydrates" needed to "sustain a peak level of performance" in today's fast-paced world, etc. etc. None of us rock climbed, or ran (without being chased), and eating Clif Bars in parking lots all day never quite felt like the fast lane, but Clif Bars, to us, were an essential food group.

The Clif Bar plant wasn't far from Telegraph Avenue in Berkeley, just west in a sketchy industrial neighborhood. The Clif Bar wrappers boasted—"So good, you'll think it's home-baked." And of course it's not home-baked, but in fact baked in a big scary fortress behind a tall barbed wire fence. We hung on the fence, looking in, the dumpster taunting us from across the parking lot. I don't know what happened—it's probably analogous to a mother, who, upon seeing her child trapped under the wheels of a truck, somehow draws up an inhuman amount of strength and *lifts* the truck a foot off the ground to save her kid. In a similarly heated moment, our emotions boiled over, we *ripped* the sliding gate off its track, and stormed the dumpster! Certainly thousands of Clif Bars lay inside! We would continue to drive around the country, eating Clif Bars forever! We dove! Bags ripped! Trash flew! The bums across the street cheered!

And when it was all over, we sat in the car, trying to figure out how to divide four Clif Bars three ways . . .

The nonbelievers will say there are some things that cannot be stolen, scammed, or dumpstered. And those people probably do not live in my town. Because, I learned, if the imagination can conceive of it, it's certainly laying at the bottom of a dumpster at this moment, or sitting on a shelf without an alarm tag somewhere nearby. "Money?" they ask, the implication being that without money our system was flawed, incomplete. When in fact our lifestyle had stripped money of its value, reduced it to an inefficient and indirect means of acquiring what we just stole or pulled from the trash. Though—at great risk of legitimizing their assertion that money was indispensable—I would mention that I *had* dumpstered money . . . once. So there. "You can't dumpster dive everything . . ." Oh yeah? ". . . not love." No one ever actually said this, the idea is too absurd. No one will ever open a Hefty bag and discover *love*. Though my friends visited the adult bookstore dumpster and came close. Still, the thought inspired long-running jokes between us—of curiously approaching the produce dumpster to investigate the rustling sound coming from within. Lifting the lid, and staring into the big eyes of a dumpster queen. Seeing her elegant form, the telltale hunch of a dumpster professional. The rising passion at the sight of Folgers crystals glistening in her hair. The arousing ever-so-slight scent of mold. Our eyes meeting and both knowing no trash compactor would ever separate us. The extravagant wedding at the city dump, with milk crate pews, the Hefty bag gown, and hoboes hopping trains in from around the country to witness the union of two strangers brought together by a love of trash. Dumpster Love . . .

Such a scenario, over time, didn't seem such a stretch. After years of dumpster diving, it came to be expected that each dumpster score would top the previous, and that there was in fact nothing the dumpster wouldn't provide. And a close analysis of my recent relationships reveals a dumpster connection to each. Because they say you can't buy love, but it can be dumpstered!

Let me explain . . .

Betty was the one that got away. She worked in the produce department of my favorite supermarket. I would see her each day along my normal route, when I passed through the store to steal juice. It was sweet how, in the early days, she would always help out a struggling derelict dedicated to a jobless existence, happy to render a peach or apple legally unsalable by "accidentally" dropping it on the ground. Food off the ground tastes as good or better than food from the dumpster! My love is given freely to any vegan, and Betty was animal-free and more. She was also involved in the straight-edge Hardcore scene. Maybe *too* involved—her boyfriend was a big scenester. That didn't mean I loved the Hardcore tapes she gave me any less, even if they were his. And in my dreams, the boyfriend was omitted—it was just her and me forever. Then I was certain I could never like her more when one morning, in the supermarket, next to the bananas, conversation turned to dumpster diving. She said she was curious, interested even, and that we should definitely get together soon and go dumpster diving. Shucks. I told everyone I knew. Betty was going dumpster diving . . . with *me*.

The anti-climactic conclusion to this story of lost love is this—we never got together. We never went dumpster diving. I never called her—I was too nervous. Betty never called me—I didn't have a phone. I saw Betty less and less. And then I stopped seeing her at all—they kicked me out of that supermarket for life.

If Betty was white, Molly was black. Betty Alien Workshop, Molly Ralph Lauren. Betty Earth Crisis, Molly Madonna—circa 1984. Molly was a comically pattern L.A. girl, by the book, reinforcing every stereotype. Heavy make-up, dyed hair, thick accent—thick *valley girl* accent. Her family was obscenely wealthy, with a big house in the hills. Our brief relationship was an almost successful attempt to deprogram her of a lifetime of upper-class training. She stopped eating meat, and that was a start. Then she stopped shopping at the mall, and started wearing my clothes. The punk transformation was underway. My habits were becoming hers. She took quickly to shoplifting at Barnes and Noble, and became quite skilled. My tastes were becoming hers. But that ended at Vegan Reich—she hated that band. My life was becoming hers. But that ended at dumpster diving. No way, she said, never. Yet, like the straight-edge condemnation of those who sell out: "If you're not now, you never were," I tell my non-dumpster-friendly friends: "If you're not now, you will be" . . .

She seemed to bend slightly. One night, as a love offering, I brought her a bag of dumpstered vitamins, many of the same vitamins her "Personal Nutrition Counselor" had recommended. "Why would they throw these away? They must be bad," she said. I told her they were past expiration date, an arbitrary date set by over-cautious regulators and bearing no indication of when a product would truly be spoiled. She took the vitamins, didn't die, and I sensed the relationship was really going places—a more solid kinship, deeper respect, the dumpster, etc. etc.

It was a dazzling transformation, a slowly progressing valley girl rehabilitation. But she still had the accent, still hated Vegan Reich, and would still never go near a dumpster. I begged her, told her if she wouldn't get in, if she wouldn't share my meals, she was still clinging to bourgeois standards—she was still one of *them*. I guaranteed fantastic treasures, made outrageous promises even the dumpster couldn't keep, and her creeping incremental progress was impressive. But at some point the line would have to be drawn and a side chosen—retail purchase price or me. Whatever the dumpster could give, she preferred the store-bought version. But when you take me, you take the dumpster too. It's a package deal.

At that time when nonbelievers are forced to look into the object of their fear, to face the dumpster, the foundation of their prejudice crumbles, and further denial of the wealth within is impossible. And so it was that one summer morning, when, on the way to the bus, we passed the thrift store dumpster. While I scavenged, she waited outside—probably tapping her toe, or nervously scanning the parking lot to see who was looking, probably embarrassed, and wishing we could just leave. Amongst the treasures I usually found in that dumpster—the toys and records and books and radios—I found a boxed and sealed Victoria's Secret makeup set. It was dumpster diving in a language Molly could understand. I stuck my head out and waved the find. She took the bait. "Let me see that . . ." I retreated back inside. Her head popped over the dumpster's edge. If she wanted the makeup, she would have to enter. Her head, then a leg . . . Hey! She was in!

Ginger could have been just another victim of two suburban kids with too much free time and an excess of dumpster food. A victim of the games that are played when bellies are full and an overgenerous dumpster provides more than can be eaten. What does one do with a backseat full of potato chips? They could be taken to a town, another town where poor people lived, and redistributed to the indigent, giving us the quieting of our conscience. Or we could do what we did do—drive around and throw them at pedestrians. We never aimed for the head, but if it was their head we hit, well it was the suburbs and they were probably guilty of something. We never let good food go to waste—never!

When we saw a girl walking on the sidewalk from a distance, I didn't need to tell Pauly what to do. He already had the window down and a bag of chips ready. We stopped alongside her. It's hard to be in motion and hit a moving target, though it should have been easy enough with that big "X" on the back of her shirt . . . wait . . . She turned to feel the force of a 16 oz. bag of Ruffles, but I had to stop Pauly. Her shirt read "Youth of Today" . . .

"Are you, uh, straight-edge?"

I gave her a ride home and a bag of chips. And today, Ginger is my best friend.

I was only looking for a good dumpster, and I found love.

* * *

Betty and I never had our dumpster date, she moved away long ago. But if I move fast and wear a hat, I'm still able to steal juice from that supermarket, the one that kicked me out for life.

Molly's last words to me were—"You're just a dirty little street rat." Click. I was sad, but my life could go on without that L.A. girl. And weeks later, I finally got my Vegan Reich CD back, and that was something to be happy about. But she got the last laugh. When I got home, I opened the Vegan Reich CD—and where the CD should be, I found a neatly trimmed piece of bologna.

Ginger lost her edge, sold out, fell off, and was just recently released from rehab. But she is still my best friend, and she taught me that there is nothing that can't be found in a dumpster . . . even love.

We were three very unemployed and broke criminals driving around the country pioneering entirely new shop-lifting techniques. It all began from sheer necessity and snowballed into a dangerous game of thrills with consumerist overtones. A reckless inter-city theft-campaign along our U.S. interstates. A crime spree inspired by the feeling that we—as thieves—were too passive, our tactics too stale and predictable. After years of prolific, indiscreet, and carelessly frequent thefts around our hometown, we began to think the local retail community was indifferent, and may in fact allow and even silently *encourage* our crimes! This, of course, was totally unacceptable. We wanted to fight. We had been going through the motions—which was always effective—but stealing almost wasn't fun anymore! The shoplifting scene was stagnant, conventional methods of theft no longer stimulating. Going out the *front* door was, like, so *last year* . . . It was time to make shoplifting a threat again!

Somewhere near death and disease, I expressed the need for militancy. I loved the bagels we had been eating for the past 3 days—bagels were great, maybe the best food *ever*—but several dumpster food groups were not represented in our diet. We needed to seize lots of nutritious food, liberate it from corporate clutches. We'll take what we want and walk. Strip away the nonsense. Because, you know, sometimes pockets just aren't big enough . . .

We pulled off the interstate and found a Trader Joe's—the west coast chain of vegan-friendly grocery stores. We walked into the back room to use the restroom and found ourselves all alone with a wide-open back door! It seemed too easy, like a *trap* for shoplifters. Reminding me of the *Hobo Trap* used by the railroads early in the century—where an open boxcar was placed in a very visible and accessible spot in the train yard as a bait for hoboes. When a bull in the tower saw a freight-hopper climb in, he pushed a button—shutting the doors to the boxcar and *trapping* the 'bo! So maybe Trader Joe's was baiting us into a big net or something. Or maybe retail management just might be *stupid!* We were hungry.

"So, uh . . . get the car."

The successful raid that followed marked an empowering progression in shoplifting—where we entered through the front door, but went out through the back! Our new "M.O." had somehow been overlooked for all these years. We had clung to stale techniques and stubbornly rejected any innovation. This must have been what meat-eaters meant when they called us "narrow-minded." This new, dangerously addictive process was straightforward—two of us entered the store, filled up a basket or cart, looked left, looked right, busted out the back door, loaded up the car, and made a screeching getaway!

It could have ended there, *should* have ended there. Theft beyond the basics of survival is dangerous and unnecessary. We had stolen food to last a week, brought clothing, and shelter . . . well, shelter was way overrated. So for several days we ate well, laughed, and saw the Trader Joe's backdoor as an isolated anomaly. But we all knew that as criminal-minded kids, our perspective had taken an irreversible shift. We had "opened the door," so to speak, on a new and wildly excessive theft technique.

It didn't help that Rite-Aid left the side gate to their outdoor nursery wide open and unguarded. We weren't looking for trouble, but really, were we supposed to *not* fill up a basket and walk out? When the side door is open, the camera department guy pulls a CD player from the case for us, and then *walks away*, wouldn't it logically follow that we'd creep out through the nursery? Duh!

Our tactics became progressively more brazen . . . The outdoor garden departments at Target and Wal-Mart became our preferred points of exit—where we could, in total disregard for safety and self-preservation, push shopping carts of food and stereo equipment out the huge, unmanned gates. We drove around the valley, laughing through mouthfuls of expensive food at the irony of Wal-Mart placing a security guard at the front door, and leaving a 30 ft. wide gate open and unmonitored in back. We were riding this wave all the way to victory! How many shopping carts of merchandise does it take to bring down the corporate empire? Who cares!

I was the coach, Star acted as cheerleader, Penny drove the getaway car. Star was working on covering her rent with portable CD players. Penny had new furnishings for her apartment. I didn't pay rent, or have an apartment, but I did have a shiny new walkman! And so much more . . .

The material world was ours. If it could fit through the door, we owned it. But there is—Krishnas will say—no pleasure in a material existence, and in three days we had regressed from righteous anti-consumerist monks to slaves of the material world. Penny was the first to address what we had all lost sight of. She called a group meeting.

"What has become of us?!" she said, ". . . of our anti-consumerist ethic?"

We lowered our eyes in guilt.

"Are we opposed to over-consumption because we're too poor to over-consume?!"

Um . . .

"Do we resist the corporations because we can't afford what they're selling?!"

I looked at my new walkman, the CD player at my feet, the CD player at Star's feet, the Electric Breadmaker 2000 on my lap . . . We had sold out . . .

But of course we weren't finished . . . Taking our rash and heedless addiction to a bold new level, we went to Barnes & Noble, picked up a stack of coffee table books, and ran out the front door!

Penny's condemnation and the sheer excessiveness of our behavior had me racked with moral doubt, leading me to seek theological guidance. During the night, in a private moment, I went outside, dropped to my knees, and reached to the sky—

"If what we do is right . . ." I screamed, ". . . give me a sign!"

Thunder roared, the clouds parted, and a vision appeared of a giant fire exit in the sky; and I knew that ours was the righteous path . . .

* * *

Our hit-and-run compulsive disorder took an unscrupulous turn when we began visiting friends and fleeing out the back door with their houseplants!

I was at the chain bookstore one day in the suburbs, reading skateboard magazines. *Pretending* to read skateboard magazines, but listening to a conversation at my right—an undercover Loss Prevention Agent in training; learning to apprehend, detain, and prosecute me and my friends the shoplifters!

"Over 50% of our losses come from this section *here* . . ." the instructor said, pointing to the pornographic magazines. My friends and I stole travel and Loompanics books, what percentage did *we* represent? Don't we get any credit?!

"Never make eye contact with a suspect, they'll know you're onto them."

Hey! *Look* at me when I'm stealing from you!

"If you suspect someone of shoplifting, but are uncertain, watch as they exit. If they touch their head, or stretch, they are probably stealing."

Dear god. I wondered how many shoplifters were locked away in laboratories undergoing testing and observation to get this information, and shuddered at the truth of it. The "nervous stretch"—an exaggerated attempt to appear casual and blasé, as if to say, "Look at me, I'm so relaxed I'm *stretching*." What else did they know?! What about slipping Punk Planet inside the free weekly paper? Or left-handing Def Jam box sets? Or removing the CDs, filling with AA batteries, resealing and returning those box sets? Did they know about *that?!*

Bernadine worked at the super-supermarket. Just outside the usual loop, but always a walk no doubt worthwhile. Perfectly centered between the chain record store and the chain bookstore—the two choicest shoplifting spots. After liberating CDs and *Vegetarian Times,* I would fade into the crowd of supermarket shoppers, retreat to the café, read, and eat leftovers. Bernadine worked in the deli, slicing meat. I held it against her. Nonetheless I would visit her across the store, though it was always uncomfortable being greeted by a good friend with bloody gloves. One day she pointed a bloody glove at a man by the entrance. She told me my shop-lifting and bulk food grazing was fully secure, and could continue indefinitely if I avoided *that man*. That man, she revealed, was the undercover security guard. The bane of shoplifters—unmasked! First instinct was violence—to bla-tantly steal a bottle of olive oil, and when he chased me into an alley, kill him with the bottle and leave a warning to the retail security profession scrawled in his blood. Blood spilled for the countless hungry and desperate in jail for that rascal's paycheck, the immoral wretch . . .

All other distractions faded into the background as I focused on the scoundrel. I moved closer and sat next to him at the espresso bar by the door. I watched as he screened each person who entered the store, assessing their appear-ance and holding it up to shoplifter stereotypes, determining the likely criminals. I took offense to entering without be-ing followed myself, my fashion apparently deemed as something other than that of a criminal. And if I looked the part of a consumer, then clearly I was one step closer to actually paying for things myself! Unthinkable!

I was the undercover shoplifter, spying on the spy, paid to spy on me. It was a rare glimpse into a secret profession. So I carried out a counter-surveillance mission, and it was the most fun I'd had that week. That time, I followed store security looking for insight into the techniques of loss pre-vention specialists. The hunter was now the hunted. As he eyed judiciously all who entered, it was clear he had no sus-picion of the well-dressed or elderly. Older people can get away with *anything*. Maybe I even looked forward to being old, and all the potential for huge risk-free supermarket heists—like "absent-mindedly" pushing a cart of food out the door. In the safety of a group, we did this as young people already; but as an elder I would definitely make it a regular habit, and if caught, play it off—"Duh! I'm old!" And even if theft wouldn't be as amusing in seniority as it was in youth, I wouldn't have a choice. I would never expect to receive social security checks—I never worked.

The undercover agent began trailing one of the less clean-cut shoppers, and I tailed them both. In bulk foods, I watched the security guard graze on M&Ms. In produce, he gobbled a peach. It was bizarre and awesome, a common supermarket scenario in reverse—following store security and watching *them* steal . . . Who was who?

* * *

That undercover security guard wore a disguise to blend in as a shopper—a bike helmet and spandex. Recently two friends were chased from that store by the new undercover agent, they told me she wears a disguise too . . . she dresses punk!

Christmas time, and Libby and I had a plan. Take the issues of "rent" & "vinyl" to the bourgeoisie—present them with a pre-written, possibly laminated list of "soft" stores, offering them anything from the aisles: half price. With this new approach, would we reach "organized crime" distinction? Walking untested waters, we found our first client—Libby's teenage sister—in fact wholly willing to *accept stolen property*! She'd get to work on a list right away!

The next morning—returning for the list and eager to "shop"—the door opened to a *scowly faced Mom*!

"Your sister told me everything."

Libby was disowned, I achieved "corruptive boyfriend" status, and we had a plan to rethink. 24 hours after inception, "shoplifting for profit"—a pitiful and smoldering wreck.

I should have learned my lesson. But sometimes, they make it too easy . . .

"Profit motive," to us criminals, was an ever-present, teasing thing. Amber ran with it, taking "illicit laptop source" towards felonious lines. Skip took it further—a fine employee-theft story losing my interest at "internet auction." And I'd never spoken with him, but suspected the clean-cut kid at the mall made untold hundreds—who knew cinema ticket-stub scams could go so far?

I stood to the side, watching them all—content with my 50¢ meals and free paperbacks. I saw this entrepreneurial approach as a distraction, and went to explore the waterfront somewhere. Profits? Groan . . . No, I don't need "profits."

Just record money.

And like I said—sometimes, they make it too easy . . .

* * *

I thought real hard, retracing my steps, but I'd never understand how I came to live *here*—with a husband, wife, two kids and a dog. Let's see . . . I'd hopped that train to Denver, almost died; hopped that train to Lincoln, almost starved; hopped that train to Chicago, almost imprisoned . . . Well it was a long way from Ogden, and the whole experience punctuated Omaha as the absurd inverse to a hobo summer. My own room in the basement of a suburban home the point furthest from my own room in the basement of a Lincoln library, the cooked vegan meals each night the polar counterpoint to the cold, stolen ones of summer. "Friends of friends" would be close. "Random quirk of circumstance" closer still. At night, with my head by the water heater, I'd count my money in the shadows. The batteries in the flashlight and mittens by the door told the story. I was suburbia's dark secret. The live-in shoplifter: fifty-cents on the dollar.

Let me back up . . .

Selling out—at that time and place—was critically close to an "option." After four months, I'd almost forgotten why falling off freight trains and stumbling through dark alleys was fun. Almost. But always, twelve hours after any such moment of infirmity, I would be on the high-school bleachers talking life with a total stranger, or riding up 101 in the passenger seat of a drunk's stolen car, and the feeling would return. If the crazy people didn't reinspire, my inevitable awakening to the warm touch of a stranger would. And when that warm touch from an angry property owner at 6 a.m. loses enchantment—check my pulse!

Certainly I'd been wet and limp in *this* town before, on these tracks. To sit down alongside the train yard with a pen and pad, maybe I could have sorted out this lapse in enthusiasm on paper. A convenient thought in reflection, but I was living it, in the rain, wondering if this is the part in the movie after the credits. I was certain the cameras had turned off when I'd made that dramatic dash onto the train in Chicago. No one wants to watch this: a dashing but wet vacationer, at 10 p.m., hobbling in the rain through the warehouse district looking for a payphone. It would be poor editing.

Skip answered the phone, building up fantastic hopes, then pulled up thirty minutes later to cut them down. A night on his couch, he said, was not to be. Visiting parents. With a 24-hour university library, I'd chosen my rainy-town-to-be-stranded-in sensibly. But explaining the triumphant thrill of twelve overnight hours in a corner chair to a domestic is hard-won, and without interpretive operatic juggling—impossible. He'd make some calls, he said. Oh yes, the "punk network"—highly efficient, even at 11 p.m. If Skip couldn't take me, the next kid in his address book would. If, at the final page, shelter remained unsecured—no one could take that corner chair from me. Because if I've proven one thing, it's—"Look like a student and the campus is yours." I don't make these rules . . .

"I'm taking you to the Jones'," he said. The Jones' weren't punk, but their kids might be one day . . .

Past the doghouse, behind the gazebo, next to the orange tree, in the backyard. The directions were precise, but said nothing of the "shack" being in fact a fully furnished guesthouse—futon, hot water dispenser, and cute little soup cups! Whatever lies Skip told to achieve me this wonder would be exposed in the morning, but now—I eat!

I don't know what happened, maybe I *charmed* them, but one night became several, the guesthouse–in-the-back became mattress-in-the-basement, and if I attempted "contributing" through housework—they'd curse at me! I'd always suspected this would happen—a middle-class family confusing clean-cut hoboism with genius, then adopting me and dragging me out for visitors. "The iconoclast as a novelty"—serving as the premise for nearly every relationship since 16, now complemented with the best curry tofu I'd ever had. Psychologists would call their hospitality a vicarious satiation of repressed wanderlust, Republicans a civically irresponsible handout to perpetuate my pauperism, but we—you know, the *rappers*—just called it "livin' large."

Somehow I never thought my adopted family would have kids—that part made me nervous. From my new place of actual residency, I stood in the optimum position to influence irreversible thought-crime in their children. But the criminalization of minors was no plan of mine. Inconceivable. I harbor no criminal-minded proclivity to "come for your daughters." Housewives are fair game . . .

Mrs. Jones was a tough read. Evasive to standard test questions, lacking any overt politics, and bumper-stickers on her car: non-existent. This was very frustrating. Our daily shopping trips ever-increasingly demanded an answer to the urgent question, the delicate confines of tact barely kept me at bay, and as days passed, issues of survivability increased the gravity of the inquest. The dam burst when the batteries in my walkman died. Mrs. Jones—

Are you down with crime?!

I stole the batteries, but her answer wasn't so easily extracted. Mrs. Jones paid grumbling lip service to an "ethical void" I existed in, grumbles falling silent when thrown a pacifier. Like, say, her own pack of batteries. Typical response. Even Mom uses that juicer I stole her—two years after Christmas, but she uses it! Most condemnation of victimless crime, at its base—I'd long felt—is only jealousy. The McDonald's cashier who threw my skateboard across the lot wished he was on my side of the counter. The beer-drinker guys who swerve to hit me on freeway on-ramps wish they had my ambition. And I'll never prove it, but I'd long suspected supermarket managers who order me from their dumpsters harbor a secret desire to *pull garbage from the trash and eat it!* Really!

Mrs. Jones had internalized capitalistic values. In her "saintliness," I saw only a soul held hostage. It demanded, like, an exorcism. Our daily deprogramming sessions—controversial in psychological circles—ran a typical course: I would be in the very pressing need for, say, new shoes, and direct Mrs. Jones to the for-profit chain thrift store. Keeping a straight-face, I would calmly ask her to pull to the door and leave the car running.

"Oh no! No no no no!"

Ha ha! Oh yes!

Her muffled protests faded to the distance as I entered the store, picked up an armload of merchandise, and walked out!

"You are a very *bad man!*" she would say, as we made our daring escape.

Deprogramming: It was a slow process.

People paying for things . . . I don't know, it just hurts to watch. Layers of resistance soon peeled away, and the deal was struck: fifty-cents on the dollar. Her children left for school, husband to work, and what happened next is none of your business. What are you, a cop?! [If so, your inability to simply *do your job* is shocking, we the criminals find you less a threat than a bad joke, and I might come for your wife next!]

Our coordinated roles were akin to a well-crafted dance, the interplay of violin and harpsichord in classical composition. She drove the getaway vehicle, did the math and paid out the unmarked bills—I actualized her shopping list. And when it was all over, it was further proof of the proven—"left-handing" success: the statistical correlative to death and taxes.

It all brought to mind the wealthy family who—two years previous—made scandalous headlines when it was exposed they employed a full-time shoplifter as paid staff! Maybe I was jealous, maybe it was *me*, but the influence of news journalism on the criminal underground is well-understood. I can't think of these things on my own. In the quiet nighttime moments, I took warm comfort in the assumed existence of other "copycat" shoplifters, living in as big or bigger houses at that moment, filling shopping lists, lacking esteem for an unjust economic system, and stealing vitamins! Just like me . . .

Socks and conditioner. Earrings and makeup. $20 for my old $40 Barnes & Noble credit slip—ancient product of that rambling and long-winded process to books more easily "left-handed." I don't waste time. Mid-September, and Mrs. Jones was already feeling festive. She crossed off half her Christmas list in one day, and I made $80. I politely vetoed her CD request for its unrealistic logistical demands, but the lard-free soap was conscious-consumption at its easiest. At night, we always made our final stop the supermarket. I was happy to secure Mrs. Jones the most expensive items from her grocery list—no charge. Mrs. Jones was happy to be saving the money. How much she saved on food I wasn't sure. I'd never had to pay for it. What *is* "full retail price?" Well, she paid me four dollars for AA batteries, which would mean . . . *Oh my god!*

Uh-oh. I'd let my guard down, was blinded by the glare from my pile of gold. I was almost actually sort of *employed*. Never before had I considered that shoplifting could ever *not* be fun. Dave had suggested it once, and he hadn't even the cruel yoke of Mrs. Jones' Christmas list. I wasn't just taking flares from construction sites anymore. This new fast-pace arena of "steal-low/sell-high" capitalism was disgracing the righteous integrity of stealing things! Impossible!

At the heart of most people's life experiences lies a rich lesson, a deep moral. And mine: punchlines. "Live-In Shoplifter"—a definite knee-slapper. They say brevity is the soul of wit. If so, I was killing the joke. Three days later I was under a bridge, waiting for my train. And what came next would have a punchline all its own . . .

* * *

Twelve months since my last visit, back home for long walks and old friends. If my fumbling hypothesis was correct, low-level retail and service industry positions will have experienced a roughly 80% percent turnover, and I could return to just stealing all my food from the university cafeteria. You see, I believe in forgiveness, wiping the slate clean. It's an overlooked perk of job market instability that new employees *don't know you're there to steal their food!*

Looking back at my notes scribbled on the train, I could see my plan was two-fold—revisit my old abandoned house, stroke the front door nostalgically, maybe shake my fist at the new owners who'd purchased *my* house at a government auction for half a million dollars. Second, find an entirely new, rent-free living situation for the winter. My friends would take care of me. And if not—I'm hard to ignore in a sleeping bag on your front porch! Ha ha ha!

Any possible psychic recovery from my time in the Midwest would be a long time in coming. Several shocking lessons were learned exploring the heartland, resonating to the foundation of my world view. Beginning when myself and a small cell of radicals *stormed a huge suburban mall*, soon choking down the realization shoplifting *can* go too far! No way! When the trunk reached 50% capacity it was becoming clear, finally solidifying at a novelty store where I stole a rad train watch, then realizing two crucial points:

1) *I almost never care what time it is*, and 2) The band was leather. I was of course then morally bound to undo my bloody mistake, pioneering the *"reverse shoplift"*—where I reached inside the store from around the corner and *threw* it at the cashier! I love cows. Had I learned my lesson? Possibly. Would I renew my heartfelt commitment to "survival only" theft? Of course. And one week later, I'd take it all back . . .

Murphy was sort of "connected." There was an unused toolshed in my town somewhere, and Murphy certainly held the missing link to it in his daytimer. We agreed to meet at B&N bookstore—the missing link to leisure, where it's often fun to spend an afternoon looking at maps, and—when the door alarm sounds—looking down from the balcony to watch the ensuing confrontation. Though, really, that store never chased anyone. Was every moment spent flipping through books for tags a moment wasted? A deep thought, with no clear answers. But that just might be the bottom line!

Murphy took the adjacent seat. He was straight like an arrow, with a computer job and espresso machine. Not part of society's 5% "criminal element."

"Do you know the Razor Finger?" he asked, tilting his head toward the music department. I raised an eyebrow. Murphy continued with step-by-step instruction on a seriously profound scheme. Lucrative, low-risk, and utterly unconcerned with their "profit margin"! Better than Skip's "free-rent" scam, and lacking the complications of inter-gender romance.

"Listen," he said, "I never told you this. It's a side of myself I would never show anyone but you." Some were magnets for post-breakup shoulder crying, some attracted gossip—I heard the scams.

I immediately walked—maybe I even *ran*—to Rite-Aid to assemble the ingredients to Murphy's criminal recipe: medical tape and razor blades. Back at B&N, Murphy offered slow-motion instruction. A razor was placed on the end of the pointer-finger—perfectly centered—and the finger then wrapped in medical-tape, leaving an imperceptible corner of the blade exposed. Why, it looked like a basketball injury! Of course, why hadn't I thought of it . . . We all knew razors took care of difficult alarm tags. Maintaining the necessary covert form was the dilemma. Murphy bridged the gap, and it was the most subversive advice a model of "work ethic" had exported so far away from itself. Retail America would never see this coming . . .

Looking down at Murphy's razor finger, I could clearly see where he was going with this. In security terms, B&N was a music retailer rogue, shunning the plastic "security shells" for square alarm tags stuck to the cellophane. Not the will of God nor the mighty arms of Colossus himself could separate tag from CD. I know—two days after the Beastie Boys CD release I could be found attempting just that.

B&N's smug confidence left their music departments largely unguarded—allowing sneaky Razor Finger kids to casually *trace* around the tag while whistling to themselves softly, stuff the tags behind the Madonna CDs, and walk! Hold us back! As outlaws, we draw heavily from all points on the historical lineage of resistance, like, say, the Viet-Cong—"An over-confident opponent leaves his belly exposed." We wait in the shadows, by the box sets, invisible but for the gleam of our razors, and the belly is looking like anything with resale value . . .

Standing at the junction of right and wrong, I went left—towards the music. First time with a new scheme— always uncomfortable for both parties. But with her gracious consent, and B&N's unwillingness to *detect* or *care* that 50% of customers under 25 *don't pay* for the merchandise—I, um, stole five CDs! With a start-up capital of 99¢ Cornnuts at Rite-Aid, the return on my investment was striking. I was the unemployed and penniless in the face of temptation, and in whatever path I shall choose, blame me not, *for I know not what I do!*

In the quiet shadow of my own glory, I paused to reflect on my B&N criminal history and the story of one kid, one store, and a lot of free time . . .

The first groundwork was laid by a very morally defunct, very *Catholic* girlfriend. I hadn't ever known textbooks to serve any purpose, until Molly began stealing them from her school's storeroom and meeting me in the B&N parking lot. Their function soon came to light. Bound by their own return policy, B&N could only look down at two teenagers and what was clearly a scam-in-progress, grit their teeth, and offer an even exchange. A beautiful thing, I think—two kids seizing their own education, presenting a stack of books and a lie. Not disposing of "their" education, just trading it, and using the difference for bus money . . .

Tactical evolution took its course. The book shelf in my house told that story—part drama, part romance, a couple chapters comprised entirely of my flailing legs extending upright from the dumpster. Waking up, many of my friends went to the university, I left for my own chair at B&N, and when we regrouped 8 hours later, I wondered who had received the better education. I harbor no jealous contempt for the formally educated, but there is a revolution brewing, and I believe strongly that the students of Cognitive Neuroscience will soon yield to the scholars of Applied Pick-It-Up-And-Run. We'll share, but you may only get the leftovers!

I broke up with girlfriends on the B&N phone, slept upright on the B&N couch, even thawed out with paid-for B&N tea after sleeping in the park. All periphery, however, to the heart of it—pulling Star Wars coffee table books from the shelf, assuming a straight face, and offering it to the cashier with a smile and a story. I swear, I would love to see old security footage of this stuff . . .

Soon Stitch and I stood on the threshold of summer—two kids and a car, a map of America's extensive Interstate system, and the unspoken understanding that whatever we chose as our next move, *a large corporation would pay for it!* Why not?! The "summer road-trip." Songs were written and movies made about such things. I'd seen those movies, absorbed myself in the characters, and say with the humblest of tones—they didn't do it right. Instead, they could have done what we did—pull a receipt from the trash, bring "The Hunter's Bible" to the counter, take the $60, open the sunroof, and drive! In tribute, we dedicated the trip to B&N. With a full palette of scams to draw from, we thought it more appropriate for *one* chain store to fund our trip. Walking out two states later with a stack of expensive books—taking advantage of and possibly *abusing* B&N's "no chase" policy—our crude plan was in motion. With the discovery of a $10-or-less difference in cash on exchanges, we thought it over, made small extensions of logic, then drove the country exchanging $80 books for $70 books. If we quietly moved to liquidating copies of the new Pearl Jam CD, it marked no straying of the heart—just Nebraska. Only one B&N.

Looking down at my taped-up finger, I knew I'd earned the promotion. From foolish acts of in-the-pocket concealment to a method of undetectable grace. I enjoyed beaming pride at my new place in the rich history of reluctant workers simulating injury for unemployment benefits. Razor Finger wasn't keeping me from a job—I had years experience not having one—but stealing CDs would certainly make unemployment an easier occupation. So while the bed-ridden forklift operator with the "bad back" was jet-skiing off the Keys, I was faking a basketball injury on the second floor of B&N in working-class solidarity. Stay free brother—this Korn CD is for *you!*

The floodgates were opened. Skip hurt my feelings with his mocking of my first unsupervised yield—a small stack of bad rap. He didn't understand, he wasn't in the trenches. Unwilling to pick a side, Skip might never appreciate the statement of underdog defiance implicit in

Razor Finger, the war cry of autonomy underlying my new Grandmaster Flash CD. Laugh, white man, laugh; I have 24 hours of free time tomorrow to prove it's more than Puff Daddy—it's liberation!

The general unforced movements of left-handing, and my blasé sleepwalking through countless return lines had effected psychic skewing of identity and purpose—I'd *forgotten* I was a criminal! The use of sharp tools and antagonistic slashing motions of Razor Finger brought me back to the comforting arms of missed sensation—yes, this was illegal . . .

Success had come so fast. Like most overnight millionaires, I knew no moderation. Looting two stores a day, I was bringing in CDs faster than I could sell them, or give them away, or present them to friends in lieu of gas money. This put me alarmingly close to what economists call a "tax bracket." I mailed CDs to friends with detailed instruction and stick-figure diagrams on bringing the Holy War to their town. Taking a page from the socialists, my approach was to tell five people, and instruct those five to tell five others. My crude math and little chart proved we'd reach all straight-edge vegans in six months, all punk-rock kids in 24, and two years beyond that, "the kids" wouldn't have to work at all! Free money . . . maybe it *was* socialist, or fascist, or something. Wait, what is it when you steal food and risk it all to circumvent employment? Do *we* get a name?!?!

It was the reckless pace of drug-fiends and amateurs. Downtown—3rd Avenue before noon. Bus #205 to the suburbs—behind the mall. #115 to "The Triangle"—second floor. Coffee at the bagel shop across the lot for tactical evaluation and self-assessment. All culminating in fifteen of the "Billboard Top 40" before 3 p.m—a $90 "street value." But was it art?! Well, it was fun, and looking at the drooling zombies working the bagel shop—necessary for self-preservation. One more cup of coffee, another look at the bagel zombies, then my CDs, then over to the "Help Wanted" sign. I shook my head. They'll have to pry the razor from my cold, dead hand. Lazy? No—*scared.*

Maintaining my dedicated pace necessitated the FBI infiltration tactic of "deep cover." Simplified, this meant no dumpstered Disneyland visor. I would have to adopt the style, effect the very mannerisms of the suburban middle class. Though, really, I had incorporated such a guise into my routine for years—and if Krishna reincarnation theories were correct—*centuries*. Even as Napoleon, I never paid for food. Still, you see, I put my heart into my work, and B&N demanded a strict code of dress. Sporting my new Tommy Hilfiger jacket, I sensed my own rebirth, an adopted identity supplanting the old—I was young, sporty, really white, and paid for everything! My undercover work and its sensitive nature inspired my soliciting from Bonnie of bleach—illegal for use by the general public—from a possibly sympathetic hairdresser. Still, there was something missing. I sought advice in Skip—himself a paying customer. He showed me the end of aisle 10, walking me through the available pomade hair-grease products. The "wet look," of course . . . Active in the underground music scene, he spoke in terms I could understand—relating each brand to members of local punk-rock bands. I passed on "Dax"—grease of choice for local Hardcore band drummer—shunning it as too forced, a pretentious and stiff concoction. The clear choice was the higher water-content brand favored by local straight-edge band guitarist—firm, but unafraid to release its grip and let the hair flail during mosh parts. Perfect for B&N—those people love to mosh. If the bus rides, taping and re-taping of the finger, the Tommy Hilfiger and my stylish hair at times seemed very laborious, I remembered the open position at the bagel shop. If ever the dumpsters dried up and the scams cut-off, Razor Finger would have its final act of liberation lengthwise across my wrists . . .

Location #4: the elusive suburban locale. Inaccessible on public transportation, and wholly untapped. If the busses don't go there—the criminals can't get there, and then, well, you know those guys are all half-asleep. Betty offered to drive. She even scribbled a Christmas-present CD list, volunteering half sticker price! Sure, I told her, I can do this. But explaining the 1" x 1" hole in the cellophane to your cousins on Christmas morning—I can't do that.

Terms agreed upon, I worked the Hip-Hop section like a graceful dance with a classy lady. At this point I had nestled myself in the very comfortable M.O. of placing all CDs behind the "Master P" divider, while I retreated to the magazines to allow any possible detection to come to light. Not crime—art. Only one thing could explain why— five minutes later—I found "Master P" empty: I had my rappers confused. "Juvenile," "Mystikal" . . . I was approaching "panic," having already cleared "denial," but nowhere near "acceptance" when my cut CDs resurfaced across the room . . . in the hands of the cashier! Ooops. Retail loyalists—scourges of the free-market. She *stole* my CDs! We really need our own loss-prevention agents for this stuff. With her contemptuous glare, I immediately assessed her condition as the common pathology of the employed in their relations with the rest of us—"Why should *you* walk free while we suffer?!" I didn't stay for philosophical discourse, to explain those CDs and her scowl as representing a timeless struggle, the very polarity of freedom vs. slavery. I could only put my head down, grab Betty in one hand, a pound of Starbucks beans in the other, and duck out of that store forever. A "defeat," I suppose. But I had my beans, and my unemployment, and—wait . . . that's not "defeat" . . . why, that's drinking coffee on a permanent vacation! I love that!

One-handed tag-cutting—the 36th chamber of Razor Finger. And the first chamber? Rubbing your face without drawing blood. Murphy lifted his head to show the spot once bandaged for a week, I rotated 45 degrees to exhibit my still-fresh ear gash. Yes, joblessness demanded more than "I quit." Sometimes, you must love the chirping afternoon birds enough to fight for them. Standing in the restroom stall, pouting, and applying a poof of tissue to my ear, I thought—gosh, unemployment is a battlefield. All out war, and there was a trail of blood from the "Fugazi" CDs to the restroom to prove it. Combat for the long, dreamy walks whenever I pleased . . . I felt that was pretty righteous. Yes, B&N was a war zone. The "Music" section the trench, and running across the lot tenderly cradling five CDs: liberation of the hostages. My exhale of victory came only in reaching the safety of the bagel shop "no fire zone." I may not be shot there, but if the bagel girl saw me sneaking free coffee, she might hit me with something. Recouping with my coffee, razor gashes in my pockets and open facial wounds, I would reflect on my fight against chain-store imperialism. Then realize, no, just against a job at that bagel shop . . .

Location #1: Downtown shopping district. A definite "10" for accessibility, and their selection of train books is first rate. Or *was*—I got them all! Ha ha! They'll special order for you though . . . Location #2: The mall. Cashier with book-guy haircut has curious knowledge of hobo literature. And though committed to abstention from on-the-job romance, I harbored an innocent crush on the second-floor info-desk girl. Altogether a bold move—placing a B&N within walking distance of five used-CD stores. Sort-of *taunting*, I think. Location #3: The wealthy suburb. My old hood, where the sun always shone and the cashiers always looked the other way. There is simply no end to the unpaid merchandise at this store. An air of exclusivity hung over it all, and Razor Finger my lighthearted response to bridge the status gap. Shoplifting: the great equalizer.

It was the four-hour work day, the two-day work week. While technology waved its carrot-on-a-stick before the humble worker, promising less work and more leisure, I was taking a small shortcut to utopia: four 1" x 1" gashes— the shortest cuts I knew of. Centuries of workplace technology had assured the proletariat an eventual phasing-out of his toil. A leisure life finally achieved with . . . a razor. The machines never did work for us, only the inverse. But razors were on our side. For my profound thoughts on the subject, I would probably have to die to earn my place next to Marx in working-class theory and practice. A good-thing—bookstore-types all know what that guy looks like. Photos of me have yet to surface! Maybe I'm in the room with you *right now* . . . It was the most thankless of jobs, one I could never admit to having. "Ridicule, violent opposition, accepted as self-evident"—the three stages, they say, of revolutionary paradigm shift; to a day when I can look my own mother in the eye, tell her I steal things then sell them, and get *respect* for it. So, what stage was it when the CD buyer at the record store noticed razor marks on 5 squeaky new Top 40 CDs, scowled, and slid them back across the counter? I have no idea, but it was funny.

At this stage in my career, I had hit something *The Wall Street Journal* tagged "the glass ceiling." My suspicious presence in the "Pop Music" section during daytime hours would eventually bring employees to raise the question "Why isn't he at work?" Soon giving rise to the realization—"Wait a minute . . . he *is* at work! Get him!" I was nervous, running out of friends to sell CDs for me, and sensed impending detection of the pattern—"When the white kid's around, *things disappear!*" This was dangerously close to the point in the story where justice prevails and the good guys triumph over masked banditry. I wished to avoid this. Traditionally, bands went on tour to support their albums. Now, I go on tour to steal them! What the heck!

Stepping off the Greyhound, I wondered if I was the only one who thought this funny. Career advancement? Or the Razor Finger sell-out tour? With the curse of success, would I "progress"? Candy-coat my technique, aim for "mass appeal," cease the unrefined slashing motions and begin *peeling* tags? No chance. For several days I slept on the roof of a church near the university, drank coffee, ate bagels, and looked at my maps. Then I folded up those maps, looked out the window with great intensity, and, you know, ate more bagels. You just can't eat too many. I'd given my plan a very polished, suburban setting, maybe the highest concentration of chain-store commerce anywhere. Perfect for skateboarding and asserting your own shock value. Towns where you sit, say, on a bench, under a tree, look at the brick planter boxes, over at the faux 19th century lampposts, then the greenest grass you've ever seen, and just want to start *taking things,* you know?

My own arrogance, at this point, is not something I'm proud of. I was one kid at a four-person bagelry table, wholly uninterested in anyone's opinion of it. In a mess of paper and lists, bagels next to other bagels, I starred key points on maps and watched a plan form. The strategy was one of escalation—connect all the little stars on my map via public transportation, and rush B&N with the cumulative rage and fury of all history's freedom-loving people—the part in the story where the revolutionary metaphors were taken *too far.* But if you'd watched the sunset off the Oregon coast from a sleeping bag, had small town families take you home, or just drank coffee and gazed out the window all day—you'd understand. Anything less was an icepick to the face. Touching a flame—you recoil. There *is* no decision. I drew my one-inch sword each day for my dreams. Yes, I thought of the college parties in strange towns, and if you'd danced with that girl, you'd understand . . .

I don't know what to say, I shocked myself that night. Awakening on the roof of the church the next morning—a smudged "Billboard Top 10" on my right arm—I was happy. And it just wasn't possible to fit every CD in my bag. On my roof, I listened to CD after CD of bad hip-hop, counting my yield and doing the rough math. OK, carry the "1" and multiply the . . . Gulp. The utter decadence of my campaign was a broadsided slap to an implicit code of moderation, building up to the absurd punchline—you know, I barely even *spent* money! *Now what?!?!*

A week later I would land in the lap of a scheme rendering Razor Finger obsolete. A stunt so rich in reward, it voided the need for most others as well, paying even my rent. And when offering restaurant food on her—Libby never took no for an answer!

* * *

It was a leisure life, selling off portions of my surplus for new records, or "left-hand" money, or to escape near arrest when I manipulated the Whole Foods coffee-girl into letting me pay at the front, and then—whoops—forgot to pay. By the time Libby and I snowballed through Omaha, Razor Finger was a proud but faded memory. By the time we returned, I had ten cassette compilations of trucker songs, twelve vocabulary-building tapes, blueprints to the under-construction library at the University of Nebraska, and a curious black cube picked up at an Omaha Ace Hardware—"The Demagnitizer." After one month of vocab tapes, we knew "proclivity," "alacrity," and "perfunctory," but neither of us could explain "Demagnitizer." Let's see, package says—"Renders all magnets impotent." Wait a minute, so that would mean . . .

I'll never have kids, but I knew the tender closeness between a man and his newborn scam. I was nervous, having so long rested on "left-handing" and the receipt scam. Without the influx of new tactics, I was having panicked doubts about my own fertility. I never thought innovation would offer itself in Nebraska. Really good truck stops—not delinquent toys. I do not wish to downplay the suffering of our pregnant mothers, but stand firm in my belief the pain of childbirth is equal to or less than the pain of Omaha. In no other town would I be caught stealing from Wal-Mart—twice in ten minutes. I hope this works . . .

Pulling the "Now Vol. 2" CD from the shelf, well, it was very exciting. Libby stood at my side, together we bit our lips, looking down at the cube with big eyes and exchanging giggling glances. We perhaps stood at the threshold of big things, right there in our favorite B&N. I rubbed the cube against the tag tenderly, possibly *massaging* it into submission. Maybe I was stepping up to earn my place next to the first kid to salt-water a Coke machine! I had borne the guilt of pioneering survival schemes before. The Milk Bottle Scam was all mine. Altering Tower Records gift certificates—I'm pretty sure that was a first. The Receipt Scam was timeless, but recruiting middle-class sympathizers to *save* me their receipts—an article of warm pride. My psychology-based free movie trick had saved me from gang attack, even Rapid City—the fate worse than death. Obtaining the 75¢ stroller machine refund by *reaching* inside and pulling the lever—a hellified classic. Maybe not of my own invention, but I was the lookout. Cutting and pasting old bus transfers to match the current days—art so crude, a bus driver had once taken the transfer, held it up to the light, and laughed at me! I think he sort of respected me after that. And heart-to-heart talks with parents laying out hugely overstated stories of hardship—no one so content had taken the scam so far. Your only child living in an abandoned house would bring a tear to any parent's eye, and the "pit of filth and decay" where I counted their money had a market-value double their net worth. Laughter roared through the mansion . . .

The alarm didn't go off. I thought that was pretty funny. I added a new one to the list: Demagnitizer.

Yes, we all drummed on tables listening to stolen walkmans in café window seats, scheming on entirely new ways to freshen the joke of unemployment. A timeline of prosperous poverty leading up to that moment in the B&N parking lot, accepting Libby's insistence that—yes—we were on to something. "Now Vol. 2"—maybe not the soundtrack to the youth revolution, but the resale value would purchase something on vinyl that came close. A 5" x 5" gilded tile on the path to . . . what? The *whole* store? Victory? I'm not kidding, this felt dangerous . . .

Holding the magic "Free CD" wand, I stood in the hazardous position of a drunk with a drink, of me at the landfill. I took the Demagnitizer dilemma back to the kids for group assessment. Baxter was stunned to silence. Sammy nodded, and said he knew of which I spoke—he'd seen the black cubes at his small town hardware store. And then what? *Kept walking?!* All agreed this was bigger than a Flying J truck stop, bigger than Razor Finger even. "Cut and Walk" was archaic, dangerous in large quantities, and if you forgot to remove the razor—just dangerous. Demagnitizer was, like, *physics* or something. The fusion of poverty and science! Although broke and without formal education, I took rosy comfort in knowing I was contributing something valuable to the universal pool of knowledge. I felt equal warmth in drawing from "the universal pool of retail," which draw from a million pools of individuality, Earth's pool of resources, society's fading pool of culture . . . wait, this was getting complicated. I just *didn't want to work*, you know? Ever!

Another trip and five CDs solidified what we were all afraid of—the black cube was the death of their "Suggested Retail Price." And when Baxter trailed me out with equal success, well, it almost felt like an actual *uprising!*

But wait a minute . . . "consistency," I had long felt, was a decisive gauge of larceny greatness. Soon after, while Baxter was in the front "exchanging" two very expensive coffee table books for a new CD player, I frolicked in the back, almost *dancing* through the aisles, rubbing five of the "Billboard Top 10" like I was above the law or something. The alarm went off. "Whoops! Can't pay up front? Sorry!" Silly me! Baxter got his CD player—and he earned it—but I was left to sit in the car, head in hands, taking out on Baxter's dashboard what should be taken out on physics, or Omaha. Anyway, I hated them both. Only the law of gravity bringing a stack of record money into my lap would restore my faith in one. And the other, well, that would just have to be bulldozed.

A week later the episode replayed itself, sending the entire "Demagnitizer—tool of liberation, or The Great False Hope?" dilemma back before the kids. Libby suggested it was the alarm tags placed devilishly *inside* CD packaging by major labels. But I never knew those to set off anything at B&N. Baxter suggested I'd massaged with the wrong side of Demagnitizer, that it was an issue of magnetic polarity. I was very upset at this point, and silently cursed them both for being stupid. First thought was to reverse-engineer the naughty cube, but soon developed a theory of my own: When magnets experience shock, magnets lose power. If Demagnitizer derived its magic from magnetic sources, perhaps I'd dropped it in the B&N restroom too many times. Or maybe this was Omaha's parting joke. Like I was the rodeo halftime show, on the monitor, and the collective residency sat laughing at that moment, throwing popcorn at my pixilated image! If that's the case, I'm unshaken. Content in my own parting joke—the one at Wal-Mart, in the hands of the scowling loss-prevention agent, and in what seemed an irreversibly doomed circumstance. Then the kicker—where I flipped the mood in record time with an elaborate lie while we shared a brief chummy moment, closing with a cordial parting and smiles all around. That joke, to this day, continues to tickle. Omaha, seriously, do I *look* like a loss-prevention agent for Tower Records? Duh!

Replacing the cube was a labored challenge. I took the question to Home Depot. Very innocently, I asked the man in the orange apron—"Do you carry the Demagnitizer?" He looked suspicious, more suspicious than the time I bought a crowbar and gloves in a single purchase. "Yeah, I know *exactly* what you're talking about." Great! So, aisle 6? Aisle 7? "The Home Depot corporation will *not* carry Demagnitizers—company policy." There was a cryptic tone to all this. Certainly there existed a market demand for magic wands.

"Why?!"

His expression turned serious.

"Can't say."

What did it all mean?! The man looked nervous. I was afraid. *They* were afraid—afraid of the cube! A long moment of silence passed between us. It all suggested I was probing a sensitive topic. Quickly exiting the store, I reviewed two gems learned: I was meddling in delicate areas with powerful forces, and their fear suggested Demagnitizer just might disable Home Depot tags!

Why would a "God" take the life of a good scheme? The current state of Demagnitizer stands as my strongest case for atheism. Until the little black cube resurfaces, I keep my first wrapped in a humble rag. It is a sad cube, pitiful in its impotence. But in its day, a light down the path of jobless justice. And the closest I'd felt to *living* gangsta rap! If you work at B&N and wondered why I stood by the listening station, making unnatural orbicular movements with my right hand—now it's clear. The kids are still in active search for a new cube source. We stand hopeful, but fear the worst—that we just might have to hop the mid-line *back* to Omaha! Insufferable . . . and a circumstance surpassed in extremity by only one other—"9 to 5"!

Yes, this was a place I knew well—kneeling at the grave of another lifeline, looking towards the horizon where maybe the schemes were craftier, choosing freedom over comfort even more fun. A locked dumpster, stricter return policy, another loophole sealed off . . . The feeling was the same each time—regret, with an eager sense of possibility. Off the record, I embraced the death of well-worn tactics—the end of that unlocked broom closet, steam tunnel entrance now on lockdown. The defeats that leave me to hitchhike to Boulder, and when the girls picked me up to shoot off fireworks at the lake—oh yes, I thought, bring on the changes. When the apartment manager found me living in that storage shed, a catalyst to my bigger, cozier rent-free house—yes, I thought, shake me from the stale. And when our favorite record store cut-off "exchange" privileges, driving us to the exciting shortcut of simply *walking out* with small stacks of CDs—yes, yes, I thought, "Out with the old, in with the new."

Taking solace in this pattern—one of flux and renewal—I laid the CD liquidation to rest . . . for now. What's next? Marketing stolen Kinko's cards? Selling CDs from the Columbia House dumpster? Book royalties?!

From corpses spring flowers. Sliding my last five CDs across the counter, I almost shed a tear, wondering where my last $30 would take me. And on that day, behind the health food store, a new scam was born. The cycle of death and rebirth was never so clear. After so many years, still we create an endless sense of newness, each day like the first. I continue preparing for the next cycle, probing strangers for the next Razor Finger, keeping my eyes open and taking notes. Because there's a "Help Wanted" sign in every window, and I'm scared . . .

THREE

MAKING IT UP AS I GO
USA ON A DOLLAR A DAY

"Find an abandoned house and live in it."

18 and a plan. The foundation for a hundred other plans: Never work. Play in the streets. Explore the warehouse district. Eat bagels. Read. Learn lock-picking. To understand, you have to stand on a rooftop in the sun, look out across this suburban landscape and call it a stage. An idyllic scene, worth taking chances for. To understand, you have to be a kid with a dream. Their sterile landscape would be my carnival. It was the plan, and if I could steal a crowbar somewhere, I'd have my ticket out of this world . . .

They said it couldn't be done. Not finding an abandoned home in the heart of the state's highest property values. Not outright joblessness. But why guarantee the outcome by believing them? It couldn't be done legally. Couldn't be done without leaving a trail of torn trash bags, without a disturbing medley of broken locks and no forensics to go on. Couldn't be done without a solid laundry scam—and 42 days from the leap, statistically—without a solid food scam. And I was certain it couldn't be done without it being the best thing I'd ever done. Because the theory is: A day unemployed is like a bagel—even when it's bad, it's still pretty good . . .

I stayed home from work one day and never went back.

The crucial "summer after graduation." While my friends packed for school, I was shaking each of them violently, demanding answers to some important questions. A lead on abandoned property—property owned by another, who then lacked the nerve or awareness to confront me when I broke in and slept there. Held up to my "earning potential," a goal tearworthy in its low aim, but I held it up to "skate in the sun all day" and it checked out. I would just run in circles sipping carrot juice! If I could secure a house. This little suburban detective game had a certain seduction. Edited properly—a really funny sitcom. No laugh track necessary, my friends had that role covered. I was a kid at a crossroads, shaking down strangers on the bus and ex-girlfriends for crude napkin maps to anything with boarded-up windows. A barrel of laughs if it wasn't so serious. I was young, dreamy, and unafraid to tact-lessly inquire on the addresses of dead grandparents! Free rent: you just can't go too far . . .

"Job or School"—my parents were chanting the demon's mantra. They said it couldn't be done . . . And if I hadn't achieved abandoned property by September 1st, they might be right! My parents' smug little date for "dis-continuation of services." The coupling of mission and ultimatum was making summer interesting, dramatic even. The practicality of my plan, at this point, was to-tally questionable. Though the allure accompanying this uncertainty eclipsed the very certain and puzzling nature of my friends' plans: "Job or School." Everyone dancing to the same played out song, without any seductive hooks or rad mosh parts. "Job or School"—Mom and Dad didn't understand. They'd never pulled an inflatable raft from a dumpster and ridden huge waves on the lake. *Pay* for a raft that sinks 30 yards out, and you'd be mad. On a dump-stered raft—just funny. Sort-of a philosophical cornerstone of my new approach. Crude allegory to sup-port my new life's absurd premise, of a seemingly backwards correlation between "poverty" and satisfaction: The less you spend, the more fun you have. "Job or School." In the ongoing bargaining process, I made the silent vow to thrive on misdemeanor theft from their jobs, and listen to records in the media rooms at their schools. "Job or School." This was the art of compromise . . .

It was a summer of note-taking. If it was free—it went in the pad. Unbolted, unlocked, unguarded or disloyal to workplace—there was probably a note of it somewhere. Preparation for unemployment was a full-time occupation. My plan to not work ever again sat on the wildly ambitious leap of faith that suburbia offered more free food options than salad bar Saltines. I couldn't prove this, but I found a supermarket that left their chip display out overnight, so, my suspicion ran deep. And if I was wrong, well, Saltines are kind of good, you know?

And further faith in the offering of more rent-free shelter than cardboard boxes and park bushes. But that too . . . maybe a cardboard box *in* a bush. Or what of a pallet house, reinforced with cardboard, in a bush, in the park?! No one ever thought of that!

I was wide-eyed and embracing it all because it was new and exciting. Because reclaiming resources and space—then juggling one and living in the other—would hang a romantic frame around life in "their" world. Because now, the games wouldn't just end at the schoolyard. It was June, the kids were hanging up the coats of youth, and mine felt curiously restored. From the roof of the luxury apartment, I thought I just might build my new life from the excess of theirs, sleep in their houses, and when heads turn—run with their soy milk! Though, if it's owned by an abstract corporate entity, no one notices it's missing, and it's in *my* town, is it really "theirs"? It was the season of philosophy . . .

. . . and hope. I put on my headphones and opened the door each morning under the spell of a flirting premise: For everything I needed, there was a moneyless means of acquiring it. I'd glimpsed enough functional housewares in the thrift store dumpster to furnish small African countries, so, I had evidence of this being the case. In addressing this issue, I felt the electro-physical rule of "the path of least resistance" shouldn't apply. I dropped physics senior year. As such, preferring, "the path of least employment." A quaintly delinquent path, where I ate complimentary chips and salsa over a menu before deciding—whoops—I wasn't going to order, and grabbed loose edibles in supermarket back rooms en route to the restroom. They never mention every option—work, school, military . . . What about *crime?!* They never mention that!

My epic summer, big eyes and big plans. I noticed a lot of free things just lying around . . . and learned to pick them up and run! Like I said, I took notes. 75¢ "refund" at the bus station for contrived anger and—"That machine stole my money!" Decorative fountain outside the pizza parlor—pleasant, pastel, and lined with change! Pizza dumpster by the beach—thick and tasty end crust, and if you brush the ants off—vegan. Small metal box marked "Candy - 5¢"—aisle 2—stuffed with nickels, quarters, and sometimes dollars. Cute, fun for the kids, and unlocked! A few small points where the crumbs fell and no one noticed. A couple-dozen more and I'd be good to go . . .

It was always a sunny day in my town. Our world was dying, and you'd never know it from my patio seat at the bagel shop. Fridays: free coffee if you bring your own cup. That was another thing I learned. This was "the sub-urbs"—unfairly poisoned with negative connotation, so when the kids asked where I lived, I said "the suburbs." They'd gasp, and I'd laugh. Blinded by their politics and prejudice, completely missing the under-appreciated stage it offered for shameless hedonism, and poolside leisure! Best to keep this my secret. Keep the young, poor people out and leave it for the old, wealthy ones. Made for bet-ter trash and cooler turf wars. Reminding me of my most guarded secret: You know what is referred to as the wealthy's "purchasing power" on CNN? It "purchased" commodities brought home, unloaded, and *thrown in dumpsters!* I swear I'm not making this up . . .

You could call it a love affair. And a scandalous one—it wasn't fashionable to love my town, and if you asked any kid but me—not even possible. Too wealthy and too sterile, too many cops and not enough action. I don't know . . . I dis-agree. Wealth meant tax revenue for extensive cross-town footpaths and the best parks in the state. A non-existent crime-rate—and consequently—non-existent supermarket security. It meant crazy and exclusive apartment buildings laid out like the finest hotels, and the only rooftop spa I've ever seen. It meant the most well-groomed shrubbery, tree lined streets, and general foliate supremacy. Sterility only meant my town was ripe for contamination, and if my plan reached fruition—full-on germ warfare. Heavy police presence only thickened the plot. And action—dear god! Let me compose myself and I'll draw you a map . . .

Though, truth was, maybe I never savored the details like I did this summer. Like, one day I was skating around and found the huge secret lot where they park the old busses! I was very excited by this. No, I never cherished my town in this way. All her finer points—the hours of fun in the newspaper dumpster, like the entire "Skateboarders" file with old interviews of my hood's entire skate crew. Or the cool middle-age "roller queen" who was *never* seen without skates—suddenly more charming than annoying. More and more, thoughts surged of long, unscripted days given to the probing for crazier dumpsters, street characters with more absurd gimmicks. I knew of the lot for *functioning* busses, but burned for small adventures seeking the building storing the bus *passes*, and the dumpster behind it. I had many plans. And now, time for them all. This plastic town never looked so fertile . . .

My world view had flipped inside a month, and this was no side effect of thrift store employees locking me inside their dumpster the month previous. I took long bus rides to forgotten neighborhoods, skated in the sun, and I was noticing things . . . Overlooked details had my sudden attention, and familiar nuances of landscape and commerce were suddenly relevant. The newspaper machine outside Starbucks—we all knew it offered pushbutton multi-quarter returns with unnatural frequency, now incorporated into my unemployment plans as a possible lifeline. The animal-research donation jar at the newsstand—always a devil jar to be hissed at, but now looking more like tax-free unemployment benefits. The phone company dumpster—almost forgotten when my hacking career didn't take off, now the wellspring of a thousand useful test numbers; numbers to give cops, and managers at the Tower Records return counter. My town was dispensing a hundred building blocks for what I hoped would be Fantasy Island—with free rent.

Each swing set felt profound. It all gave rise to new feelings, exciting but unfocused. "Life is in the details."

That may be it. Eyes off distractions like "GPA," they drifted down a little, and to the sides. To the unlocked grain elevator at the bakery. "Life is in the details" . . . I understand now. Hello rats!

Most common urbanite response to seeing my town for the first time—"Looks like a board game!" I heard that three times. "Looks like," building up to this summer when I decided that was in fact what it was. Roll the dice, land on "Unlocked CD caddy @ drug store"—advance 3 spaces. Draw "Rad dumpster fun to push and release down parking ramp into busy traffic—now chained" card—go back 2. Pass "Go," collect $200—$250 with dumpstered baseball mitt. Now if I could secure one of those "Get Out of Jail Free" cards, I'd really be set . . .

A thousand inspired plots and schemes, all of it between Mom's paid-for meals and my very comfortable bedroom. Parents are so counter-revolutionary . . .

It was one of those "good-news/bad-news" chats. To celebrate graduation, we—the family—would leave for a vacation stay at a waterfront hotel on the beach! Another setting to pillage . . . Definitely the "good news." They would pay for the ticket, and the room, and everything else—well, "Good luck!" Yikes! A gentle nudge toward the economic realities of adulthood. Both awesome and perilous. Seen for a moment as "the bad news," but I don't know . . . Broke and on fire in a waterfront carnival? Why, that's just a sunny "Choose Your Own Adventure" novel in the streets! Let's go!

The plane ride was smooth and the room elegant. An opulent backdrop to two smug parents, exchanging furtive jabs over their clever plan. Yes, their boy would now become a man. Looking out at the vibrant hotel lobby spectacle, certain elements of their scheme gained my support. Mom, Dad—your "tough love" is touching. I love you, cherish this withholding of food as a lesson in maturity, and now cross the threshold into adulthood . . . and table scraps! I saw a real future in this approach . . .

An actual active role in the American Dream: "self-sufficiency" and the economic realities of the capitalist marketplace. I had mental notes on this. Buy low, sell high, and when supply exceeds demand—lick your lips and pull it from the trash. I had at times viewed clear evidence of edible food carelessly discarded by white people. I'd found it in dumpsters while looking for books. Once or twice I'd eaten it. The collective middle class clutched their chests and took a step back over my new strategy—to, um, *subsist on garbage!* Ha! I picked up my skateboard. There was food in this town . . . If they tried nailing it down, there was probably a hammer in this town too. And if they nailed the hammers down, I was dead . . .

The pavement was smooth, the pedestrians rich but barefoot, and did people ever look at their watches in this place? There was no reason for it. This—I thought—is where the "work force" slipped up and showed me too much to ever go back—beachfront sun gazing and directionless leisure walks in the shade of palm trees . . . For real—"nine to five," after this? Employing a policy of "non-cooperation," really, was the only choice here. I skated the boardwalk. Now *this* was a place a kid could forget his "responsibilities."

Where humans congregated and ate food, I surmised, they just might drop it! Or turn their heads, or throw it at me . . . I was new at this. But hope burned red for the truth of it, putting me on a skateboard down every street, hunting down patio crowds, grumbling for people to hurry up and leave, you know, while there were still fries on their plate.

It was so exciting, standing before the very colorful Carl's Junior salad bar. Stepping to the trash, I tore through it all looking for what I knew lay under an onion ring carton here somewhere . . . Excellent. "Pull plate from trash and eat"—functional advice from my favorite zine. It was good salad. Maybe the best salad of my life—hung, the way it was, in its evasive frame. I immediately began broad and visionary applications of styrofoam plates as a lifeline. No reason I couldn't initiate an endless *circuitous tour* of my hometown, collecting plates, filling tupperware with pineapple and eating unfair amounts of salad at a different fast-food salad bar daily. Or with clever rotating disguises—the same one. "Free food tastes better"—I'm not the first to say it.

I skated all day in the sun, my head on a pivot, rubbing my palms and scheming on all new ways to exploit the landscape.

"Sir, there's no swimming in the fountain."

Call the cops jerk—I'm on vacation!

Let's see . . . strawberries in the supermarket dumpster . . . gosh. Tortillas behind the natural foods store . . . crazy. Another freakish fountain in the mall, where small girls could be found closing their eyes, making a silent wish, and tossing forth quarters. I closed my eyes and took a private moment by the potted plant to plead for world peace and record money. I got half!

Looking for adventure upstairs, I bumped into something else entirely. The singer of my favorite straight-edge band.

"Here's my number, we'll hang out."

That's it. Experiment's over. Rick Rodney—*the* binding legal pretext for everlasting unemployment and travel! Look at me and tell me I'm wrong!

I would wake up uncontrollably excited and immediately scan the landscape for the curious drama which surfaces when you're young, free, and, well, *broke!* The correlation was puzzling, and I feared analytic thought would kill it. People left much food on the beach. Like a sprawling 5 p.m. buffet. A tragic waste of food while children starved in Africa. The starving children in beachfront suite #203 shed a woeful tear at the injustice of it all, and let no chips go to waste!

A week of sun, sand, and skateboards. Gilded with the glory of not a dime spent nor a moment employed. My plot to put the course on "repeat" for—oh, I don't know, *several decades*—was in effect. And the agent of a dangerous paradigm shift. Like punk-rock plate tectonics. My volatile experiment was crude but conclusive: "Paying is optional." I sensed eventual eruption into irreversible dependence on the crumbs of the upper class. I felt neither shame nor pause, and asked only—*is this wrong?!*

Back home, I found my town still disquietingly void of unemployed poor people. Not for long, Mr. Town, just you wait!

Reinvigorated and back on familiar streets . . . My evolving scheme for "Spring-Break-52-Weeks-a-Year" was almost military. Initiate covert operations deep in hostile territory (hotel banquets at 10 a.m.), neutralize traitorous agents of the Red Menace (retail management), further strategic diplomacy with officials of high-rank in sensitive political climates (counter girls at bagel shops), and fund (suburban) terrorism with taxpayer dollars! Mobilize the troops—I'm hungry!

A few dozen lists and torn trash bags told the story of one kid who'd read a book on the waterfront, and wasn't willing to just *turn away* . . . then forged a gift certificate for your business and stole your garbage. My upsetting strut towards *full suburban parasite status* was progressing nicely. One day, in the sun, I found a whole dumpster of baked goods! And if September 1st arrived without shelter—nearby delivery trucks to sleep in. Not much of a home, maybe a slumber party or something . . .

Each day, the environment hurled these possibilities and loose edibles my direction. I would look at them, write them in the pad, beat my chest, then slink home for the prepared "crumbs" and "debris" scavenged from Mom's china. Like marijuana for the subversive, neutralizing mechanisms of the opposition come in enticing forms. But I'd seen the inside of a dumpster, and more and more, I was eating it. Like Mom's meals, but glossed with that "beating the system" allure . . . I chewed the food slowly on public transportation, and thought—when dining is an adventure, only adventurers *really* dine. The rest are just lining their bellies . . .

I think my parents were a little concerned. Like, where was I getting the pizza crust and expired chips? Mom, Dad—forensic criminologists explain that humans leave an unseen trail of hair and skin cells everywhere we go. It's like that, but with commerce as the scalp. I can't explain it, but it feels so right!

My parents casually dropped reminders of the cutoff date—September 1st—"Job or School." A cut lock on the cage, then an attempt to lure me back. They needed better bait. And I needed abandoned beachfront property in, like, six weeks! Tick, tock . . . I could almost hear the tune from Jeopardy . . .

Six weeks . . . It took about six minutes. Through the park, past the tennis courts, beyond the very unsecure corral where the ball field chalk-marker is stored, and under the interstate. It seemed "too good to be true"—an abandoned waterfront mansion . . .

Or that's what the kids told me. The ones I shook down for information in my campaign, approached menacingly with my rent-free plan and held in headlocks for answers. My first lead—I was electrified, an aspiring escapee ablaze. And a *golden* lead—huge and on the water! A million-dollar home, at least. But when I loosened the straps on the chair and put down the whip, each told a different story about that house. Usually ending in arrest. Something about "police patrols," but I was already lost in the injustice of it. Had I come this far to let my dreams lie stamped out under the boot of a cop?! Mean ole cops . . . Wretched guardians of "property rights"—never human rights. The going plan was a blunt burglary tool to one for the other. The right to disregard law—the only one they can never take away! Hand me the crowbar!

I hung on the fence. Pastel, shiny, and massive; like the kids said. But if one cannot approach nearer than 50 yards without wire cutters, and a night on her floor is a morning in a cell—is it really a home? I looked at a mansion lost, sad but empowered. This was it—seven-figure evidence of the imperial citizenry discarding a *whole house*. Groan . . . White people—sort of a "love/hate" relationship.

I continued skating my hood. Skating, scouting, chasing down unnoticed corners, architectural design flaws, *bigger* crumbs. With no frame of reference—or evidence militant unemployment *had* one—I questioned if I was "doing it right." I wondered if Robin Hood ever subsisted for whole days on salad bar breadsticks, or loitered beside the free produce samples. And where *were* the university showers? You see, the questions were many . . .

Erica had none of the answers, but looked up to her ex-high school sweetheart, his sad descent into the pits of squalor . . . She wasn't helping by holding my hand, towing me uptown and to the register of a buffet-style restaurant one evening—then continuing past without stopping! Outright interactive instruction on a promising free-food scam, the best I'd ever seen. Ok, so, sclf-serve pasta and salad? Seconds permitted, *encouraged* even? Quick math confirmed it—oh yes, this was free! I retract what I said, Erica had one answer. So much suffering in the world . . . and visible from our perch above the drink dispenser—so much citrus fruit! My simple challenge to anarchism—who will slice the kiwi?!

Erica complemented the free meal by confessing to knowledge of one very abandoned, very *haunted* house! After, like, five plates, she took me there. White picket fence, vacant, and occupied by hostile dead people. The abbreviated history, she explained, included a revolving door of residents, each the victim of violent paranormal assault. Live there? No way, I said. Don't laugh, shut up, and no. That's it.

So it was a dead-end lead, but with rosy implications. Like, further evidence for my eventual lawsuit against suburbia for setting 9/10 of the world ablaze, dragging its carcass home, and throwing it away. And inspiring evidence that—in the case of failure in this life—there was hope for us all on the other side: Eternal free-rent. So, really, by crowbar or razor, the kids can't lose . . .

Then—I found it. A house. All summer, my search had too narrow a scope. Suburban youth had let me down, forcing me to the highest echelons of DIY wisdom—and they came through. Thanks Grandma! She directed me behind Safeway, and there it was. At the end of a hundred impassioned shakedowns of friends and strangers for leads on abandoned property stood a giant, structurally unsound ball of trash. Behind the strip mall. Call it a disgrace to America's proud architectural history, call it a house, just don't call it up to code! You could point to the broken windows, hold up an empty 40 oz. from the porch and look to me with a raised eyebrow; but you'd never convince me the boards weren't trimmed with gold, that this wasn't hope itself . . .

I crept through a hole in the fence behind Safeway to introduce myself. She was a boarded-up beauty—with boards where windows should be, a splintered frame where a deadbolt should be, bad graffiti where kitchen walls should be, and I felt perhaps this is where I should be. Like maybe this *could* work. I couldn't believe it, and it felt like victory . . . with a really weak infrastructure. Don't sneeze. Like all trash, Trash House needed positive reinforcement and restored self-worth. I could hear her sad song, that sad song of discards that echoed through the West—"Give us respect!" Imagine the betrayal . . . She was a sad house. I rubbed her beaten walls, knowing this symbiotic partnership would elevate her to grace, and me to disgrace. Polar goals, singular path. We shared the bond of outcasts. Perhaps I was yet to be discarded-and-spit-on societal trash, but if my plan blossomed, I was on track to be just that!

I threw out 9/10 of what I owned and put the rest in storage. Time for bigger things . . .

When the apartment complex next door left a broom by the pool, I stole it, and spent long days clearing debris. Beer cans, fragments of smashed walls, items of female clothing telling an uncomfortable story. If I could install a lock on the door and put up a few posters, Trash House's décor would rise to that of a proud punk-rock home. But now? Horror movie axe-death scene. A morose thought in my beamish glory, but look in the bathroom mirror reflection at the two words on the adjacent wall: "Red Rum." Chilling in a house without sunlight. Like one of those fear-instilling tactics of a Scooby Doo villain in his crude attempt to scare the gang from the site of his illicit crime operation. I was the "meddling kid"! Well, it sure was scary. Better close the door . . .

Further torment came in Grandma's town—not my own. A thousand miles away in aesthetics and charm, if only a dozen by car. A suburb lacking enough huge and elaborate jungle gyms to get respect from the others. Or me! No public fountains, waterfront leisure or highbrow sophistication. Only a sprawling paved stage for thousands of burned-out youth to walk in circles bumping into one another, smoking, and spray painting *my* house! Oh well. A few weeks and I'd own this town. I could wait that long for a college to explore.

. . . but not garbage. My Trash House lay in a town with the anomalous quality of not hosting any trash itself. Not in dumpsters. In a one-inch thick layer on my living room floor—not dumpsters. Just alley after alley of outrageously poor city planning. I hate trash compactors. This was the summer I'd committed to permanently confusing trash with food, so, this was doom. Barring military intervention and emergency airdrops of trash—I was dead! Help!

Though new to poverty, I enjoyed a very vague and unfocused conceptual grasp of a "beggar-in-the-gutter" backdoor: crime. This isn't Kerouac. I'd always been a little obsessed with scams. High-school leisure crime had taught the "Tower Records return scam," the "Open, Remove Contents, Reseal and Return," "Super Dollar," and "Payphone Refund Check." At 18, translating respectively to "No Longer Welcome," "No Longer Relevant," "No Longer Works," and "Blacklisted." My belly grumbled.

When heads turned, I borrowed two empty dish soap bottles from Grandma's cabinet. My favorite zine offered guidance from this point. I had no record money, and followed step-by-step instructions with the frantic attention associated with this condition. "Fill with warm water," Ok. "Saturate water with salt," Mmhmmmmm. "Shake it up," right . . . At 2 a.m. I crept down to the seafood restaurant, looked the Coke machine up and down, let out the war-cry and emptied the bottles into the dollar slot! Apaches hurled spears at freight trains, we stab at Coke machines with saltwater. Circuits sizzled as the backlit display flickered. The machine and I entwined in conversation. She buzzed, I squealed. She hissed and sputtered, I giggled and bounced. She spewed smoke, I clapped. She looked at me . . . then spit out all her quarters! It was so exciting! My pockets bulged, and a cute improvised shirt pouch held the same. She gave a distant stare, seemingly dazed, and after an awkward moment of silence—hiccuped. A Coke fell out. Then, she closed her eyes forever . . .

She is remembered by several vinyl LPs in my Mom's garage, and this profound lesson: The system is ticklish, rub the right spot and the world is yours . . .

I'd never admit to it, but owned claim to one consistent free-food scam: "Grandma." My reluctant co-conspirator. Although guilt over the assistance grew with steady increase. It just wasn't nice My guilt rose at pace with my mounting distaste for its ease. The belly demanded food, but demanded it be *dangerous*. One night I snuck into Albertson's, picked up a bag of chips with a straight face, and, um, walked out! Proof the shortest distance between two points is in fact a straight line.

That night, from my seat three blocks north at the bus stop, I watched the Saturday night craziness, and ate my chips . . . seasoned with danger. Busses came, but I let them pass. The town had my attention. On that bench, I sat firmer in my belief that all anyone needs is free food and wide eyes. It was a summer to learn both.

The night was young and inviting. I took a few busses to my old hood, my familiar mall. I owned this town. The rear door to the buffet restaurant read "Alarmed," but didn't go off for me. Came with the town. I ate their soup, defiled the scenery, and unsportingly occupied a whole booth. Mark this as the summer the kids stole it all back. "Private commercially owned space" seemed a necessary start. I laid out my zines and notepads. There was hope in this landscape, the country clubs and restaurants . . . none of it created for me, but I was in the choicest position to pretend it was. Like, Albertson's left unobstructed passage from shelf-to-door as charity for the criminal-minded. Roof of apartment with view of city: commissioned by city hall as nighttime perch for the unemployed and dreamy. And this salad bar . . . no pretending necessary. Look at the rear door and say it's not charity. Now *look me in the eye* and say it!

"If paying for food changed anything, they'd make it illegal." Not paying for it was changing everything. Thin walls around what I knew to be excitement. The flavor of the food itself. Implied threats of doom towards the unemployed—now a "ha-ha" funny joke. I raised a glass of tea to the memory of a time when the Man had us all mortified, and held our consumables hostage! The leafy greens were brought out alive that night, but the context of doing it on a Saturday night in the state's trendiest suburb just felt *wrong* . . . and consequently—so right! A sense of triumph psychology can't account for. My freedom lay in their food. From this point, what I want—I take. That's it. I received severely empowering brain damage from this meal . . .

But the risky holes in my approach were clear. Picking up food and running, assaulting Coke machines on busy streets, crashing the salad bar every night . . . and in its wisdom and sustainability, "merchandise in pants/backpack" was close to wrapping oneself in barbed wire and stepping on a landmine. Continuing this course, the "law of averages" would soon threaten an imperial entanglement with the other "law." Friends with this amateurish approach were getting picked off by "The System," neutralized by the courts and in criminal retirement by 18. No way. My rough near-future timeline presupposed the existence of good books and warm sun for at least the next ten years, so, this was unacceptable. I was flailing for answers to this "longevity" question. Knowing only—"Time to go underground," or at least under the radar . . .

Crucial parts of my research: 1) steering every conversation to scams, 2) making abrupt demands for information from people I met in and around dumpsters, 3) lifting crumbs of advice from a hundred obscure zines, and 4) inducing starvation and watching my next move closely! Research is awesome.

Only hunting for "longevity," then uncovering outright criminal immorality. I gasped, and it was the last thing their world would ever hear from my direction . . .

The answer lay in my favorite zine. A document of one kindred spirit from the other coast, for months affecting me in profound ways with touching stories of, well, sunshine leisure and sledgehammers to the streets! Buried in the handwritten pages was an unnoticed gem—the "left-hand technique." Somehow overlooked the first twenty reads, it sat humbly on the page—demanding no attention and making no promises. No, to notice it, you had to be desperate. "Militant bulk-bin grazing" was enchanting, but was it a *threat?!* I want it all!

With great attention to detail and poise, I walked into Albertson's. I brought a small bag of chips to the counter, held them casually at my side—below the counter and outside the cashier's line of sight—paid for a banana with the other hand, gave god high-fives in my head, and . . .

"Hey! What about the chips?!"

Ooops. The parts left out of the zine. The cashier felt it was an honest mistake, and I feigned surprise at being "reminded" I was in fact, you know, *holding* a bag of chips. It was all very pleasant.

Returning to Grandma's, I reverse-engineered the mechanics of left-handing, uncovering hints of genius . . The crime and I had sort of an understanding going.

Approaching the counter at Albertsons the next day, I don't know what to say . . . Security camera tapes would reveal a smiling kid with an apple, bagels, great posture, and—wait a minute—Virgin Mary mother of . . . *what's going on?!?!*

They were good bagels.

It was a new dawn . . . Every block hosted a supermarket, and I ran in rabid circles, taking food I didn't need and shaking bottles of carrot juice at the sky. With an apple and a quarter in one hand, I'd place in the other—oh, I don't know, *whatever I wanted*—complete the transaction, make a cryptic comment loaded with arrogance and insult ("Thank you"), and walk out! Too subtle to appear criminal, too simple for the uptown intellectual, too free to be legal, and just too *right* to be wrong! I was "single-handedly" going into the vegan food business—low overhead, room for advancement, and retirement benefits . . . well, retirement at 18 *was* the benefit.

Unimpressive on paper, the subtleness of "left-handing" didn't translate. The genius was revealed in the act. A dozen successes inside a week and it was becoming clear. The logic and psychology of the left-hand technique was almost brilliant—*not* concealing an item struck far outside the retail world's frame of reference, their shoplifting paradigm didn't allow for it. "Left-handing" seemed the criminal's cutting-edge response to undercover loss-prevention agents and high-tech video surveillance. Very 90's . . .

Who, what, where . . . I understood these things. But *how* did it work? Scrutiny revealed simple brilliance. Once a person stepped into line, really, they are no longer suspect as a shoplifter. It would be assumed by suspicious eyes that a person intends to pay for what they are holding. The cashier never sees what you're stealing, "loss prevention" is no longer interested, you never conceal anything, the cashier's happy, you're happy . . . A true warm-hearted middle ground for both parties.

Once trained in "good form," I knew this was something like that dreamed apex of shoplifting fantasy—*the risk-free crime*. On the warpath, the 1-in-50 episodes of detection were invariably played off as an honest mistake. Say, the counter was too low, or the cashier too tall, they spotted the food in my hand and said—"Oh, did you pay for that already?" Ooops! Heh . . . I would sSammy my forehead and say—"I forgot I was *holding* this soy milk!" An honest mistake—exactly what it looks like! Cashiers and I enjoyed several touching moments of laughter over this. Oh dear, where is my head today . . .

Epilogue: Juice flowed, profit margins plummeted, I owned everything, etc. etc.

The nickel-and-dime capital demanded by my new line of work was a compromise. In conflict with my scheme to spend only pennies—dropped in bus fare boxes for the convincing "clink" effect. Vexation compounded by Tower Records becoming stubbornly rebellious to a kid pulling a receipt from the trash, the corresponding CD from the shelf, and kicking me down $16. One long-running high-school campaign taking its final breaths. Consumer groups were unresponsive, and I was left drinking decaf in Burger King, looking out at the rain, getting all wistful for the days of three-figure weekends. Toward the end, the granting of a "refund" was impossible with out firm demands and indirect threats—"Let me speak with a manager!"— and in the final scene of defeat, as I slipped $16 in my pocket, the loss-prevention agent unmasked himself, pulling me aside to whisper he'd found my return "suspicious." I feigned shock and dismay in the aftermath as the cashier drowned me with apology, "I am *so* sorry—that man was way out of line!" Closer inspection reveals not a defeat, but encouraging testimony from the "Man" himself! Even when they "know," they don't really *know*—and they'll never prove it! I found delinquent joy in the smoke from his ears.

Burger King made bad coffee. My window view offered the archetypal scene of western suburbia: Safeway and Rite-Aid. And the trash cans outside . . . It was a pivotal time. My Earth Crisis tape wore thin, and a replacement cost $8. Mouthpiece would make it $16, Undertow $24 . . . It was all too much. My proven Tower Records theory spoke: Where people shop, people have receipts, and where people have receipts, people drop them, or throw them away, or turn them over when confronted with suggestive neck-slashing motions, or something. I had no money.

Soon after the thought, I was pulling two boxes of Cap'n Crunch from the shelf, setting them on the counter, presenting my trash can receipt with a smile, and exiting with $10! Gauging from my recent crime statistics—the closest I would ever come to learning the price of food. The cashier's receipt: legal proof of purchase in all 50 states, respected everywhere chain stores value relations with kids who just didn't want their "birthday presents." Or corn-based cereal *without* Crunch-berries! No way—I demand a refund!

Of course, drug stores and supermarkets . . . Parents say—"Pick something you enjoy and do it for a living." Pleasure in this season of post-graduation came in suburban shock-value—ransacking trash cans, throwing trash around, making loud clanging noises from inside dumpsters, eating discarded food in public places, and assailing employees on trash-duty with obnoxious comments from *inside* the dumpster. This stage of adulthood brought thoughts of just what I would "do with my life." Family asked it, and finally I could sit up a little taller with my answer—"Dig through trash cans." Any confusion over the "profitability" of gar-

bage would be allayed at explanation of the finer points—
"Pull receipts from the trash, steal the item, return it" etc.
My slowing influx of vinyl—and the lucrative nature of on-
hands-and-knees parking lot foraging for that
mid-two-figure prize—both begged my attention. I felt no
need to "do the math." The job? I'll take it! This was the 4-
hour work week, at most. When shopping, please look
under the car before pulling out—there might be a receipt
underneath. And you might take off my arm!

"Left-handing" and "The Receipt Scam"—twin pillars
of the unemployment edifice. Call this the answer to my
last question, or just call it the end of work. Life was rich
with options, the stage now set for any dream. And in this
new world, anything seemed possible . . .

Grandma was very sweet. My furnished room offered
floral scented sheets, a squishy mattress, TV/VCR combo,
and other counter-revolutionary distractions to further
Grandma's agenda of bourgeois Grandson. I felt my temporary exploitation of the middle class as a stepping stone to
poverty was justified. The sun would rise, and it was a small
storm of notepads and footwork—stealing locks, wondering where to take showers—lining up the intricate particulars
of my plan. Gosh. Actualizing bumhood was hard . . .

A week into my preparations—fixing Trash House,
crude "refund" attempts of dumpstered merchandise, and
eating discarded movie theater popcorn—Grandma asked
my plans. I had avoided this. Plans? More of a feeling than
articulable blueprint. Reduction to a language of human
construct would be injustice itself, an insult to life for attempted digitization of the rawest of emotion to the crude
vagueness of spoken exchange . . .

"Live in the abandoned house behind Safeway!"

Linguistic genius. And I think Grandma had heart
palpitations.

Walking through the parking lots and side streets of
my new town that night, it felt the stage for delinquent
possibility. For anything. Good books and bad graffiti. Wide

smiles and narrow escapes. Probably it had been here all along—this obscure path of living off the excess, of exploiting the loopholes. All along, just under the surface. Like the steam tunnels below UCSD without a widely circulated map. I drew my own—"X" marks the unlocked door. Mostly I felt my way around in the dark, insulting business owners and ending my proud ancestral lineage in a flaming wreck. I'm never having kids, and barring priorital collapse, the closing chapter of my family name will be . . . "Dumpster Diver." Future genealogists will fall out of their chairs, but yellowed documents and obituaries miss the nuances. I mean, I found several hundred books and LPs in the bookstore dumpster. Family descendants won't extend my memory and status the warm eulogy of, say, "President," but really, wasn't this *better* than growing up to be that guy? Presidency is overrated. He has to pay for books.

I called Molly. She'd ended our romance the previous May in a touching moment—

"I know your life philosophy—it's wrong!"

Hugs not drugs?! That one's timeless! Wouldn't she melt back into my arms at hearing of my Trash House. Poverty, Trash House, eating trash . . . I whispered all the right things in her ear. You could say we were back together.

Molly was a "Valley Girl"—the myth, the legend, the zip-code to prove it. Big house and big hair, and the blue streak didn't fool you for a minute. Fooled me—not you. A Hollywood "industry" father kept the stereo upgraded and the cupboards stocked. When Dad wasn't in Hollywood—and I wasn't dragging entire bags of Hollywood's product from video store dumpsters—I crept to Molly's to eat that cupboard food. And when I finished, use that stereo to put CDs on cassette. "Where to plug in the stereo"—a possible flaw in my blueprint. Notes on the subject offered one untested solution: "Luxury apartment exercise room after midnight." Entirely consistent with my new world view stating I owned everything. In the interim, Molly was my answer. Molly was the answer to many things. Deep questions on the priorital disarranging effects of wealth and suburbia. Simple ones on the truth of what they say about Catholic girls. Mostly she answered questions of food, off-and-on shelter, and the value of a support network for the class fugitive. If she looks familiar, her only wish is you please not approach in the mall asking if she is in fact the teen celebrity you mistake her for. She gets that everyday. Molly had never acted professionally. Except at the Barnes & Noble return counter—she earned obscure awards for her work there. Molly: 10% punk, and the rest, well . . . that can be explained. You see, her dad had this credit card . . .

Molly wasn't love at first sight, just second sentence— "Dumpster diving . . . that's cool." We met in Tower Records months previous—on the floor by the magazines—during the filming of my art-film project. I gave her the test— what am I up to tonight? "I'm here to dig through trash and film it!" Look them in the eye and say "dumpster"—I love that test. My friends and I captured some stirring dumpster-diving footage that evening for our documentary, returning home with a car brimming with stolen garbage . . . and the number of one suburban girl who didn't run screaming when I showed it to her . . .

I wondered how far her "open mind" would stretch before exploding. "Molly," I said, when we met, I dove for CDs—four months later I dive for food, and I look at it, and I eat it. Molly thought on this, then offered support. Sweet Molly—my future plans include occupying a piece of trashy trash called Trash House and it's a big piece of trash!!! Molly thought on this, then offered support. Fascinating . . . Trash House scarcely supported itself. How far would she go?!

Molly was in high school, status concerns were the dictating force behind every thought and action, and I had no idea why she gave a vagrant space on her bed—or when her father returned early—under it. Molly was smart. Her friends boasted of *their* boyfriend, *his* new car . . . Molly turned up her nose at them all—"Car? My boyfriend has his own house!"

When she saw me next, Trash House sat up straight and proud. I had teased death-blows to my criminal record and family relations to assemble for Trash House a modest first-aid kit. Hammer from Grandma's garage. Nails from credit-card-to-the-door of apartment maintenance room. Padlocks from crude-but-effective theft at drug store. Dumpstered doorknobs and deadbolt mechanisms. Screwdrivers and latches. String and cardboard. And one wooden ladder from a condominium parking garage, riding my back several blocks to be placed humbly at Trash House's feet. I laid out my kit, puzzled. Well, what now? This was total improv. I checked my notes, looked at Trash House then flailed about—waving my arms, making crude stabbing motions with stolen tools, and hitting things. When the dust settled, she was—yes, still a barely upright Trash House— but now sporting a functioning lock. I welcomed guests—the lock was for cops, and trendies with alcohol. Cardboard over the window held back the wind. Flashlights hung on strings. A small radio in the corner of my room inched "trash" towards "home." And I dedicated many nighttime hours to picking up several dozen milkcrates behind Safeway, looking over my shoulder, and running. The dairy industry: They exploit cows, vegans steal their crates and make furniture with it. Proof two wrongs do, in fact, make a right. Grandma, at this point, had collapsed into limp complicity. She donated a mattress.

She was a sweet house. Was I her first? Certainly not. But sweet Trash House didn't respect the others, the rent and mortgage payers. Those relationships were exploitative, reducing a dignified house to a shell, a middle-class TV-watching box. Sort of tragic, you know, a thing as a shield from the world—Trash House was my gate to it. "Shelter" from one end of the ladder, and from mine: "experience." I reached out to touch her beaten door—together, it was us against the world. . . .

They had thrown me food in their dumpsters, left tools in broom closets behind crude locking mechanisms, placed a fruit bowl in the TV-station lobby—and rubbing their chin for ways to take this charity to extremes—threw out an entire house. So many gifts just lying around, looking up at me with sad eyes like I knew where to go from there. This was very confusing. Bringing edibles to the mouth and chewing—that was straightforward. But what of the streets themselves? Was I in fact free to skate them all night, listening to my walkman and climbing their rooftops? Like, without regard for adult form or "the future"? Evidence was mounting to suggest just that!

Pondering the context of the late-20th century on a stolen skateboard, playing in the streets seemed the true threat. And not buying anything . . . hold me back before I have a rich experience or something. These moments "off the clock" were volatile ones. Anything can happen. And when I stopped going to work and stood around a few minutes—it did. A lesson becoming clearer under bridges, on the waterfront probing for forgotten boats no one would mind me borrowing. I never found a boat. But I was excited by the possibility of it. Excited by everything. Because at the "bottom of the ladder"—those were my options . . .

It was a real big affair, stepping into Trash House with a sleeping bag over my shoulders, creeping past the hole in the living room wall, the other hole, a few dozen more . . . The flashlight brought me upstairs to my milk-crate bed, where the night's tentative plan was to lie down and sleep on it. It was a warm bed. During the quiet moment of my "big break"—every sound was a cop and every draft a ghost, but still, had any night ever been this absurd and awesome?

That first night in Trash House, I like to think Big Brother threw down his hat and shook his fist at my image on the monitor. The path to this place shared genes with blood relative "poorly choreographed barefoot dance down trail of broken glass." Not always pretty, but well-fought. At the end of this road to unemployment victory lay . . .

well, a big empty room strewn with beer cans. The seduction doesn't translate.

I could hear the kids' hushed words of my small-scale suburban scandal. I did it all for the books on the beach. They called it extreme, or just sad, but I only knew it as the logical extension of several basic premises. Life's "masks-down—hoods-up" approach. You always think there's a foaming-at-the-mouth scowl under those masks, but maybe we're laughing . . . Maybe we're laughing at *you!* Did you ever think of that?!

"We *have* to find you a new house."

My housewarming slumber party. I had forgotten to warn Molly that Trash House was more trash than house. I think she was a little traumatized. Well, which end of the crowbar was she on?!

I'd never been in a "love triangle," but knew one corner always got hurt. Best to keep the rivals for my love apart. And to diffuse tension, downplay to each my feelings for the other. To Molly, Trash House was only a stepping stone to better things, an abandoned house in a more exclusive suburb. I didn't need to convince Trash House of anything. She knew Molly's interest in my novelty value would soon fade. Probably just after her blue streak washed out. I sat in the eye of the storm, blushing. Caught between a musty housing felony and a slightly underage one. I felt comfortable there.

"We *have* to find you a new house."

Molly was tough. She slept in Trash House that night, and feigned excitement. Mine had to be contained. Illegality, general context, touch-and-go risk of structural collapse . . . Romantic in theme, if not ambiance. We lay in bed under the light of a street lamp, savoring this absurd antithesis of the "American Dream," and the actualization of a dream more relevant—mine!

Risk it all to chase life, then clash swords with its most listless non-participants: drinkers. The attempted break-

ins began Friday night. I would be swaying gently to a pleasant song on my little radio, and the house would shake;
upsetting me greatly. I would yell at Trash House that forceful demands for my attention would get her nowhere, that
I couldn't live with such a needy woman, nearly peaking at
broadsided slaps and tears when I heard the voices. From
my broken window I could plainly see packs of frustrated
youth with six-packs—taking blows of great fury at sweet
Trash House!

Good thing about shoplifting: one's able to select the
most expensive option. Fiscally counterintuitive, but the
legal opposite is just, I don't know, it's just *wrong*. Trash
House was adorned with only the best—the thickest locks
and thickest latches. They might break the stolen lock on
my stolen door, but they'll need a stolen crowbar! Peering
from behind the cardboard, I watched the dramatic escalation of tactics, held my ground, and made the heartfelt
commitment to never again approach abandoned property
without sporting a white flag, or dumpstered pillowcase,
or Kleenex from the hotel lobby, or something. All repos-
sessors of forgotten homes would be polite to take
note—I'm probably inside.

Thump thump thump . . . A tense standoff. But the
kids fell back, went home, quit drinking, or who knows,
and I could turn my radio back on and feel tough. In these
poignant moments of forced-entry, property owners had
police protection. Property liberators had . . . well I don't
know what we had. Flaming Nerf arrows. That was my only
idea. And I had no idea where to get them.

Boom boom boom. The mob—back in 24 hours. Reminding me of the university library sign: "If you don't eat
in our library, we won't study in your kitchens." I'd never
slept in or around someone's liquor cabinet, and didn't deserve this. Respectable dedication, but their beverages were
just *so* cliché. What's an effective scarecrow for drinkers?
Standard issue? The beer cans I'd swept into the next room
had told the story I'd been scared to hear. Yes, I'd found

the youth drinking spot—and now, I was living in it. Look, I still think this is cooler than rent . . .

The whole of my drinking knowledge: "They do it on weekends." The pattern was clear, and it scared me. Next Friday I skated my new downtown, tapped my toe, made unrefined Kinko's trash collages, and raided the Goodwill donation center, putting off what I knew was coming: the kids and their bottles. If they drank on my porch and left those bottles, the redemption value would go towards sand-bags and big nets. I'm not a pacifist. Creeping into an apartment rec room, I philosophized in the hot tub, dove into the pool, then went in circles stopping up the jets with my palm. I always do that. I would then cease my flailing arms and splashing, the water would come to a still calm for an absorbing moment while I thought it over in the shallow end, and I'd jump back in the hot tub! My eyes soon grew heavy on the couches in the TV room. I imme-diately rose up to challenge the necessity of a conceptual societal construct known as "house," stole every cushion from the couch, locked myself in the bathroom, and went to sleep! I swear it's our civic duty to do these things . . .

The kids expanded their trendy campaign to weeknights. Grandma began locking her doors while at work, effectively cutting off half my food supply. I bounced back . . . until she began locking her windows too. Molly stopped calling—I didn't have a phone. Trace amounts of trash were eventu-ally found within the town's sparse dumpster array—most of it pornographic and none of it edible. My only local friend sank into the rave scene, then twisted the knife by not surrendering her old straight-edge shirts. More and more, Trash House was sharing me with Apartment Restroom. My heart grew homesick. Then other body parts joined—unused vocal chords and grumbling belly. The towns' *other* secluded Coke machine—at the apartment pool—displayed offensive corporate loyalty, staring at me with smug silence and stubbornly denying me its quarters, though I smacked it with saltwater twice weekly. Coke machines can't be philosophized with—I tried. And in a shameful act of feeble escapism, I ran from big chunks of falling sky to the Toys R Us video test display to play Super Donkey Kong 3. Mid-game—the machine reset. Programmed timer perhaps, but I suspected power-politics. It was too much. I called Molly.

She lamented over my grievous condition sweetly as I cursed the sinister forces conspiring against me. Expecting heartrending words and a falling tear, she instead offered ten days in her hilltop palace. The quarterly Hawaiian vacation . . . I had totally forgotten. Golly, my own house in my old hood. I held the scene up for any possible flaws—OK, pleasant neighborhood, near the huge beverage distribution center where after midnight the cool forklift guys kick down free drinks on request, CD player, on major bus line . . . I'll take it! Why, this might lead to a deeper level of commitment in our relationship, as glimpses to the soul often can—yes, I was certain her diary was around there somewhere, and I was going to read it! I couldn't wait! And food—could I eat the food? "No food," she said. Her parents would know I'd been there. "Bye"—the back door is unlocked, don't touch anything, no girls, kiss kiss.

Love blossoms and civilizations fall in ten days. My ten days baited me forward with hints of both. The plan was to exploit the labor of Molly's father, use his house as a launchpad to find my own, break in, and live there! Heck, while I'm young, let's make it huge and near the beach! I'll be "practical" when life isn't so rad.

Ten days to find a house . . . I find these dramatic "life-or-cardboard-box" episodes fascinating. Like one of those 80's films where the guy has exactly 24 hours to spend one million dollars, except mine was a moneyless race to spend no money for the goal of spending no money on anything ever again. So, really, there's no analogy there. Planned tactics rested on an esoteric premise of hit-or-miss theoretical statistics—skating every street searching for a house, with faith in the probability of eventually seeing it, tripping over it, a thousand monkeys in a room for a thousand years typing a story about it, or something. I don't know, I've never done this before . . .

One "All Expenses (not) Paid (for)" vacation in my favorite town. Molly's vacation, I felt, was a little misguided. Side-by-side, I suspected "Hawaii on $10,000" lacked half the fun and all the drama of "Hometown on passion alone." I held this theory dear, then opened the door and ran with it . . .

At the bottom of a dumpster: one whole bag of Nintendo games, my first night at Molly's. "Every experience is enriched by having to fight for it"—the most overt lesson of self-sufficiency. Two elderly volunteers as combatants didn't make it less of a fight—they were ready to throw down! Well I got their games anyway. My theory was the fight also enriches *the games themselves*, but I'd never test this theory. Nintendo was two-dimensional, necessitating two senses at most. 18 and voluntarily broke—I had surrendered to a new addiction: full sensory experience. Maintenance of most fiendish addictions demands money. Mine begged the absence of it. The Star Wars game was tempting, flirting with me from the bag. But outside the TV, I had a fun little ongoing (intergalactic) war with growling (Imperial) security guards at the (Star Destroyer) mall—like sliding down the gap between escalators in my socks ever hurt anyone . . . I beat that level every time. Advancing to . . . well, that was the best part— I never knew!

And those fun crazy fights I mentioned? Breaking out everywhere, making suburbia fun again. Small furious clouds of dust where you see only flailing arms and heads, surfacing in a flicker at unnatural angles. The cloud dissipates—and I have your food! Actually I would never take from individuals. Food on store shelves not bolted down is, however, considered public domain, and I'll probably eat it.

When a storm broke, my games and I ducked into the chic mall to find a bizarre and unnatural ritual of wealth—

hundreds of people, dining on gourmet international cuisine in the upscale food court, then standing up mid-meal and just *walking away!* Couldn't explain it, but I could eat it! My fighting effort was enriching more than the experience, but also the taste of food itself. Mmmmmm . . . French fries fried in peanut oil. The peanut oil is key. Tactics escalated to actual cross-room reconnaissance on specific meals—first peering over shoulders, identifying meatless items, confirming vegan status at the respective counter, then just mumbling vague threats from across the room. Please sir, hurry up and just leave . . . stop teasing me. I never did disguise myself as a bush, but it would have been really cool if I had.

Bulk-food bins up the street plainly reaffirmed a newfound understanding: America's unwillingness to make starvation difficult. There were, like, 400 choices! No free food is insignificant—I believe this with my heart. This was the same store where friends of mine laughed to themselves softly while marking bags of $7.99/lb nutritional yeast with the P.L.U. # for corn meal. Total reformists. I grabbed the carob and ate it!

Attention that day was claimed entirely by suburbia's obscene amounts of free food—picking it up, looking at it, and pondering whether to place it in backpack or mouth. This led to completely losing track of time and purpose. Only after raiding the Wendy's salad bar, convincing the supermarket cashier the two unwrapped burritos I'd heated in the microwave were not the expensive vegan ones but in fact the 50¢ ghetto brand, and pulling entire bags of bagels from dumpsters, finally collapsing in a booth at the buffet restaurant and looking up to see *still more food*—did I realize I'd found no house. Better grab a plate and think it over . . .

Maybe I privately longed for missing the last bus that night, and a six-mile walk in the rain. Skating large hills and side streets, enjoying intimate contact with my surroundings. Richer approach than sitting in a box, moving through it. Such an insult to the world, our boxes. Degrading landscape to a burdensome gap between two points. Usually two boxes. Interacting with my environment had brought to surface the drama I'd always suspected was there, in every construction site and rooftop. I knew why the sensations so long eluded capture: 18 years—all boxed up. The world in a square block—I was seeing it clearly now. Six miles would bring . . . well, I couldn't say. But I did the math and was a little concerned. One block=one world, four blocks to a mile . . . It was, like, whole novels, entire rap albums! Dear lord . . .

My favorite department store lay at the three-mile mark—where, a year previous, I'd dumpstered 400 cans of Pepsi. Grateful Dead fans are characterized by heavy eyelids and having the vitality of zombies. But yell "Pepsi—25¢!" from a shopping cart at their concerts, and they come alive!

Still mid-epic, the rain poured for dramatic effect, or maybe just to remove fingerprints. The town was on my side that night. Like, behind that department store, I found a row of metal walk-in storage units. In celebration of my profound "Box Theory," I looked the very box-like units up and down, unwrenched the lock, filled whole bags with Christmas lights, and ran! Simply *months* of return money! So much trouble to get into . . . "Only 24 hours in a day": God's cute little joke to the unemployed.

Three miles left to Molly's. I wished it was a hundred.

On my last night, I laid out my paper and pens, and sat to write Molly a "Ten Days in Review." Perhaps there wasn't enough paper in the world. Then I picked up a pen. No, perhaps one sheet was too much. The experiences didn't translate. Any attempt was almost an insult to the profoundness of it all. I gave each day one line and turned the page.

If it was thrown away or left unchained during those ten days, it was probably stashed under Molly's bed. If it was unlocked, I probably opened it, crept inside, and rummaged through the boxes. If it was black, I probably painted it white, then danced on it. If it cost money, I probably evaded that part and took it anyway. Probably I did it all that stay. Everything but find a house . . .

OK, I found one. Huge, nice neighborhood, and permanently unoccupied. Claiming owners who scarcely acknowledged the structure as their own, and never went inside. Also perilously close to the home of its wealthy neighbors, twenty feet from the daughter's window. All sounds would be heard, all movements seen. I was desperate. My extreme condition demanded an extreme response. So I shrugged, packed my bag, walked twenty feet, and moved in.

More of a barn than a house—that was my thought stepping inside. And my thought upstairs—"More fun than both!" One floor—all hay! A house of four-figure amusements twenty feet from mountains of hay . . . I just didn't get it. More hay for me! And it really was like being a child again—stacking bales in the corner for my own *hay fort*. A few stuffed animal bombs for intruders with cooties and I'd call it home . . .

Possibility was the sentiment of the time. Crime the means, suburbia the stage, hay the safehouse, and "practicality" the unmentionable. Molly left for school, her parents left to earn *my* rent, and my day began—wholly unaccounted for by any state or federal agency, traceable only by noseprints on the windows of a few tattered homes. My other trail—of left-hand meal receipts reading "Bagel - $0.59"—had gone cold. I began saving them for humor value. 59¢ meals—that joke would never grow stale. At day's end, when I was certain life could never be more absurd, I crept into my barn for a sneaky midnight date. Molly wasn't always punctual, but she always brought food.

It was punk rock love—cheeseless pizza and big plans. Molly's tender hopes for a life together in the abandoned shack she'd found had crumbled—I saw hints of activity— but tell us ours was a doomed plan and we'd gasp.

"Analytical thought" and "statistical evaluation"—unsporting words of war. No way, this was a feeling. Possibly the rebound effect of a TV childhood, my last job, or both. "Find an abandoned house and live in it"—I never thought to hold the dream up for holes, but I held it up to its opposite and that was enough. And I had *hay,* you know? Truckloads!

Maybe this life-addiction secured me an everlasting dependence on "someone else's" house, "someone else's" everything. That was part of the charm. While I drank "their" juice on "their" newspaper boxes outside "their" supermarkets, I took smug comfort in the one thing called "mine"—you know, whatever came next. They warned I'd adopted a dangerous approach entirely dependent on the labor of others. Sir, I too long for a more equal partnership in which we walk together as brothers . . . First step: Quit dropping things! And tone down the abundance, or cover it up a little or something. Duh.

Danger, I felt, was a crucial element of romance—thematic or female. And Molly's love was dangerous. Felony in age and physical hazard in daughterhood—caught by her father, she said, and . . . well, just *don't be.* He'd beaten journalists on sets before rolling cameras, and there were no such deterrents pointed at Hay Fort. The point was swallowed, and at night I sank a little deeper into my bag at slight sounds. Childhood had taught DIY forts to be fortified against girls, sometimes lobbed furniture cushions. Parents knocked them down and sent you to your room. So it was on our date one night at 2 a.m. that something went critically wrong.

"MOLLY!!!"

Eviction. They call what happens next "homelessness," but I only knew it as sleep getting a little more *dangerous* . . .

My vision for idealized homeless form was me, and a boom box, all day in a public setting, listening to distorted hip-hop tapes. Like maybe on the lip of the fountain outside the mall . . . Or heck, *in* the food court, eating *your* leftover fries! Call me a dreamer . . .

I made the all-day bus trip to Trash House one last time . . . only for the boom box. Any extended life in her arms was not to be—the bottle kids would have their house back. My sights had fixed on waterfront dreams in more promising neighborhoods. Turning the final corner, I let out a nervous laugh, and turned back for the bus. City "Public Works" department perhaps, but I detected "Revenge of the drinkers." And where they got a bull-dozer I have no idea . . .

I stumbled about my hometown in a daze, certain only that I wouldn't "grow up" and "be realistic" short of Death's Door. I had faith in finding another house that night, a tougher house, where the wrecking ball would just go "chink" and bounce off. OK, I had no idea what I was do-ing. Probably I'd become one of those guys under the bridge! Anyway, time to find a place to sleep . . .

My options were many. University, "work force," mili-tary . . . College would distract from my very profound studies inside the public library, supplemented with field research at Barnes & Noble where I, you know, stole books and read them. Working inspired thoughts of time cards, and effective downward strokes for applying them to my jugular. It's a point of great pride that I've never seen my own Social Security number. And military . . . I was cur-rently on the frontlines of a near-armed struggle with the thrift store manager over his dumpster. I needed no for-mal training for this—only bolt cutters! Leaving only plan "D," whatever that was . . .

On the surface—lacking shelter or capital—perhaps my situation seemed a little desperate. Perhaps in the arms of extremity, men do extreme things. Convictions fold and slogans fall. The insurgent is brought to his knee before the slavemaster. I don't know what to say . . . I went home. Like, to my parents' apartment. They welcomed me with open arms, we embraced. They perhaps sensed closure to a son's deviant phase, and that everything would be "OK." I looked them in the eye wistfully . . . then ran to the complex rec-room and went to sleep! Couches, TV, and under the sink—tea bags! It was great! The suburbs claimed much private space—now, I make it my own. What I want—I take. When I'm tired—I sleep. And if it's on the couch in the lobby of *your* apartment, well then . . .

My new approach had Molly a little concerned. So I flung open the double doors for a little dose of truth. It was all there—plush couches, several weeks of *People* magazine, ping-pong . . . and the residents really respected the room as my own, I said. Or didn't know I was there, or had their own couches to sleep on, or something. Anyway, I owned it now. We set up the hot-water dispenser, tossed back cups of tea, watched MTV, and fell asleep in each others arms. It was all very sweet . . .

At daybreak, we awoke, looked at each other, then at the manager standing over us. She threw us out.

At 8:45 p.m., I called Molly at home, giggling.

"Molly, the library closes in fifteen minutes . . ." ha ha ha ha ". . . and I'm going to *sleep here!*" HA HA HA!

Molly was confused. Like all humor, if it has to be explained, the effect is lost. "Hide in a restroom stall, and when the custodians leave—run up and down the aisles." It was the plan. Not my own plan, but I gave a nod to its pioneer—whose zine lay in my bag—before stepping into the stall. An hour passed and the question remained—when the custodians leave, what to do first? Collect change from the seat cushions? Slide the tile in my socks?

The head of a Mexican woman came under the stall door. We looked at each other for a tender moment . . .

"WE CLOSED AN HOUR AGO!!!"

"Oh! I'm very sick, so sorry. . ." I said, clutching my stomach. Ugh, groan . . .

The suburbs were mine that night—maybe *forever*—and if I had to break minor laws to claim it, well, that was the seductive part. I was tired. Let's see . . . *bushes*, I felt, were dangerously uncreative, a threat to no one, and really, the embodiment of conformity itself. I suspected the answers lay outside the confines of custom, beyond even my imagination. I wasn't sure, this was all new. If this *had* been don\e before, it wasn't within city limits, and not with a Transformers sleeping bag. I rode the bus to a familiar neighborhood and took a long, hopeful walk. I looked at the skate park, the recycling center, a couple construction sites . . . A path taking me three miles, to my ex-girlfriend's window. A window best crawled through another night— right now, I had sort of a little point to make. My old high school lay twenty yards north, a stage begging for a statement—like, say, *beating* the door of a trailer until it caved. My alumnus status clearly legitimized the property damage in this case. I dove behind a mound of football equipment and went to sleep!

Living in a trailer behind my old high school . . . I thought that was awesome. My daytime hours were committed to following up leads on abandoned houses, hit-or-miss residential searches, and eating salad. And did *you* know the supermarket left out boxes of bananas on the loading dock? Did you know *why?!*

So many houses, each with its own unique disqualifier. House by the library: dangerously proximate to active construction sites on all sides. House by mall: seemingly inspected routinely. Entire neighborhood of abandoned houses: slated for demolition in 6 weeks. Broken into helmet-and-pad storage trailer near 10 yard line: nothing wrong with that! I keep my head high in these uncertain times. Still, the selection was totally insulting. The terms were: Empty, unchecked, by the water, four walls and a roof; with owners either dead, never returning, or not returning until I was dead.

My demands were met that weekend. I'd known of it for weeks, or known it was coming. "Inside" knowledge of an opening in the real estate market. Carpeted, rent-free, and not on the water—but close. Totally abandoned, and the residents—relocated. How had I forgotten . . . my parents' apartment: vacant.

Digging deep in my bag, I couldn't be certain I still held the title of ownership, but I felt around, and . . . oh yes—the key. OK, perhaps not abandoned in the strictest sense. Its "up for grabs" status more one of philosophy. You know, if it was suburban and unguarded I owned it. Doomed to certain eviction perhaps, but a mindset supporting thoughts of "tomorrow" was dissipating, yielding to an urgent sense of urgency. Every morning I awoke was a rent-free night they could never take away . . .

My own rent-free apartment, I'd always wanted one of those. I really loved #208. The whole complex in fact. All the cool secretive doors opened with a pocket knife— the meter room, door to the roof, janitor's closet, elevator room . . . all unmarked, and I never knew what lay behind. Sort of dramatic. Like, would I take door #1 (dusty books and a ladder), or #3 (puzzling room of pharmaceutical promotional items)? The answer was, of course, both, and afterwards, through a third—to rock out in the spa with a view of the city . . . I had plans for the empty storage unit on floor one—remaining a rent-free fantasy until answering the question of "how to lock from the inside." I thought on this daily. But until then—free batteries (door by restrooms), and my stylishly carpeted, stylishly *empty* apartment. One way in and one way out—if I awoke to a shocked prospective tenant with a furious manager demanding my exit, well, they'd just have to step aside! And be schooled in lock-picking—I slept in the bathroom. And if an eventual brawl erupted over property rights, I came strapped with "Prozac" promo pocketknives (4th floor), making a gory mess remedied with a steam cleaner (5th), altogether an exhausting struggle for freedom requiring recuperation with hot tea (5th), while reading strangers' mail (5th), in a dark and quiet room of buzzing wires (4th), with a borrowed flashlight (1st), and when the SWAT team arrived on a homicide call sending me flailing for an escape route, I'd found the blueprint room—it's on the 4th floor!

Molly and I met three nights later in the parking lot of Barnes & Noble. Her hopes of a quiet night at "my place" were put down gently. The tape I placed over the keyhole in my absence? That evening—admonishingly *gone*. I mean, yes, the apartment was mine, I was philosophically the owner, so long as I evaded detection by the legal ones.

Molly was stubborn and tough—if the mean ole suburb tried claiming a victory over her boyfriend, she'd hold my hand until we got even. When I felt her warm tender grasp soon release and fall away, I felt no betrayal—stolen food demands both hands! Three trays of food at the mall later, we saw this as a rebound victory of sorts. The mall closed, we filled my bag with pretzel bread, and threw ourselves out into the big, crazy Saturday night social frenzy. I wonder where two kids and a bag of stolen food sleeps in this town . . .

Back on "the streets"—a term weighted with doom-filled connotation, but in my town only meaning lots of fountains and public art. We walked the polished streets. U-Haul got all subversive and donated two blankets from an unlocked truck. Or said nothing when we picked them up and snuck away—two things, lately, I'd committed to lay aside all prejudice against and call equal. Molly was plainly looking to me for good form and sharp ideas—a transient power-move pulled from my hat. We passed the mall fountain, the office complex fountain, pizza parlor fountain . . . dead-ending at the park fountain. My favorite. Colored lights—breathtaking. We sat down in the park with our blankets—in the shadow of luxury condos—and, well, went to sleep! "Sleeping vagrant in park," I think about those guys a lot. And since that morning, suspect several frightened joggers think that about *me!*

Blankets over shoulders, Molly towed me up 2nd St. the next morning, to the lobby of the big hotel to recover from the trauma of it all—stabbing points and cold stares, shame only death could wash away . . . Definitely the last time I ever *pay* for Molly's phone call. Embarrassing. We fixed our hair in the mirror, checked for overnight damage, and left to explore the hotel. Soon after, we discovered whole worlds behind unlocked doors. A room of office equipment for the "business traveller"—with fax machine, computer, and phone! I didn't know what a "fax machine" was, but the "free" part ignited a desire to learn, then use it in unfocused ways. On the exclusive "top floor," we jiggled doorknobs and ate fruit from room-service trays, taunted all the while by a smug, pompous door by the elevator— "VIP only." Brushing past an exiting VIP, we stepped inside—and out of mere *leftovers* forever! One huge, colorful buffet for criminals! Soy milk and Frosted Flakes, kiwi and cantaloupe . . . We placed napkins on our laps, assumed dignified poses, and choked down laughter while averting eye contact with other diners. By our sketchy logic, *Vagrants In Parks* were VIPs too. Let's see . . . Wendy's salad bar Mondays, the "all-bagel" Tuesdays, VIP lounge Wednesdays . . . Yes, there was hope in this town. Maybe I'd always known these free amenities lay just below a thin surface, and needed an encouraging hand to hold. Molly had pretty hands. I took her left in my right and stepped to the balcony. From that 25th floor perch—the highest in town—I could see the town and all it could be. The bagel dumpster, the other bagel dumpster, the record store, the rooftop of the mall . . . and, well, there seemed no reason I couldn't subsist on those dumpsters, steal *every* CD, and play on that rooftop; and do it all as a full-time profession. No reason I couldn't see it all and do it all. Own this town and dance in the streets—*forever!*

. . . if I could find an abandoned house. In the heart of the state's highest property values—a thought akin to the punchline of an absurd joke. And near the water—the *whole* joke. Laugh along, they all did. I laughed. In the quiet morning moments over microwaved bagels. Ha ha ha at night—back in the apartment rec-room. Riotous laughter everywhere the thought occurred—circumventing a lifetime of work and mortgage payments with a crowbar. And doing it all in that zip-code: impossible. My life-plan—at that point—was analogous to a children's cartoon: raise questions of its realism, adherence to known laws of physics or the like, and the joy is lost. I'd suspended pragmatism for the dream, resting on the theory: My prolonged community presence would soon create abandoned property by inspiring residents to actually *run screaming from their homes!* I'm not going away . . .

Such a sweet girl, Molly, stepping off the bus with a bag of stolen tools for our big day of forced entry. Sweet, and *tough*—even if they were only her father's. Maybe I had run out of ideas, run out of streets to walk, or run out of "youthful idealism" boosting hope for that empty and forgotten mansion. Maybe Erica's ghost-assault stories no longer scared me like thoughts of restless sleep on apartment roof shingles at a 45-degree angle. I mean, it wasn't *bad*, I'm just saying . . .

So did it all come down to *this?* Young love and illicit tools, lingering knowledge of that still vacant haunted house, then throwing up one's hands to just break in and *live there?* It was the day's going plan.

Everything was perfect, the snapshot idyllic: a girl in one hand and a crowbar in the other. Some scenes define times, entire generations of the sick and tired. Others just scare small children. Our strut was sincere, winding our way through the park, past the cool lookout perch for quiet nighttime introspection, the rich white joggers . . . Erica had really come through. I'd seen the house already, but closer scrutiny brought more promise. Like the yellowed slip on the door—"Condemned." Sounded *permanent.* Was this it? Like, had I *won?!* We weren't in yet!

The rear door sat stubbornly unresponsive to a crowbar, and my obnoxious and unrefined blows only brought the occupying spirits inside to roars of laughter. With new roommates, I saw this as "starting on the wrong foot." Here it was—my first prying motion of a crowbar. A tool weighted with revolutionary symbolism—and like most celebrities, a snob! It doesn't do anything! I handed Molly Mr. Hotshot and shrugged. Molly raised the crowbar to the sky—as lightning bolts rained down with all heaven's fury—then brought down the tool with all the shame and rage of a girl with a homeless boyfriend and *smashed* the window! *MOLLY?!?!* We stared at the jagged hole for a profound moment . . .

Uh-oh—the cops. We fled.

We ran out of breath blocks away in the town's largest park—one of those rad, lawless belts you instinctively run for in tense moments. And I'm almost certain at this point most kids are *born* knowing of that cement perch by the tennis courts as "World's Best View of a City."

It would be cool and tough to say I'd reached "the end of the line," but really, I could drag out this standoff for years—long walks with dubbed tapes, crowbars and nice grrrls, apartment rec-rooms (coffee on Saturdays) and sunpatio lounge chairs . . . I think the appeal here was lost on Molly. She wanted to go. I wanted to take my crowbar to anything with a door. So maybe I *was* disappointed. But we sat on the grass in the world's most pleasant place to be so. Face it—five blocks from the water, this park was the garden of cheer. Rad jungle gym for the kids, big grass, near downtown, beach access, bordering previously undiscovered huge and abandoned house—uh—wait . . .

* * *

"Find an abandoned house and live in it."

My faith in these words remained solid, while after that day the plan itself unfolded in less than ideal ways. Despite the sacrifices, I held my head high for the next two years.

Yeah, that half-million dollar palace wasn't on the water, but I'm telling you man, it was close . . .

More plans than time. Train tracks and donut shops. Good books and small town kids more impressed with you than you are with yourself. My summer at this point was perhaps summed up best as one crazy month of glory, shock value, and upright university library naps below the "No Sleeping" sign. And I'll never forget that thrift store, with the employees who welcomed a struggling writer into their place of work, giving me free run of the back room and first pick of donations—then waving with a smile as I put it all in bags and walked out! Thanks guys!

Then there was the amazing place I'd found *here*—in Little Rock—where the community conspired with "lost" copy cards and public seating to support a struggling writer, and his effort to spend all day writing about them in smugly insulting terms! I almost felt bad about this. God, I still can't believe they let me sit here all day . . .

I hadn't always occupied a "Customers Only" table in Little Rock. I began other places. It all started in May, building on the rough premise to recreate every hobo book I'd read over winter. To lose myself in wistful reflection under bridges, land upright in daring dives from moving boxcars, always triumph over cops, eat unpaid-for merchandise, and savor it all. I'd tested this recipe once or twice. All I will say about the experiment is: Don't believe what they say about blondes having "all the fun"—it's really the dirty guys in train yards! I was both, so either way this was going to be a rad summer . . .

Over the years, I'd read many books on this subject. It was roughly about the time I read, oh, the *first one,* that I grabbed my walkman and decided to *live it*. Books are dangerous like that. Incomparable to the landmine and shrapnel of a summer at home, but still dangerous. One book of infallible truth and romance by those more daring than you, and you'll never sit still again. Several dozen in four months and you're back sitting still—to write your own.

I'd just cleared this phase. Five months in a basement, surrounded by pens, used books, and stolen everything, resting on the assumption the other guys didn't do it right. I'm not proud of this artistic swagger, but as an amateur outlaw—I had disputing opinions on the subject. Alcohol was the hobo's first problem. Stealing from each other another. Eating animals, exploiting societal abundance in unambitious degrees, general grumpiness, etc. . . . As my hobo reading mounted, my friendly literary project evolved from graceful movements of the artist's pen to the vengeful hacking motions of a ballpoint knife. I knew custom, and I wished to kill it. The paper storm settled, and I invented a subtly shrewd plot to legitimize the work by completion *on the road*—in truck stops and bagel shops—wherever vagrants enjoy themselves all day and are wholly unconcerned with your opinion of it! I was a little obsessed . . .

My pen and I were on tour. We caught a few rides and rode a few buses. I edited in the rain, proofread on Greyhound, and manipulated your sister into kicking down free coffee. I evaded Nordstrom's security in the tenser moments, fought for the perfect word in Cineplex seats during those more soothed. And I ate a lot of bagels—though through masterful contextualization, my summer meals took on frames of romance. The whole bag of food from the college town health-food chain was "Tortured Artist" extremity, eating it all by the maps in the university library was the "Offending Hobo" . . . with nowhere else to go! Such was the idyllic lens I'd affixed over my crazy summer.

The plan to authenticate my art exposed me to an under-the-surface support network for authors—girls saying "no charge" at coffeehouses with a grin, and copy store cashiers giving 95% discounts with a nod. And thoughts always returned to the back room of that thrift store, and the very rare and free poetry book I sold for $50! No surprise really, I'd known of such workplace corruption for years. Artists don't need "grants," just *you* to look the other way!

The charity grew to absurd levels upon discovery of an incorporated design flaw in the library of a major university, where—not only was I able to study maps all day and run up and down the stairwell—but now, live inside!

My long running campaign to steal back "private" space and sleep there brought me on another bus, to another university. Smaller library, but with longer hours—24 of them! They never closed! I find places do things like this for me quite often. So, at the point in my work day when I would have crawled onto the nearest roof, I crawled on the nearest couch. Was it progression? It felt that way, and the hobo books I'd studied during winter made no mention of such things. The less-groomed men that campus police dragged past me each night probably didn't write. This was only to be a stop on the way to something better, but the library hours had me momentarily stationary. Long enough to crash into an outright brick wall of the best hobo book collection I'd ever seen. Soon after stapling me to the furniture with an equally absorbing collection of sociological texts on shoplifting! On the cusp of my layout phase, and it was all there—cut-and-paste quotes on the communist implications of retail theft, and pictures of old guys under bridges! Twin themes of my work.

Reading a book a day, my obsession snowballed to unhealthy extremes—taking long walks to distant bookstores for coffee table hobo-pictographies. My possessed research evoked fantasies unrestrained by reason, while life outside imagination was utterly bookish. Late May . . . in a library? Unthinkable! I stormed from the double doors, stole some luggage, threw my project inside, and hurled myself at summer! I'm a tramp!

Stepping off the bus into Little Rock, I carried a humble thrift store suitcase, brimming with notes and scraps, photos and stories. I chanted a mantra to myself softly, from the mind of the author who'd given me literary life—"You have to suffer to create." Greyhound had inflicted the necessary first half of the equation. Little Rock was my stage for the rest. No good books, distractions, or "open-minded" lenience towards shameless loitering—only Southerners, and me: the hobo threat. It was a well-researched role . . .

I took my little suitcase to the waterfront, the park, several attractive benches . . . I found what I was looking for at the natural foods chain grocery store. Dexter worked the deli, was my only Arkansas contact, and stood in staunch support of hoboism and those who wrote of it from privileged angles. Maybe *too* supportive—I couldn't fit the food in my mouth fast enough. It was a warm greeting—first with smiles, then tofu. We wasted no time discussing the important issues, and I humored his confirmation of what I already knew—aisles of food: *all free.* Well duh! "Arkansas" perhaps, but still inside U.S. borders. Then, I was shown the tables by the front—for the loiterers, he said. Get busy. I looked at the table by the door, the one closest to "Vitamins" . . . the plain pick was extreme northwest payphone seat—with clear view of all other tables, the leftovers on them, and a straight path to the coffee bar with little room for misdirection. I took the table and made it my own. A loiterer of hobby and sport—I knew the unhealthy attachment occurring at times between kid and public seating. I embraced this. But not before the Little Rock health food store had I premeditatedly *set-up* the romance. I sat down. Gosh, room to suffer, and create, free coffee, and orbited by paid staff of questionable workplace loyalty! I laid out my papers, scissors, notes, and white-out. A strange town, deep thought in public space . . . It felt like summer now.

I was learning vagabond triumph is often predicated entirely on employee disloyalty—solicited by hungry eyes, direct questions, or in this case: both. One eight-hour day and employees glared suspiciously. Three days and hushed word of the hungry tortured artist was moving counter-clockwise around the store. Five days and I had a small "free food" support network. Throwaways were donated, cashiers were "forgetting" to ring up 9/10 of my purchases . . . Ten days and I owned the store! Although bashful, I had strategic alliance with two cashiers, one kid in produce, the entire deli staff, and the vitamin girl. The coffee girls bridged the perimeter gap between deli-case and books. Their allegiance to my free-coffee-confederacy was never expressed, though unpaid gallons left the self-serve dispenser without comment, so I think their partisanship was clear. The bulk-foods manager was an introverted mystery—possibly sympathetic, though his eyes told nothing. I ate his fig bars when he wasn't looking.

So . . . if you neutralize the leader and the army falls, does consorting with the leader yield *free food?* I operated under the theory, clearing a space at my table for Dexter during his lunch breaks. A captain of sorts, he knew the entire staff, and served as ambassador between my table and paid guardians of the five food groups. One well-placed connection, and within hours, food most have to leave their chair for—even pay for—was delivered to my table with a sly nod. And plastic utensils. Conversation centered on militaristic analysis of floorplan, camera placement, content of the back-room "free box," and criminal proclivity of the entire staff. No cameras on aisle 3. Sonny was a loyalist. Managers gone at 5. Vivien was untested. Dumpster fruitless. Danae harbored no loyalty to her white slavemasters. Dexter flowed the internal reconnaissance, I was the tactician, the smoke cleared, and we were in the parking lot—eating cookies!

The commute from office to home was agreeable—half-block east, on the right, United Artists Cinema, screen 5. Or rather, under it. Screen 1 was unkempt, a mattress of JuJu Fruits and trash. Screen 3 was dangerous, threatening exposure with a four-inch gap between curtain and floor. Unaccommodating, both of them. A testament to society's betrayal of "The Artist" as a pillar of culture, the negligent dismissal of literature as an edifying moral compass, a tragic discontinuation of nurtured artistry by a neo-conservative administration . . . then I found screen 5 and took it all back—first-class! Squeaky clean, a row of speakers to nest behind, and somehow always hosting the best films. My product of trial-and-error, late-night screen hopping, and predator/prey evasion of ushers in my shopping for a choice 6 1/2 x 3 foot vacation home. It's a buyer's market!

The path to this American Success story suffered broken bridges, near defeat, and sleepless nights. At first it seemed without flaw—who but a rat or hobo would crawl beneath a screen? My first night at 3 a.m., with three inches separating giddy kid from huge empty theater, everything seemed perfect—just me, a little bag of popcorn, and one small rent-free triumph! Then the custodians rushed in with leaf blowers, flapping the curtain up in a storm of trash and popcorn! They were "blowing" my cover! A tense moment, and while I rushed to stabilize the curtain with a foot and a backpack, I wasn't sure if this was a prelude to eviction, or just the most fun I'd ever had at the movies . . .

Perimeter penetration of the theater was my little joke. Dexter called it "an insult to our skills"—unlocked doors, beyond sight of usher or concessionaire, beyond the satisfaction of "challenge" even. From there it was a simple matter of finding a bag of popcorn in the trash, and choosing a 10:00 film. When the movie failed to stimulate, I could wander to empty screens looking for a housing upgrade, dig for more popcorn, or think on—but never quite implement—my untested supplemental income scam of stealing movie posters for their often overlooked resale value. You can look at the posters, touch the glass longingly, but you might never know the frames open on a hinge—fastened only by Velcro!

The film would end, the lights turn on, and it was a quick move to exploit the sliver of time between last moviegoer and first custodian. Then a dive over the speakers to exploit a forgotten design nook. All of this just after exploiting the labor of Hollywood and the hard working actor, offering no monetary compensation for the favor. Made possible by an exploitation of publicly accessible monuments to passivity, of unsightly sprawl I had no say in creating. From all angles—parasitic exploitation! It was great!

My literary project was coming along. Facial white-out stains marked that progress. There was a subtle thread of order running through the stacks of paper and photos, even if the cashiers just thought I was making a big mess. Dexter cheered me on from the deli. He's followed the course from casual acquaintance to the hand that feeds me—then the head that tells the other heads to look the other way. Soon after promoting himself to "literary agent," forcing workers and customers into the adjacent chair, shoving small stacks of paper into reluctant hands—"Read this." Embarrassing. I didn't need "support" or an "audience," just more double-sided tape every six hours, fig bars every four, and coffee every two. But Dexter roped in the "reading public"—and reviews trickled in. Review #1: blank stare. Review #2: blank stare, etc. etc. Demo editions were handed to casual friends, who then never spoke to me again. All suggesting I'd released from it's cage a novella so crude and appalling, it lay beyond the courtesy of feigned praise! Like, they were *upset!* Obviously there existed no "target market" for dumpstered VCRs and small-town drama. If disowned by all others, I took comfort in one assured following: the rear five rows on Greyhound. They love me there.

The relationship with food holds deep distinction for those who must look over shoulders to get it. I never actually do this—poor form. Nonetheless, edibles were close to my heart. Yet even food was losing importance as my cut-and-paste tornado grew more intense. Even *possessed.* A trend developed away from table-by-the-payphone to copy-machine-in-the-corner. Cancer by caffeine to cancer by Kinko's. Soon I was only seeing my agent after his shifts when he brought me food. Though only a mile in distance from my grocery table, Kinko's was an entirely different climate. This was a raw, behind-the-back, hit-and-run art-attack. It felt good. On my first day, I was feeling out the store—opening cabinets, sizing up employees, spinning on the computer chairs . . . Then Dexter found a $14 dollar copy card in the reader! He donated this to my project. Soon, keeping my layout phase afloat rested entirely on suited guys rushing in, flailing their arms and throwing papers around, looking at their watches, running out, and leaving their cards in the machine!

Ten hours in Kinko's, ten in the theater, with the balance offered to pools and busses, side streets and paperbacks. And if I timed it right—an appearance at the natural food store for the throwaway rice and tofu. A poetic time carved out of a southern town with retail defectors, unenforced vagrancy laws, and the selfish belief I deserved to do whatever I wanted—forever!

My little art-war in the corner of Kinko's was escalating. I had first entered as "customer," dozens of hours later bordering on "resident," and as I put down roots, learned to fix the machines, and put up my own stickers, it became a full-on "takeover." There was a line from the card dispenser to the courtesy phone—west was an occupied autonomous zone, east lay the hostile loyalist belt. Contact between us was limited to me approaching the counter with a scuffed and unreadable card, demanding a replacement, them asking the amount on the card, me saying "$90," and them then *taking my word for it!* Next time—a *hundred* and ninety!

I stored papers in the drawers. I shaved in the restroom. I acquired technical knowledge of copy machine mechanics. I spent more time assisting customers than most employees. And I can state with a glow that my ungodly "24-hours-in-a-Kinko's" experiment was a success! Applying a possibly *communist* logic to my art, it was my feeling that since I put in more hours than most employees, I was entitled to *free copies*. Dexter agreed. Together, late one night, we noticed an even numerical match between "us" and "them," and *raided* the auxiliary counter! They didn't even notice! We escaped to the autonomous zone to count our new stack of copy cards and giggle. We fed card after card through the reader, and giggles turned to stunned silence. I'll never admit to the numbers we saw. I'll say only that artists' grants this large cannot be applied for. They're beside the register—and you have to reach!

I went back the next day, and the next . . . Backs would turn, and I don't know what to say—it was in the wrist. And when backs wouldn't turn, I employed distractive questions and smokescreen. No, the smokescreen isn't true, but the lesson remains—if you pay for anything, you're not really trying.

Many social lives center on school, others on the weekend punk shows, then there's me—social contact occurring entirely with random Kinko's customers. It was a slow scene. And at 8 p.m.— just me and balding conspiracy theorists. So when the blonde bombshell walked in—heads turned. In a moment, I was certain I knew her story. In ten minutes, she had told it to me. Gosh, a real newspaper reporter. A woman of letters. Rides, handouts, and authorship—the quickest ways to my heart:

"Cheyenne? Get in."

"One refill—no charge."

"Here's my zine." Or my byline . . .

Shoulder to shoulder, we shuffled through our papers, getting closer, soon shuffling through each other's papers. I read her painstakingly researched and penetrating report on the Whitewater scandal, she read my tearful accounts of digging through trash.

"What are you working on?"

It is, in fact, a manifesto of the unemployed, my statement to a world gone mad. Thanks for asking.

"Show me more."

Golly. My first voluntary reader. Together with my first audible review—on the same night. It was all smiles and applause, and she didn't even ride the Greyhound. No, she was straight champagne-in-Amtrak-window-seat, I was certain. She read, and I watched, certain I was seeing the radicalization of a reporter. And when she read my "free food" scam—maybe even the *criminalization!*

I inquired on infiltration techniques used by a reporter for access to exclusive and newsworthy events. She probed my philosophies on life and seizing it. When we finished, I'd learned that to get to the other side of the velvet ropes, sometimes you just have to look the Secret Service in the eye and *lie.* And she'd learned there was a big world outside the cubicle. But I stopped just short of bum-rushing the capitol building. And she stopped just short of full commitment to unemployment. Somewhere in the middle, she slipped me her card, and that was something . . .

Days later, with a rough copy of the manuscript in one hand, the plainly-typed address of her cubicle in the other, I crept into her office, handed my work to the secretary, and walked out real fast.

During my ongoing isolated and withdrawn "tortured artist" condition, I would pull out her card, look at it, put it away, think of the girl, ponder the potentially scandalous political implications of our mingling worlds, and look out the window. She was a face on the "corporate media," a blonde, big-business mouthpiece, manipulating public thought and controlling boundaries of debate. I don't know, the "corporate media" was sort of pretty. And gauging from her willingness to *accept* and *use* stolen Kinko's cards—shockingly uncommitted to the System! I understood the complete arrangement of socially-constructed barriers to shield the possibly fragile set of internalized capitalistic values of reporter and suburban child from ruin, debasement, and influence by radicals. Safeguards included gated communities, train tracks, prisons, and a generally insular class structure. But sometimes "they" wander into Kinko's while we're stealing copies—and the seeds we plant aren't always "good for the economy"! At night in the theater, I began constructing wildly delusional out-of-touch schemes for exploiting the contact to commit irreversible thought subversion, maneuver my position to *radicalize* the girl, influence news stories, and use her office supplies! Oh, you loved the manuscript? Dinner? Beer?! 6 o'clock?!?! Gosh . . .

At the coffeehouse counter, she reached for her wallet, offering anything on the menu—on her! Under any other circumstance, contact between pseudo-vagrant and blonde reporter would only be conceivable in an interview through inch-thick plexi-glass—but during the hobo-summer: they take us to coffee. Kinko's is awesome.

I raised the mug to my lips, and she whipped out the manuscript with highlighted passages and notes in the margins! She dove into the questions, my back was against the wall—it was full-on ambush journalism! How did I justify my parasitic behavior? What was I doing with my life?! Help! If a microphone lay buried in her hair, we were all certain to find out in the paper the next morning. Free coffee's always great anyway . . .

Dropped off at the movie theater and sitting against the wall outside, a very intoxicated gutter-punk stumbled over and sat down. I gave him a banana. He dragged himself to the ticket window and returned with two tickets. I'd never really been drunk, but paying for tickets at that theater—I suddenly understood "impaired judgement." Golly, an untorn ticket. Good for a $7.50 refund in the next fifteen minutes, with a made-up story . . . if I could shed the drunk, but he was right on top of me until we sat down. The movie started, and he began screaming at the screen, shouting at moviegoers, belching, and jumping around! Coming into *my home*, and disrespecting my guests! Embarrassing. But taken out to coffee and a movie inside of two hours . . . "Southern hospitality" or statistical fluke? *What's going on?!*

Kinko's was a flaming ruin, my suitcase scaled down to a trim 108 pages, and the tortured artist was on hiatus.

Manuscript finished. For three weeks I had fought with pens, tape, and white-out, insulting paying customers and abandoning my only readership demographic: vagrants. What next? Fame? Girls?! Maybe, after revisiting my window seat at the natural foods store, my books, small town punk rock shows, all new reasons to avoid "pulling myself up by the bootstraps," all I found amazing and important in life.

Back at my window seat, the struggle for all new ways to not pay for food was taking an urgent turn. Dexter had put in his two-week notice. Film, history, and literature—all laden with stories of men with nothing to lose. At 5, the manager would leave, Dexter would pass my table slowly, and without making eye contact mumble out the side of his mouth—"The store is yours." A waving of the checkered flag of theft—yo, let's go! Dexter threw down cases of Clif Bars on my table! I grabbed arm-loads of food and just *sat down!* Dexter slam-dunked food into my backpack without shame! I took more than my fair share of cantaloupe samples! The erosion of everything decent and godly! Pass the carrot juice!

I almost felt bad for that chain store, and considered consenting to an equalizing handicap. Like maybe I should wear a blindfold or something. No use. The path from table to freezer—I could do that blindfolded. To cope during my crippling episodes of guilt, I would walk to the end of a register, pick up the pitcher of wooden "5¢ donation" nickels given for each reused paper bag, and just dump it in the "Rescued Animal Sanctuary" jar! Compassionate crime, and a great karmic equalizer!

Dexter really *was* quitting his job. "But how will you eat?" they always ask. I knew the answer to that question, and asked one of my own—*"How will I eat?!"* Unemployment was a move to be applauded, but there was the more urgent issue of chili and trail mix delivered to my table twice daily. That's it, I thought, back to the left-hand, or rationing movie popcorn, or both. I had burned bridges at the two accessible supermarkets, spent several days on the all-movie-theater-popcorn diet, and in an unholy Kinko's marathon—I *ate small children and white-out!* So Dexter's job was very meaningful to me. Dexter out of work translated into a more traditional food-gathering ritual, where I would have to, like, get out of my chair. I thought about how I visited San Diego for books and beaches, San Francisco for records, Boulder for discarded manuals on "how-to" car theft, and St. Paul to write letters. Little Rock was "copies, free shows on the river, and food delivered to table." I'd finished my copies and broken most of the machines, no upcoming shows, and soon—"self-serve" free food! I dumpstered a case of soy-jerky and thought—it's July, and if you're not diving off trains, making waves in small towns, and hanging out at mini-marts with kids from different schools each night, is it really summer?

"Hi, I'm looking for info on the Chicago train."

The unspoken alliance between hobo and train-worker: they put us on the right train, we leave their children alone.

"Train? What about it?" he snapped.

"Well, um, is it made up yet?"

"For what?" What? "You mean to *ride?*" He looked upset. "Tell you what, how 'bout I call the Special Agent and have you hauled to *jail.*"

"Gosh, why would you do that?" I asked. A stranded and crying hobo—is that what you'd like to see?!

"What I'd like to see is for you to *get a job* and *raise a family!*"

Ha ha ha ha ha! If his life-view was correct, I must have been wallowing in the opposite: a pit of anguish and squalor. Then I found a cool abandoned truck to sleep in! And I thought, no, I have it right . . .

The next day, *all* day, I paced the huge train yard and thought—this is it, just like the books! Dust and drama!

The bum on his bag in a cozy ditch, and the train in motion is the one for him . . . It always seemed the dusty old hobo books painted this yard-side "waiting" phase of the saga as full of eager possibility—the will to risk is a ticket to ride, and the grass is *always* greener . . . My ditch view of the Little Rock yard was one of wide-eyed hope and promise—hundreds of shuffling trains transporting coal and hoboes to new towns and a better day, Kinko's where you're still welcome . . . Soon, like the books, the housewife-with-vacationing-husband would assign me the guestroom, blackmailed cops would be taking orders from *me*, or I'd find the end of the rainbow in my little bush . . . I had no idea what I was doing. I just hoped they left one of the boxcar doors open. The doors were supposed to be open. I'd done the research on this and more, and watching the trains, sat beamish for what came next—the part where I win, and stand in the boxcar door before a glowing sunset, smile on my face and fist in the air! I read a lot that winter . . .

Disappointment lay in the books too, somewhere. I never retained those parts. But now I could write them! Dexter had imparted to me *really bad train advice*. For two days I sat in one spot, in precise accordance with his directions—watching trains rocket past. Was the world laughing at me? Are *you* laughing at me?!

On my second day, two hoboes outside the nearby gas station gave me a "what's up," which always makes me nervous. Like, what gave me away?! At what point—I often wonder—is "hobo" no longer just a role . . . The two hoboes volunteered the worst train advice I'd ever heard. Everything west bound for Austin? Even as an amateur, I knew it false. For another day I walked the yard, finished my book on the history of prison riots, and committed to a small hobo riot of my own. Forgoing any pretense of restraint or safety, I marched into the heart of the yard and simply *stole* my train. The first train that moves: *always* my train. There. After several missed chapters—back in the books, where the hobo always wins! My train brought me towards the edge of the yard, away from that place, and forward to the hopeful pastures of . . . 300 yards west. Even my own advice was wrong.

Among my most cherished train lessons—above "patience" and "boxcars *steal* and *eat* cassettes"—stood "always ask." I sought train advice—specific and sober. From experience, I knew bad advice in bourgeois life to exist in a narrow margin of error, causing scuffs on a still-intact structure—cramped airline seats, dull films, depreciated stocks . . . Bad train advice would alter the very fabric of the hobo summer, bringing hazardous script rewrites like "arrest at border," "death in desert," and "Council Bluffs." So when a huge, senior hobo came forth from the shadow of an inviting boxcar—offering advice and hobo partnership—and I then *accepted both*, it was a knowing firebomb to structure and design. I was going to hop trains with drunk guys and tear up the South! *Awesome!*

"Big Man" was my ticket to a secret hobo world, where life isn't always pretty—and we *never* are—but that's quite alright, because we have each other, *our* culture, and if you're a little shocked and offended, we only ask with great humbleness that you accept us as people, suspend judgement, and approach our little fire to sit with us . . . yeah, so we can *spit in your eye!* Sheep! We hopped to Texas . . .

We met up with others. Two became four, and we were an army . . . Culminating in a shocking moment where I looked up, blinked my eyes, and found myself *before a can of Sterno in a circle of tramps under a bridge*!

Big Man was a Deep South hobo storyteller. One of our great undiscovered folk heroes. He would dive into a heavily embellished tramp-drama and not come up for air inside an hour. Sort of the mentor I never had. "Millionaire for a day" sagas, "beating up train cop" romances and "dumpstering diamond ring" epics. Big Man always triumphed. When the sinister switchman knowingly put him on a train going a thousand miles in the wrong direction, we had doubts. But a return trip with fabricated accusations of sexual harassment evened the score, and we all gave a silent cheer. When I stood nearly awed to silence, I asked his favorite dumpsters—"Rental Storage Spaces." Storage companies, what an incredibly brilliant idea . . .

"Shoestring" was just . . . he was just *drunk*. A shameless handler of the "Will Work For Food" sign. Profits went to beer, excess to gas station cookies. Well, I admired the means. "Will Work For Food" . . . I'd always wondered about that profession. Watching Shoestring "work the sign" at a distance gave rise to an obvious question, and when he returned, I asked it—"What happens when they *do* offer work?" His response—well, maybe it didn't occur this way exactly—but it seemed the moment when the circle all look at each other for an awkward moment, then bust out laughing. Fine, I was an amateur. *Not* "working for food" is, of course, the goal. And in the insulting scenes of drivers offering yardwork, his standby line? "Can't ride in cars—claustrophobic!" Yeah! Unemployment—no approach is sacred!

"Strawhat" swore he didn't do it. The dead guy at his parents' house? It wasn't him. It was that other guy using his name. He was innocent, innocent . . .

I closed the circle, around a can of Ramen, on a bed of cardboard, under a bridge, in Hearne, Texas.

Big Man—"Did I tell you the story of . . ."

Strawhat—"I didn't do it."

Shoestring—"Burp."

Me—"You shouldn't litter, guys . . ."

From high-school outcast to hobo *nerd!* This was very depressing. When you *try* and *fail* for acceptance by a group of drunk illiterates under a bridge, time to start threading a noose . . .

Walking down Main Street in a small Texas town with two drunks and a fugitive . . . I love summer. En route to the supermarket, a police car passed slowly. Strawhat panicked, ran, and disappeared forever. Life was unpredictable, the townsfolk scared—two themes I could really get behind. Shoestring endured a tense moment buying beer at the gas station when the driver who'd given him "food money" showed up behind him in line! Panhandler drama!

Something about sleeping under a bridge among beer cans, cardboard signs, and vagrants . . . Mom—take a picture.

It was a time of stolen chips and tag-team story-telling. I believed in these things. White and employable—I think the Unabomber would call my obsession a "surrogate activity." But you could never convince me I was insincere—under a bridge, 33% of a small hobo army committing small-town emotional terrorism , eating out of cans and then *throwing them over our shoulders.* I didn't support the last part. I pass on the 40 oz., and you doubt my authenticity. But then I take a spoon of that peanut butter, and you know I'm solid . . .

Trains came and went, and Shoestring and Big Man never raised an eyebrow. Two days later I was still looking for a cue, some strong leadership from the ranks of seniority. I sat confused. This wasn't "tearing up the South" . . . just beer, Sterno, and hugely exaggerated train stories. And, hold on a second . . . *we were just three bums under a bridge!* Hey, who's been sniffing my glue?! The most mythic of scenes, and at the same time—the most real. The brotherhood! The cardboard! The improvised cookware! Three tramps in the shadows of "their" world. Society? Let me finish my glass of hairspray, then I'll tell you what we think of "society" . . .

Shoestring was averaging a dollar-a-minute in that little town, with a 30-minute bridge-sign-beer-bridge turn-around. Inspiring. A train pulled in, and Big Man and I left Shoestring behind . . . for what? Take a picture of me and an elder hobo icon, on our train, before the Texas sunset—then look at it. That's my only answer.

There is something subversive about stealing back a means of transport. Something radical about self-navigation after a lifetime of chauffeured rides and school busses.

Something dangerous about jumping on a moving train. (I only board the stationary ones.) And something crazy and amazing about free rides to all relevant points in North America. These are my thoughts each time the train pulls out, when I achieve small town celebrity status waving to packs of kids outside gas stations from my boxcar. I have many thoughts riding trains. Crazy, exaggerated ones in the quiet moments. I think of myself as keeping the light on in a fading culture, rich with the history I've researched in a dozen university libraries. Then I think of my shameful and fraudulent place in the lineage—how the hobo was traditionally a proud migrant worker, trains functioning as a long-range commuter bus—and that I lose my breath at the mention of "work." I think on why I'm the only one in these lonely train yards, and why I can see the flicker of TVs and computers through the windows of each house. Leading to an almost deep thought on the cultural epidemic of passive entertainment over rich experience. From the opposite side of a boxcar, the door offers a moving image, proportionate to that of a movie screen. You can watch it, lose yourself in the fast-moving plot, and when the train stops—jump in and participate! Fun, a stimulating date activity, and you get to write the ending yourself!

Big Man said this was Dallas. An obscure yard in a forgotten corner of Dallas. We sat in the yard to take in the gritty scene. This wasn't Laguna Beach. Stay in the shadows, Big Man said—this was a bad neighborhood. A hostile war zone where rogue forces wanted to strip me of what was mine. Just like the supermarket. For our on-guard session Big Man offered a can of soup—no charge. This really was like the supermarket.

I was familiar with only two city types: those vibrant and volatile, where you stumble off the bus—all fiery— storming into a town that hurls forth culture and climax in unfair amounts. I looked at the pavement cracks, the cop demanding my ID, the upsetting scene of a dead turtle . . . Dallas was the second—"So bad it's good." Gritty and unforgiving, lots of weeds and soy milk nowhere. It growls, and you laugh, because it's just a big, stupid city. It presents its most menacing packs of angry youth—you laugh harder. It presents endless eight-lane chain-store strips, all leading nowhere—you're doubled over. It puts a huge guard at every retail door, you eat its food, etc. etc. Sort of a "win-win" deal either way.

From our shaded fort—yes, under a bridge—I threw rocks at trains waiting for them to move, traded a few more stories, then *demanded* a faster moving plot. Hitchhiking wasn't the quickest of plots, but it was something. And besides, Big Man was beginning to repeat his stories . . .

After two hours around the corner with my thumb, I'd gotten googly-eye faces, "thumbs up," near-miss swerves to hit the white kid, and every point on the longitude of uncreative hitchhiker responses. Everything but a ride. Each scowl-faced driver wholly unaware that *I too hated white people*. I should change my sign . . .

Back under the bridge, Big Man had secured a gem— "Track 1, 1 a.m., train to somewhere." When it pulled out, I sat balled up in the corner, happy but sad. I left part of me under those bridges . . . I wondered if this Sterno and drunken company gave something close to "credibility," or something closer to irreversible bumhood. Maybe smartest to leave a short rope of identity to this side of the page, fearing the day I irreversibly penetrate the "fourth wall"— waking up prostrate across railroad tracks, cradling a bottle of wine . . .

Everyone loves surprises. That morning, Little Rock was mine. Big Man caught a train to Memphis for a welfare check, and I was sad . . .

Problem with establishing office space and residence in public is the lack of any real legal standing for smacking someone when they come near it. Revisiting the natural foods store that day, a dreadlocked hippie stormed my drug-free table, cornered me with the rumor of my departure by train that evening, and asked to share my boxcar. Problem with being a vocal proponent of militant poverty for white people is sometimes white people like to get militant on weekends, and need a hand to hold. I tried tactfully evading commitment—"I'm going to a show at the riverfront, if I see you there . . ." Who would have thought, I *did* see him there. With a friend. "Ready to go?" Now *I* would need drugs . . .

That right there? That's a train. This right here? A bush. Shortest path between them is a straight line. Those guys in the tower? We close our eyes each night to dreams of their burning bodies. This isn't Amtrak . . .

This was a place I'd been—guiding the uninitiated, a flashlight into the intricate structural support of perpetual vacation and adventure. Taking an innocent bourgeois and smashing their earning potential under a dumpster lid. Offering the first corruptive train ride, an encouraging nudge into a dumpster, interactive shoplifting instruction . . . One on one mentoring that plays a decisive role in "societal debasement." I wished to further that. But I think back on my own path, from starving and skill-less, to where I am now—you know, starving but *good at it*. When I saw a hole in the fence and ran for it, having no help on the outside provided 1/2 the allure, 3/4 of my commitment, and 9/10 the fun. One jailbreak, a couple faded zines, and a thousand questions needing answers before I was rained on, or starved, or collected dust in a Columbus parking lot. No hand to hold, no instruction manual or guy behind the bread rack with cue cards . . . Yes, I was one of the lucky ones. Because how-to advice whispered in one ear blows charm and fun out the other. You say you'd rather hold out for another person, another day. I say that's a curious stand. Because if I had waited for a friend with a clue, I'd be a kid by the phone . . . with cobwebs.

I love train yards at night. Sneaking around all sneaky and tough. One victimless crime perhaps we're all glad is federal law. Gives good context. Beneath a tree beside the yard, I faked *actual knowledge of freight trains,* and offered the hippies very safe, sanitized train instruction. The height of disservice for two novices, bleeding the soul from it all. Then conversation turned to one of heartrending regret for having left *good* 'shrooms at home, and I guess I stopped caring. I answered a thousand questions, accumulated hours of on-camera interviews for their possibly drug-inspired documentary project, and ate their food. It was 1 a.m.— long shadows and ominous creaks conspired to create a series of profound moments. This was a train yard at night—maybe it gets better than this, but bringing bagels had slipped my mind completely . . .

We fell asleep on a train . . .

A treat every time—awaking to an all-new huge and crazy town. Not knowing which one was the treat. I sat up, looked around . . . uh . . . the hippies were *gone!* Guess the 'shrooms lifted them to a "higher plane of reality."

Chicago's south side. This must be one of those "look back and laugh" stories; the kind where you don't die, but get hurt really bad, then point at the stab wounds later and laugh. Standing alongside the yard, I looked at the huge abandoned buildings and wiry old stray dogs. I was still tough, yet uneasy enough to know if one of those dogs made eye contact—I'd run! As a nervous white person in the ghetto, I knew this was no small victory for the prison-industrial complex. You know—glimpse it from the yard, then run to tell the other blue-eyes how scary it was. I thought about it, then lay down in a vacant lot. That lump between that charred and decayed log and pile of dirt? Visible to all sidewalk pedestrians and crack zombies? That was me. You never get used to the vulnerability of outdoor sleep, just better at laughing it off.

Waking up—I was still alive, and still very disguised in that lot as a big piece of trash. I was good at that. My record of being inside a dumpster, then having trash dumped on my head by employees, yet remaining undetected *as not being trash myself* was untouched. In this phenomenon, I saw paralells to what they say about owners growing to look like their dogs. I'd *become* a Hefty bag!

I had a guilty secret. In my backpack, behind the books—a hand to hold, a cue card . . . Besides acquired drug slang and a headache, the two hippies had left me with one thing—the elusive "Crew Change Guide." A detailed, city-by-city guide to navigating every relevant train yard in North America. In my world—a photocopied jewel with the mystique of Greek mythology. Looking for direction, I felt around in my bag . . . Ooops. My crew change guide—gone. Left on the train. What an incredibly inspired move towards danger and romance. I impress myself with my own mistakes almost daily. I once made the faux pas of forgetting obligation to society and just ran around for 6 years doing as I pleased! It was totally cool. And I had no idea where to catch my next train.

I enjoyed a long walk . . .

Bananas, peanut butter, and bagels. It was close to brilliant when I invented the recipe right there in the aisle of Cub Foods. Free food—in addition to caloric value—offers the additional fuel of "glory." I would ride my wave of energy all the way to a train yard . . . just after shaking down every drunk in every abandoned storefront for directions. I hoped for the usual inebriated and somewhat cryptic response of great profoundness, like, say—"Train yard? Follow the tracks!" I could think all day on that one . . .

Five miles back was the vacant lot, the boxcar, probably the graffitied corpses of two hippies, and what I had learned was not a train yard. After a very stylish and well-fed four weeks, I craved what I knew was coming next— long and random wandering through a huge scary city, sleeping in piles of lumber and sharp metal, and a general assembly of scenes that would make my parents cry. As kids, we're products of structured tour-guide "adventure" and "on-line" convenience. So there's a certain seduction to sleeping in industrial waste. And sometimes, a certain need. Like that incident of heartbreaking pauperism in Santa Rosa, at midnight, in the rain, where I spotted a mountain of discarded carpet behind a carpet store, became uncontrollably excited, unrolled one of the more high-end choices in the parking lot, laid down at one end, clutched the edge, and *rolled* myself up! This of course shocked passersby, but for me, a major victory. Then a girl pulled up and began loading me into a truck! I stuck my head out to tell her of other unoccupied rolls nearby. She screamed, then offered money and a place to stay. Trying to ruin my near-genius housing triumph with a couch, groan . . . I'm going back to sleep! The moral? Exploit their mess and put it to work for *you!*

I confused several people, scared others, but eventually picked up one very specific lead on a train yard. Legend and lore held up Chicago as a train black hole, a hobo mouse trap—ride in with ease, but the gates close behind you. Most of the city's 30+ train yards were "hot," populated by rogue mercenary yard police in jeeps inspecting trains with spotlights, growling, chasing hoboes up trees, and then *shaking the tree* until they fell out! Like most good vs. evil chase scenarios, there were tactical answers for underdog victory somewhere. Usually in cartoons. The hoboes had done their research. We all knew the dazing flat-headed effects of a 50-lb. anvil dropped on the antagonist from a tree. The additional time bought from a spherical black bomb down his trousers. And if the cop chased me into a carnival funhouse, it would get good . . .

On the edge of the train yard, just as I finished Woody Guthrie's *Bound for Glory*, the last word of the triumphant ending where a sense of promise was never so poignantly committed to paper, and Woody is leading a boxcar choir singing "This train is bound for glory!"—a switchman offered help.

"Help me to the first train *away* from Chicago!" I said.

"Ah, running from the cops, huh?"

Well, no, but I liked the thought of "fugitive" status. So far that trip I'd engaged in "theft of services" on railways, trespassing, petty theft, jaywalking, let's see . . . I lied to the ticket seller at Greyhound about my name, stole that train map from Barnes & Noble, um . . . went up a "down" escalator, went unpunished for copious vagrancy violations . . . What does it take to be a "wanted fugitive" anyway? When the worker radioed the tower for train times, he was "aiding and abetting a fugitive" . . . as far as he knew. My quickest way to the state line was on track 23, he said. He didn't know its destination, "but if you need to get out, it's your best bet." So I caught that train, one step ahead of the law . . .

My destination? Was there a place better than this place? A moment richer that this one? There were friends that way, urban hipness this way, but I was pretty sure there was more adventure over here—in the fringes. The place the train always goes when you don't know where it's going. That museum inside the gas station off the two-lane highway. Where the farmer drops you off when he's "only going thirty miles up the highway or so." That truck stop in Nevada, MO; where the high-school kids will drink coffee with you all night and hang on your every word. They're drunk—and you're a star . . .

A pleasant ride in a smooth riding boxcar. And when the train stopped, it felt great to jump off, stretch, be out of Chicago and in . . . East St. Louis! Gulp! Following gangster rap closely, I'd always found it chilling how East St. Louis was always lyrically situated near "homicide" and "murder," and the two didn't even *rhyme!* Was East St.

Louis in fact "just like Compton fool" as DJ Quick warned? Was I *down?* Are you?!

Small fires in abandoned lots, barred windows, and packs of kids pausing mid-hustle to watch the blonde bum. Perusal of "E. St. Louis" in my lost "Crew Change Guide" at this point would reveal the ominously abrupt "in dangerous neighborhoods." I wondered if underclass solidarity would triumph over, you know, most white people actually *deserving* the force of blunt objects. I walked the residential blocks of East St. Louis for the charm of it all—people in the streets just kickin' it, bouncing balls and riding rusty ole bikes in the sun. I'd long understood "poverty" as synonymous with sunshine leisure on corroded implements of little or no resale value, with hurling yourself to the streets and *doing things.*

There was an unspoken underclass bond between myself and the huge guys drinking on the corner, the guy in the rocking chair . . . but not the little girl on the bike!

"You're not from here!!!" Yikes!

Life felt dangerous, and I could put off guilty feelings of succumbing to minority crime-hype until the train. Right now I had to watch out for broken glass, and little girls on bikes. I looked at the packs of kids against the brick wall and guys lifting weights on porches. This was all new. Though obvious parallels existed between East St. Louis and my hood. Between gang warfare and the relationship I shared with the manager of my favorite dine-and-dash restaurant. Overgrown and decrepit abandoned buildings and the sparkling suburban ones I lived in. Graffiti and my wet cement etchings. Bug-eyed head turning for the white kid and bug-eyed head turning for the trash covered Phoenix rising from the dumpster. "You're not from here!" and "Pay your fare or get off of here!" I'd once survived 2,793 miles on $4, I'd survive East St. Louis . . . if I can outrun the girl on the bike!

..ck of kids looked curiously like the one on the
.. This abandoned house like the last. Hold on . . . I
. in the hood! A scene often used for comedic effect
ı. .ım, usually involving a broken car, and in the next
scene—stolen hubcaps. I found the hugest toughest guy
I'd ever seen lifting weights on his porch.

"Excuse me . . ." He sat up and flexed his muscles.
"Where's the train yard?"

He answered, filled my water bottle, offered food,
then gave me a smile . . . and five dollars! Lightning bolts
of bad rap music thundered as the Snoop Dogg lyrics became instantly clear—"East-side St. Louis, Spokane, *getcha
money man* . . ."

The situation degenerated. I mean, yes, I wanted to
suffer, but I wanted to live to write about it. The yard
was an impossible maze of police and fast-moving trains.
Passing townsfolk thought me crazy—"Don't go in
there—they'll arrest ya! Yup!" I soon realized—wait, I
am crazy. Car loads of kids would pass slowly and pull a
quick U-turn while I scrambled to hide in shrubbery.
Counters at the grocery store were too low to "left-hand"
anything. I soon understood what was meant by the
"other side of the tracks"—the side where you have to
pay. The sun began to set, shadows grew longer, the
empty lot fires larger. The mosquitos were eating me in
the ditch where I slept. I ran out of water and the store
was closed. The next day was the same. I began looking
up to see a dark cloud of bad luck and insomnia hovering over everything I did. Surely, consistent with the
trend, the cashier at the gas station would hand me my
Fritos, my change, and hit me with an axe. So when I
bought a $23 bus ticket to the next state, was I *selling
out?* I never would have paid for *anything* in 1995. Maybe
I was "maturing" . . .

"Ooooh . . . that's *not* the best part of town." The
gas station cashier held up my train yard address. She

looked concerned. "Not the best part of town" was becoming a trip theme, probably part of an elaborate practical joke. And when I wasn't being chased down tracks by Springfield, Illinois' rabid dog colony, I was laughing along.

Twenty-three dollars . . . I couldn't get over that. I held it against East St. Louis, or Snoop Dogg, or somebody. If the woman was correct, twenty-three dollars less the savages would pull from my dead body. Next year I'm taking the monk-like "table-scraps-and-Saltine-crackers" tour, where I spend *no* money, go nowhere near Greyhound, use fake tears to make blunt demands of pink-haired cashiers, and explore my theory that if you stand by the magazines and *roll* a cantaloupe out the door, it's not really shoplifting!

A car of girls waved to me, and I was feeling rosy. My smile carried me six miles to a small cluster of tracks, gravel, no train action, a tumbleweed blowing past my feet . . . On a lonely stretch lay a single boxcar. I crawled inside to sleep. One of Springfield's true enablers of train-addiction approached my boxcar, stared at me slumped in the corner, the troll in his cave, all crazy, raggedy, and fire-breathing; and returned soon after with a bag of meatloaf sandwiches—for me! They're still in that box car if you want them . . .

Deep in the night, I awoke with a flashlight in my face. A nice train wo rker, looking for a friend . . . He gave train advice, brought me water, asked if I was cozy, building up to a very real fear he would move to tuck me in. Soon, he said, they would hook up the engine and take me to . . . well, he was nice enough to not spoil the ending by saying where. I thought back to my East St. Louis ditch and dehydration, and that the engine would soon tug me to better things. I thought of new towns of possibility, I couldn't wait to turn the page—Kansas City? Denver? Council Bluffs? More than ever I believed in happy endings. Even gangster rap songs had happy endings.

When I awoke on the train the next morning and looked around, I listened for the canned laugh-track to the hobo sitcom I was clearly starring in.

It was East St. Louis.

TWO

The worst town I'd ever visited, but still pretty fun. I found several rustic but cheery old hoboes outside the abandoned strip mall, had poignant conversation on American excess with a Trader Joe's employee from knee-deep inside his dumpster, and nodded my head slowly over obscure old books in the university library. The girl from the basement show never did write, but girls somehow always lost consequence at the first line of a good book. Which is why I came to this town . . .

It all started in the bookstore. My path from university to bookstore was fixed and intentful—I wanted books, and I wanted books of instruction on fringe acts of evasion with winking disclaimers. That's it.

One night, right there under "subculture"—two such books. Books we all hoped for, but *knew* hadn't been written. I was more nervous than happy when I found them. Nervous about two books voiding any excuse for a night at home ever again. "Don't judge a book by its cover," they warn. What if the cover pledges the secrets of *sneaking into everything?* Can we judge *those?!*

Looking at the cover upset me greatly. *"No Ticket, No Problem! How to Sneak into Sporting Events and Concerts."* Great. A quick scan of the table of contents confirmed what I was afraid of—I had work to do. "Press Passes," "Backstage," "Luxury Boxes". . . If it was out of reach, it was in the book. The author—a slick, middle-aged Robin Hood for the uninvited—explained his thankless freelance work as "hotdog vendor," "press photographer," "employee with charming smile and flashed high school ID," "hurried man of great importance with cell phone," etc. etc. He kicked it backstage with Billy Joel, and I was impressed. He infiltrated the Academy Awards, and I was amazed. He exited and re-crashed using a second technique, and I was stunned. He snuck in a third time to then occupy Whoopi Goldberg's spot on stage, and—I don't know—I couldn't take it. I was *jealous*. My head still spun as I closed the book, and thought—"Time to check the concert listings . . ."

I was sort of traumatized at this point. Yes, I was full of hope that there *is* always a way in; but still pouty over being looked in the eye and told I wasn't doing it right. Like I said—traumatizing. I pulled another book from the shelf— *"The Gate Crashers."* What kind of bookstore *was* this? *What's going on?!*

It was all there—a thousand amazing anecdotes of sneaking into things! The book detailed a secret underground I fiended desperately to join—profiles in the dozens of men and women not willing to take "Ticket Please" for an answer! Where we find the author casually dropping personal anecdotes of dabbling in weekend pastimes like, oh . . . *sneaking into nine separate Academy Awards!* I was disturbed by Dionisio Dominguez— who'd crashed a thousand weddings, and "kissed a thousand brides"! Who would win my heart? Let's see—Stan Berman, who charmed his way into the Presidential Box at the 1961 Presidential Inaugural Ball? Or the guy who crept onto stage in Radio City Music Hall's exclusive "Night of a Hundred Stars" show as #101? The guy who conned a path to the stage at the Oscars and presented Bob Hope with an award? My own life remained exciting, but really, was this an excuse *not* to dive into the life of "Party Guy"— who clocks out of his office job Friday night, puts on a tux, drives to Hollywood, and just *walks in* to celebrity parties? I reject all such celebrity and idol worship. Nonetheless, I believe it's important to live a life full of doing things just so you can say you did them. So . . . better start taking notes.

I bought them both. Then skated to the library real fast.

The two books were read and digested, and I soon settled in to the fact I was—uh—an amateur. So, it wasn't too upsetting to be on an Orange County shopping spree of sorts, and find a third—*Catch Me if You Can: The Amazing True Story of America's Most Extraordinary Liar in the History of Fun and Profit!* An autobiographical account reminding us of one neglected fact: Genius often manifests in strictly criminal ways. How soon we forget . . . We all sit reminded of the fact in the book's pages, a true story of a con-artist who—with a convincing pilot uniform and confident pose—scams airline flights around the country! With free travel as a launchpad, he runs around in a medley of scams and free everything . . .wait, this story sounds familiar . . . Anyway, he evolves into the master of impersonation, to whom no doors are closed. Such lofty feats put me in the role of drooling spectator, the idiot non-participant thinking only—"Someday . . . " He then—when finally caught—*talks* his way out of jail! In my aim for a free Madonna concert, I felt there was real applicability here . . .

Profound. A few hours in public seating bringing down whole walls in the mind. Small boundaries around possibility gone unnoticed for a lifetime—exposed, implicated, and killed. "Act like you belong and no one will think otherwise," "You are who they think you are," "Act like you own the place and you own it." Physical points of impasse revealed as mere psychological boundaries. "The gate"—an ominous, guarded thing—stripped of its might, laid bare as submissive to resolute confidence and crude props. Maybe with these books, anything lay in reach. Every concert and record release party. Industry conventions and high school proms. Urban life never swelled with such possibility . . .

It was outlaw psychology, "the suggestion factor"—a merging of firm untruth and feigned charm. The power of a ticket was transitory, isolated in time and space. But shrewdness of the unwilling ticket buyer, wired-in flaws of the human mind, and security guards being universally *stupid*—all timeless. Maybe it made *too* much sense, and I sat feeling a little foolish at the oversight. The practical applications of these lessons amplified greatly the old feeling of "not enough hours in the day." It was then I knew the obsession was a worthy one . . .

A man with a handcart and a smile, yes, it made perfect sense . . . A society of privilege based on the surface and material: the intimidation effect of a flashed badge, and freedom of passage for the rushed man with suit and briefcase. I thought of UPS uniforms, Whole Foods aprons in the back room. A society of obedience based on the petrifying effect of the self-assured: hotels offering room-keys to "pilots" on layover, and the demon-eye of my ex-girlfriend. I thought of dropping the bosse's name at obscure doors, service-gate passage with a brisk pace and large box. Overcoming swarms of competition and the high security of the fertilization process, we come into this world as gate-crashers. You could say we were born to sneak in . . .

* * *

The theory was: "Act like you belong, and no one will think differently." Hand the door-person a paid-for ticket, or approach in EMT uniform hurriedly and watch them step aside. Outlaw psychology, "Social Engineering." That place where charm and poverty come together and conspire to fling open doors. For years I'd known it as the only way to raid a hotel reception buffet table. Flaws of the human psyche, well-written rehearsed stories, good props . . . I placed hope in these things. Is lying for hedonistic pleasure ever right? Are free rap concerts *ever wrong?!*

I think back to the early days. The crude duck-and-slide motions made when heads turned . . . wait—I *still* do that! And pleasantly poor and uncool—surely I always will. The tragic reality of capitalism is if you enter your house through a broken window and eat trash—*you probably can't afford a GoGo's ticket!*

Probably it *always* begins at the back-door of the cineplex . . . and for too many, it sadly ends there. A "gate"-

way activity of sorts. When the girls passed us their stubs over the velvet ropes, we felt sneaky. And when I took the extra one to the window for a "refund"—it felt *gangster!* It had begun!

My favorite dumpster. Such luck, such fertility. Each dive surpassing the last, and did any of us foresee Tower Records *outdoing* the $20 gift certificate? I held them up to the light—five very shiny, very *blank* TicketMaster tickets. The big empty white space in the center seemed to whisper "use your imagination." Pauly used his, holding the blanks up to his own ticket for that weekend's Anthrax show. Glassy-eyed, he broke toward the typewriter. I played Nintendo, Pauly stomped his feet giggling, and when we regrouped, I recognized this as a fitting insult to the band who attempted *copyrighting* the "New York Hardcore" logo. One crude forgery with imperfect font and bearing-little-to-no resemblance to an actual ticket. Like the photocopied Greyhound Ameripass that delivered no-one-I-know from Greensboro to Gainesville. Sloppy felonies: we always laugh about them later. The bouncer held up the forgery, squinted, looked at the long line of impatient metal guys, back at the ticket, I lifted my shirt a little to show I was packing, and he waved me in! If free food tastes better, do free concerts "*rock*" better? That turns out to be the case!

I put my thumb out for free and often disturbing rides, hopped my first train, and crawled beneath the cashier's window at the public pool in a small Wisconsin town . . . All less-advanced gate-crashing actions, crude but effective for advancing our cause of a "ticketless society." Sort of like our campaign of "full unemployment by 2005," but lacking the tedium of hostage negotiation. Amateurish—as insolvent uprisings go—but really, can utilizing the "wet stamp transfer" at a Sex Pistols concert in defense of a proud culture being bastardized, then sneaking behind the stories-tall inflatable bottle of corporate sponsors Budweiser and yanking the plug, bringing the huge stupid thing collapsing on concertgoers and sparking brief chaos—ever be downplayed? Punk itself may be "dead," but the shrewd Trojan Horse approach to "ticket price"—and belly-laugh value of scurrying ticketholders fleeing large inflatable objects—remains eternal.

A consistent theme of the books—the something I'd always wondered about, and at times flirted with: "Unwavering self-assuredness as a weapon." Effectively proven in the chain hardware store the day I set a $2 pair of gloves on the counter, next to an expensive power drill. The gloves were scanned, and the cashier reached for the drill. I pulled it away and feigned annoyance, placing the drill under my arm—

"Just the gloves."

She gave me the change, and a smile, and I walked out! Like the books, in reverse—a confident pose to get *out* the door . . . I knew I'd stumbled onto the shameless exploitation of a psychological loophole—"Everyone is insecure and submits to those more confident." Manifesting in the absurd scenario of a customer firmly requesting to *not pay* for 95% of his purchase!

Sitting still, after the books, was analogous to reading *Steal This Book* and *not* immediately doing a crude tape job on a size 14 washer and dropping it in a payphone. A cackling laugh comes over the receiver. It's Ma Bell. The washer scam's been obsolete for 25 years. But could guards stepping aside for the telephone *repairperson* ever be obsolete? I could put the books away, but not the tugging awareness of missed opportunity, and backstage pineapple stars. Of slick and confident militants in hard-hats *at that moment* holding thick-gauge speaker wire, coasting backstage three hours before showtime like they really *were* setting up a live feed for K-JAM.

I think the problem with most poor people is our readiness to look at an upraised palm demanding money, and not just push it aside and go around. Revisiting the books, I thought—when the story enthralls, living it is *probably more fun*. I checked the concert listings. Life was beginning to look a lot more exciting . . .

* * *

It was summer—classroom for the applied physics of whatever-I-learned-about-over-winter. The always-uneasy season for bridging the gap between thought and action. But I was nervously avoiding the free weeklies of each new town. Or at least the music calendar. Venue ads sat with mocking sneers, divided into hundreds of little squares for hundreds of bands, each one saying "now or never." Stupid ads. What happened in Seattle would be what scholars of chronology term a "historical inevitability": perusing the free weekly and—uh-oh—turning one page too far. The ad was big, harder to ignore. For that band, *the* band, the one I'd for months bounced to on the back seat of public transportation, the soundtrack to winter's gate-crashing studies . . . on a reunion tour. You could say I had a plan.

I stood outside, grumbling. In the books, dramatic episodes of genius played out, supported by suspicious miracles—paying customers *dropping* tickets, vendor uniforms hanging unattended, the guest list always conveniently angled so as to be visible to the gate-crasher . . . and no one ever stood outside a waterfront Go-Go's concert in the Seattle rain, trying and failing to sneak in. Putting naïve trust in the miracles, I had no plans. No Domino's Pizza uniform or large boxes—just hours of accumulated talk to live up to, and burning love for Belinda! Together with Stiles & Cindy, I stood in the rain, penniless and eager. They say drugs open doors to the mind, but not like poverty . . .

Some band called "The Lunachicks" was opening, and we watched their roadie move freely between tour- van and backstage gate. Crazy hair, obnoxious clothes, that punk-rock snarl . . . I think I had a friend.

"Hi, um, *have any extra tickets?*"

She gave me a sneer that said I was the king of fools . . .

And a backstage pass.

"Abrupt requests"—it wasn't in the books, but it will be in mine . . .

The mythic "backstage at arena rock concert." Where, I learned, the real performance is. Dozens of slick, well-dressed pseudo-celebrities sipping wine and making all the right moves. And one punk in the corner, pondering the limits of "All Access Pass" while raiding the fruit platter. I couldn't be certain, but I think this was rubbing shoulders with "industry"!

In the form of currency, laminated security-clearance badge, or backstage pass, most status—at its base—is simply paper. My paper—beyond admittance—gave the added benefit of "coolness." For the first time in my life, man, I was *down!* Hole-ridden shoes from a summer of trains reminded me I would never win their approval . . . but I could eat their food!

Fashionable moderation, I felt, was, like, *so* bourgeois, and I built shocking fruit mountains on little plates in the banquet tent. At the exact point of the pineapple apex reaching maximum geometric sustainablity, I would pour a big cup of coffee and sit to take in the pre-show party. Subtle social signals in that room told me I'd burned all bridges by not using tongs. I fired back the message they should just hush. Most of their passes were red—"Limited Access." Mine glowed blue and said "ALL" real big in black ink. Simplified, this meant I could eat kiwi with my hands, drink all the coffee, insult their ancestors and dance with their women!

Security checkpoints lay at every turn. Approaching each huge, muscular off-duty cop I watched their eyes grow big at sight of my pass, step aside, and wave me through! They even called me "sir"! After years of police harassment, it was fun to just walk in circles, forcing cops to "move along" and get the heck off my path to more fruit. Oh how the mighty have fallen . . .

Exploring the venue, I could isolate four chambers of rank, and my unearned place in it. Paying ticket holders were the bottom-feeders, disposable, mere dollar signs and hopelessly un-chic. Beyond the first checkpoint lay a small courtyard for the radio contest winners and second cousins—never cool, just lucky. Moving further, the literal backstage—a vast expanse of equipment, frantic activity, good food and strong coffee. For road crew and VIPs only. You could cut the exclusivity with a knife—possible leakage from the two other camps evoked fears of what the VIP call "cross-contamination." Standing in the epicenter—like, by the non-dairy creamers—one could truly feel the tension from both sides. 40-year old women with cell phones, pleading with security from the ticket-holder side, swearing they were "with the band," then just swearing. "You let *him* in and not me?!" In defense of the pecking order, I spun around—"I'm with the Lunachicks!"

I ran in circles, double-fisting coffee and spring water, wide-eyed and fiery, peering around corners and making unreasonable demands of paid staff. Mr. Uninvited with the "all-access" pass—an anomalous fluke with dangerous implications threatening the absolute core of capitalist caste systems, of society itself . . . I would only cross this bridge once, may as well burn it.

I cornered my punk-rock benefactor by the bar—"Am I blending in?" I asked. She turned and walked away! Ha! I was sort of flattered.

One last exclusive corner existed, where the cop looked more rabid, the cloud of mystery over it even more thick. "Band Dressing Rooms." Like, where the Go-Go's were. I covered the holes in my sweatshirt and approached with an exaggerated sense of authority. I'd learned that even cops, although illiterate, can apply rudimentary phonics to "A-L-L," and make color associations often displayed by the lower primates. Continuing on a truly consistent course—eyes grew big and red carpets unrolled for the white kid with the blue pass! Probably a retarded younger brother, beneficiary of an approved proposal to the Make-A-Wish Foundation, or god knows . . .

Doors were closed and curtains drawn. But I took joy in knowing that although not the Go-Go's "biggest fan," I was closest in proximity at that moment. I paced before the trailer, waiting for an invitation, or shouted demand to fetch a napkin, or something. I thought of the books, and how it never ended with mere unpaid entry, but always something closer to the cheering triumph of an arm around the frontman immortalized in photograph, or a celebrity kiss on the cheek! I paced, huffing at the frustration of it. This must be what they call "stress," I'd always wondered about that . . .

At the base of the stage steps, I watched the Lunachicks fix their hair, bounce in place, pat each other on the back, and—as the announcer called their name—charge the stage! Then I got to run around and watch it from the front! Fifth row center. This was the city that brought me to near-arrest for fishing quarters from an unlocked arcade game with a plastic spoon, so infiltrating VIP seating at one of its concerts was a major victory.

It was a slick crowd—middle-aged, highbrow, and curiously well-dressed. All around, men in suits and women in gowns sipped champagne from glasses and danced. Turning around, it was a scene of thousands of bouncing bourgeoisie, cheering and screaming for *me!* It was that kind of night . . .

Lights dimmed, the Go-Go's rushed the stage, drumsticks went "click click click," and that was it—the musical Holy War. Yuppies kicked over chairs while I spun in circles without regard for style or grace. The ad said nothing of lightning bolts striking us all from the instruments, the death of my comfortable world, revolution itself. At peak fervor, like, the climax of emotion when it was either start burning things or watch the pillars of society and commerce fall, the collective VIP rows brought down the velvet ropes and—yo—*charged* the stage! Full-on insurrection with a *really cool* soundtrack! The chorus to "Vacation": a curious catalyst for just brushing the cops aside and running for it . . . Met by Seattle P.D. with the "pressure release"—a necessary pacifying tactic for volatile population control. Give them a protest sign and a place to stand, a joint, the ten feet between stage and partition, and quiet the revolution. I burned to enlighten the crowd, to address the need to stand our ground at this crucial moment—the breaking point of art and scenery sparking the fire to burn their whole world down. To the stage—no! To the streets!

I'd overlooked another pacifying agent: pop music. I chose the stage. And I'm not proud of it.

Ten feet and felony stalking laws—the thin sheet between us. An innocent but sincere crush. Then Belinda made eye contact! Though, if your eyes have in fact become little cartoon hearts, is it really "eye contact"?

Every classic and one cover. Then—it was over.

Oh gosh. Me and Belinda, together—the quiet eye of the after-show party storm. Beauty and the Beat-The-System. So close I could touch her if I leaned over real far. And, um, I almost did!

There was a place in life I chased fiendishly, risked it all for, jiggled doorknobs to find, and sometimes did at the bottom of a ladder beneath unlocked grates at the university. The exact junction of a chance taken and a lesson learned. Where statistical improbability and "getting away with it" align in ways I'm glad my parents aren't always there to see. More than ever, I'd found that place in the 5th row. The big beautiful sun setting behind the Pacific to my right, five women singing me a song directly ahead, and behind—several thousand tragic reasons to put away your wallet, take a deep breath, and consider the alternatives. Because experience is as much context as content. I learned that in the 5ᵗʰ row. And learned with a blunt request at the service-gate—honesty isn't always the best policy, but now and then the best tactic!

I gave my summer a new theme and ran with it . . .

I celebrated our nation's independence on the high-school bleachers in Ashland, and three days later fell off a bus onto the streets of San Francisco. Did I have *friends* in San Francisco? Just one. A punk rock girl. And if my timing was correct she was backstage, unloading equipment . . .

Predicating 1000-mile trips on fragile expectations . . . I know this dysfunction as "summer." But "failure" . . . she was a stranger. Until two hours before showtime at the Maritime Hall, and still no girl, no blue pass . . . Buildings can be wide open until several hours before the event, and I was scanning the lot for a last-ditch window of opportunity. Looking for "clever and boastworthy," I settled on "crude but effective"—a wide-open back door. The best kind.

They chased me.

I soon sat back on the curb, wiser knowing that without a suit, "I'm the pizza man" only gets you so far. And without pizza—nowhere at all!

Fast forward a little . . .

La Jolla, California. Wake up in a UCSD broom closet, throw your bag in an empty locker, then step outside to find yourself cornered—in the upsetting confinement of a community offering the youth no creative outlet but to, well, hang out in the sun! Endlessly! A magic place. Sammy and I were the unknowing pioneers of a subversive new cultural threat, where we just run around on the beach bodyboarding all day! Really!

It all started in a Longs Drug Store, slipping very large and expensive bodyboards under our arms, and approaching the counter with our 50¢ water purchase in a bold "left hand" move. The cashier scanned Sammy's water, then got testy—"What about the board?" Sammy looked her in the eye, and in a moment of sheer charismatic brilliance, said—"*Bleergahbaluba!!!!*" and walked out! Yeah! Never mind the legality—*let's surf!*

Sammy was the spirit of youth. Unchained by middle-class ailments like "Restraint," "Caution," or the fatal "It Can't Be Done." The last time such vulgarity flew his direction, he asked the Radio Shack clerk to kindly remove a police scanner from the case, looked at it, and ran! Perfect for road trips, oceanside water sports, and co-strategizing at the now-legendary La Jolla Whole Foods café. Where guys with cell phones make business decisions condemning small African children to squalor over lentil loaf. And where, in the next booth, two kids in shorts thought real hard on truly relevant issues of strategy and logistics—delivery man costume or Spin magazine photographer? *Walk in backwards?!* Worked at the movies . . .

I styled out my hair. Showtime was in four hours. The B-52s were opening for some dear old friends . . .

It was something I swore I would never do again. What I only knew to stand at the junction of the roads of desperation, uncreativity, and self-murder. Only Sammy's support and the pleasant setting of a waterfront patio overlooking the Pacific seduced forth the courage. The virgin canvas of atrocity was picked up at the front desk of Harbor House Seafood. I took a deep breath, and I did it. I filled out a job application.

We walked next door.

"Whoa boys! Where you goin'?!"—Go-Go's front gate security.

Well sir, that hinges entirely on you *not* noticing the "Harbor House Seafood" logo at the bottom of this paper! We held out our applications.

"New hires for barista position." I had no idea what that meant.

"Bob!" he shouted into the radio, "I got two new hires here!"

He scanned us head to toe suspiciously in a dramatic moment . . .

"Send 'em in!"

It was a great show . . .

It was a common annoyance at the grocery store—I'd have my 50¢ bagel, the exact change ready, my food to steal snugly in left hand, a big smile, then arrive at the Odwalla fresh-squeezed juice case to find the Odwalla delivery man restocking, blocking my path to the Mango Tangos. I'd stand to the side, tapping my toe. Behind me was the restroom where—in the old days, richer with struggle—I would lock myself inside with an armload of food and have lunch. To my left, the microwave where I heated my bagels—six each morning. No kidding. Directly ahead, the manager's booth. He never seemed to recognize me, though he'd kicked me out of the massive dumpster in back at least once. Most employees bought the "looking for rabbit food" line, but not him! And the orange produce-pyramid next to me. Absorbing, but didn't touch the towering, geometrically precise pyramid of empty Odwalla bottles in my abandoned house. A project in utter gridlock until the delivery man finished. I mean, I appreciated his work, needed it even, just wished he'd accommodate my schedule, or leave the delivery truck unlocked or something. I mean really, are you or are you not "down with the kids"? Sheesh! Well at least the juice was free. . .

Blackberry Shake, Rooty Fruity, Carrot Juice . . . He filled the cases with fresh juice every morning, then filled his crates with "expired" juice. Juice certainly slated for the dumpster, a big dumpster far away, a dumpster filled with every West Coast Odwalla discard. A dumpster I would find one day, and live in. To us—the health conscious criminals—Odwallas were our kiss of life, invigorating, something to drink on the bus while we gazed out the window at the pleasant landscape and got all starry-eyed. And really, reading on the waterfront all day just wasn't a postcard without a Piña Colada. My clichés are very important to me. It was tasty juice, but also serving the functional purpose of offsetting the unhealthy "Bagel Diet"—hotly contested amongst dieticians, the chic dietary regimen of pulling whole bags of bagels from dumpsters, selecting those with fruit, eating them, then going to the record store. So, in our world, the Odwalla man was, really, the "Giver Of Life." Above the employees at Tower Records who threw out whole bags of CDs, above our noble creator continually manifesting the hospitality of strangers in desperate times, above even the friendly brakies at the train yard who put us on the correct train, and not the one to Council Bluffs. That one's never the right train. And anyway, does Odwalla *deliver* to Iowa? Why take a chance?

He'd storm in the store pushing his handcart like he was in a real big hurry. He'd rush the cooler and assess the stock at a glance. Quickly, he'd jot a few numbers on his clipboard, pull the "post-dated" product, and dash out with whole crates of juice—simply *dozens* of bottles! In pitiful form I was never proud of, I'd reach out longingly at the tragedy-in-progress, shaking my head in despair. "Left-handing" two bottles, for me, was standard. Three some days. Four could be done. Amber claimed to have done five. We'd even taken to filling reusable canvas grocery bags at times, then left-handing those. At two trips a day, it was a lot of juice. My quart-a-day carrot juice habit troubled Ginger, who at each meeting demanded I show her my palms—"They're orange!" Bagels aside, we were approaching the "All Liquid Diet." Still, each morning I'd be reading the paper at my table by the latte counter, watch the Odwalla man come and go, and wonder—"What gives him the right?!?!"

I was pretty sure it was the coveralls.

Twelve hours after the thought, I was in Kmart, paying for sunflower seeds and holding a pair of coveralls and mesh hat below the counter. Ten minutes after that I was creeping across the loading dock of the supermarket, my sights fixed on the unguarded handcart. Sammy had donated two genuine Odwalla crates his records were stored in. Baxter had assembled an impressively phony list of invoice slips for the clipboard. The next hour I was suited up, my cart aimed at Safeway. Libby was the getaway driver, Baxter the lookout—yo, it was on!

Zipping up my coveralls, I thought—gosh, I look like a real "worker." A dangerous compromise, but so is a day without juice! Wearing a blue-collar noose for ten minutes was, nonetheless, a greatly lesser concession than years of supermarket visits allowing only *two bottles per trip*. At 59¢ a visit, the established power structure had us locked in a ruinous cycle of spending, dependence on *their* dimes and quarters. The bottom of the economic ladder was a comfortable place, but what of being off the ladder altogether? What's *that* like?! I burned to sever all ties. Libby said I was bananas. Pulling my hat real low, I tilted my cart, high-fived my getaway driver, and *rushed* the Safeway!

Filling my crates with juice, I really felt myself merging with the role. I *was* the Odwalla man! And if the real Odwalla man walked in, with *his* cart, I wasn't sure what I'd say . . .

So, if I looked like the Odwalla man, and veteran employees thought I was the Odwalla man, then I filled two crates of juice and pushed them out the door like the Odwalla man, was I, in fact, the Odwalla man? Could you prove otherwise?!

Throwing the crates in the trunk, Baxter and Libby just shook their heads. I think we all took a moment to digest the profound applications of falsified identity. Then we just drank a lot. Hand me a Protein Shake . . .

Was it psychology? Or physics? Or the same force behind the receipt scam—magic? No doors were closed, no merchandise out of reach to a hurried man with coveralls and a clipboard. Proven in 1997 when a man/woman team assumed the role of ATM repair-persons, pushed a cart into a mini-mart, and pushed out the ATM! The employee even held the door! We didn't need money, but what of phonographic stereo equipment? The *whole* Odwalla case?! Since spotting a shiny new cellophane-wrapped case behind Whole Foods one day, I've been sort of obsessed with owning one of those. A little logistical fine-tuning and this was really going places . . .

The juice flowed in our house that week. When the last drop of carrot juice left the 50th bottle, the kids began shooting me—the house criminal—thirsty, impatient glances. "You know what to do," the looks said . . .

Libby zipped my coveralls, Baxter took his lookout post by the bananas. Burglars and arsonists, they say, always return to the crime scene. Poor form perhaps, but I was thirsty!

Avoiding the appearance of outright *burglary,* I left one in each row. Everything else went in the cart. Shoppers reached over me to get *their* juice, walk to the register, and pay! I don't know, I can't explain it either . . .

50 bottles later (50 x $2.99=$149.50), I pulled my hat down, jotted meaningless numbers on my blank invoice sheet, tilted the cart, and walked. It was so dramatic! Baxter and I exchanged knowing nods as I passed the bananas, and the final stretch seemed a cessation of reality beyond my fixed path—just me, my juice, and the door! Nothing between me and victory but ten feet and . . . a pair of feet. In dress shoes. Help.

"Ah, what's going on?"

The manager. He looked suspicious.

"Uh, restocking" I mumbled, scribbling on the invoice.

"OK, ah, we just got a delivery this morning . . ."

Tone, body language, steam rising from head . . . all suggesting my identity as being something *other* than the Odwalla man! I just might cancel this account!

"So . . . what's going on?!"

After a brief footchase I lay slouched in the car, shaking my head. Time to steal a new cart . . .

Libby voted for Greyhound. Baxter for the Oxnard train yard. I voted for a good story—whatever it takes. Finding totally free transport to get Libby to San Francisco for work in 24 hours—a plot I could really get behind. Hunched over and limp, the three of us were the single greatest eyesore in the Tustin Metrolink station at that moment. And the brokest—the panhandler by the payphones? You could clearly see at least 60¢ in his cup. Maybe our "poverty" lacked the hard math to back it up. Maybe we had hundreds of dollars, maybe *thousands*. Maybe we'd adopted the obscure condition of internalized, psychological poverty; marked by crawling on your hands and knees below the cashier's counter at the nickel arcade to evade the $2 door fee the night previous. They threw me out. Well, this sense of mission had been lacking in my life lately, and all themes of recklessness and urgency supplanted entirely by free coffee at no less than a half-dozen points in town, and stealing entire stacks of vinyl from the chain record store. Ok, hold on, I've been doing that for years . . . I needed this trip.

Greyhound or train yard . . . Greyhound, I felt, was played-out, a non-event. I didn't even save my ticket stubs anymore. And I'd finally accepted that there is one punk rock girl on every bus—*and she will never sit with me.* Oxnard train yard—"Track 3, weeknights, 10 p.m. to

Oakland—guaranteed" an old hobo once told me. We all knew it, maybe we were born knowing it. More of a mission than Greyhound—we could take over the Amtrak patio by the yard, throw rocks at passing boxcars, capture our train at 9:45, wave to the prisoners in the Soledad yard, and be in Oakland by noon. But looking at the schedule, we'd missed our last Metrolink to Oxnard. A silent victory for me—proponent of a plan "C": Where, as a unified force, we push the boundaries of free transport, break new ground, aim for a good story and settle for spending no money. Usually one in the same. More of a feeling than a plan. It was the virtue of non-compromise— because I swear on everything, we'd throw ourselves in front of a moving Greyhound before we'd buy a ticket . . .

An hour later we stood at the Anaheim Amtrak station, rubbing our palms. "The feeling" had materialized into a pioneering plan. Like all great plans, it bore direct congruency to *Ferris Bueller's Day Off*. The part where they steal the Ferarri? It was sort of like that. We all agreed that, yes, Amtrak would give us a free ride. This was overdue. A delayed inclusion to the history of my life and "their" transportation. I'd crept into their boxcars, zig-zagged the country in their passenger seats, squeezed long distance rides from $7 Greyhound tickets, invented the free Seattle Ferryboat scam unknown by actual residents, hopped subway turnstiles in two states, and harbored sincere intent to fund future air travel by stealing my own luggage. So really, wasn't Amtrak the final unexploited option? Did we really have a choice?!

Our train pulled in, stopped, and pulled out—with us on it. We'd held a brief conference, pooled our collective Amtrak knowledge, and detected a glaring loophole: Ticket-holder status was validated by a small card placed above the seat. Baxter said a card above the seat was as good or better than a ticket. Three-letter codes denoted the riders destination—"SLN" for Salinas, etc. But why

would anyone *go* to Salinas?! The friendly stick-family en-
campment by the I-5 on-ramp—it was the only
justification. But we sought no answers. Just cards.

Libby took the middle cars, Baxter and I the front.
Speed was crucial. Faking a sense of destination, we would
have to navigate the aisles, identify the northernmost cards
in an instant, and to make them our own—carry out the
"yawn and stretch." A trashy, unsporting move employed by
sleazy jocks to put their arm around your sister, but applied
to Amtrak—totally righteous. We were going to "put the
moves" on our U.S. railways—all the way to Oakland!

We regrouped in the rear car and took over our seats,
stifled laughs boiling over as we affixed our borrowed
"SBA" cards. Our Amtrak dream was coming to fruition.
So many years, and I still couldn't believe it—our very
self-serving worldview that big business owed us something had come through for us again. Never fails . . .

This opened all new doors. Maybe I'd even mapped
an epic summer trip before hitting the seat. From Oakland, I'd palm a "PLD" card and savor the smooth, entirely
free ride. Portland—known by most as a hotbed of en-
lightened leftism, was known only to me as "hotbed of
redeemable milk bottles," and with $200 more than I ar-
rived with I'd be set for the summer. In Seattle I would
meet a crazy rad punk girl, like, in line at the REI return
counter. She'd spit on me, punch me in the shoulder, pour
trash on my head, then take my hand and together we'd
catch our train. In Minnesota we'd sneak into the mythic
"Net Park," then, still dizzy, Scam-Trak to Chicago for
the equally legendary vegan donut company dumpster.
With simply no end to the drama, and our idyllic wave of
youthful enterprise inspiring whole novels written in
Amtrak window seats, I would nonetheless suffer—at
each station—a tugging emptiness, an incommunicable
void of colossal scale sending me flailing for answers, only
realizing in the darkest corner of my emotional pit that—

wait a minute—Amtrak hosted no filthy old hoboes drinking wine! I miss them! Such was one of the obligatory casualties of "efficiency." There was only one solution. And how to sneak a half-dozen winos and their cardboard on the Amtrak, well, I had eight hours to think it over . . .

"Tickets please."

Ooops. Chilling words side-by-side. Similar to a 'Nam flashback, "tickets please" evoked the reliving of every circumstance where I'd entered without a ticket, and was subsequently thrown out. Every concert and city festival. That train in England and the police-science convention in Anaheim. "Tickets please"—a precursor to doom. I held my breath, hoping Amtrak was more lenient than the Golden State Warriors' security force, and closer to the bus drivers back home who back down at a menacing stare. And to the very core of my being I hoped it stopped short of the outright brawl that ensued after "tickets please" at my hometown cinema. Broken glass would be taking this too far.

We were asked to follow them downstairs. Libby was passed up altogether. She could get away with anything. I mean, remember the day the police rented out Raging Waters for "LAPD Family Day," but she still got us in, and we spent all day riding water-slides with 5,000 cops? Superwoman!

I'd accepted what I knew was coming, maybe I even embraced it. "Kicked out" . . . always something of a charmed novelty. Often bearing moments where I'm outside myself, uncontrollably excited and giddy, wondering—I wonder what I'll say! Will I *charm* them?! Well, we'd laugh about it later, right? I looked over at Libby. She was laughing about it right now.

"You know, boys, this is a federal crime."

We lowered our heads in shame.

"We're throwing you out at the next intersection. But first, the conductor would like a word with you."

The conductor stepped up, and for a train-fiend it was sort of an honor. Nose to nose with Mr. Untouchable.

"You going to school in Santa Barbara boys?"

We nodded. I spent more time in the UC Santa Barbara library than most students.

"There are, boys, other ways to Santa Barbara than breaking federal law."

I ran it down in my head—no freight yard, inaccessible by public transportation . . . Sir, we've been *driven* to this!

"Boys, train people are good people. If you're in a pinch, find a conductor and he'll help you out every time."

Hard luck stories worked at the rear door of bagel shops at 6:15, sometimes even with parents. A well-rehearsed story yielding free train rides was a tip so staggering in its potential, it surpassed even the time Sammy and I broke new ground by approaching the Odwalla delivery driver with big, woeful eyes; and leaving with a crate of juice! A firm lie for a free ride—that seemed like a pretty good deal.

"Boys, I was your age once. I'm-a let you ride to L.A." To save face, he explained, he would have to kick us out there. He then gathered us into a private huddle, and in a confidential tone, said—

"Tell the conductor with the white beard at the terminal your story, tell him Berman sent ya. He'll let you ride."

At this point I stood silent, enjoying for the thousandth time the clear understanding of an outlaw maxim—"The victory is in the attempt." Somehow, fulfilling our commitment to the attempt, cute little angels took it from there. Doesn't disprove karma—just whose side she's on.

The train pulled into L.A.'s Union Station, we shook hands with heartfelt eye contact, and faded into the exiting crowd. Does crime pay? Jesus Christ. 2001 A.D. and I can't believe we're still asking this question . . .

Our "broke college student" story and dropped name hardly raised an eyebrow. The conductor smuggled us onto the next train and hid us away in a dark corner. His agreeable nature and the smooth course of the process made us nervous, but also full of warmth towards the hope that maybe we all can come together—the gate-keepers and gate-crashers, both sides of the bagel counter—like possibly we can both declare a cease-fire and they'll just start *giving us stuff*, you know?

Train guys are simply cool. Stepping into Santa Barbara, I confessed to Libby my pangs of conscience at telling our shameless "college student" lie to a nice man. "Biology major"—there was no excuse for that part. But the balance . . . If I spent dozens of hours a week eating, reading, and even sleeping at universities, was it really a lie?

In my obscure lexicon—shared with only a few hundred bearded guys cooking over a Sterno can outside Northwest food-stamp offices—Rapid City was synonymous with profanity. Choose a word. And Santa Barbara—what I cry out when, say, I discover an alarming number of door locks at the university open with a small knife. Anyway—bliss. Santa Barbara was all things carefree and leisurely. I was happy to have made it there. 16 hours until she was scheduled to work, Libby wouldn't hush up and let us enjoy the old Spanish architecture, reminding us that her situation was, in fact, desperate. Employment, I agreed, was a desperate circumstance. To be immediately corrected with a circumstance of unemployment. I pulled a newspaper from the trash, glad it wasn't 16 hours until *my* job . . .

Libby was a little upset, pacing the terminal, but I didn't understand. We stood in the choicest municipality in which to be stranded, think it over, then just throw up our hands and start a new life. Why leave? We stood

30 yards from the world's largest fig tree—you've never seen that before! And I owned proud claim to a circuitous Santa Barbara leisure route—where you ambush the coffee place on State Street, walk 50 yards and lounge on the beach, repeat several times, then recycle your cup, walk 20 feet south to the seafood restaurant, crawl on the roof and sleep! A hundred-yard round trip, at most.

Our assumed roles in the dilemma bore the suspicious convenience of film script, and I was pretty sure there were cameras rolling somewhere. Libby—the sole vehicle for drama, her approaching deadline offering the only hint of a plot with motion, and serving as the only delicate partition separating me and Baxter from running 200 feet and just living on the beach for a month. Baxter— the quiet, indifferent, tactical genius, with all the ideas, but none of the desperation to run with them. And me— I just shoplifted a lot. And this was wholly unapplicable to the plot.

Life's most precious chapters are born of absurd, sketchy plans. Such was the premise of Baxter's plan. We'll take over the Amtrak "Sightseers' Lounge"—absent on the previous commuter train—where Baxter was 80% certain no one checked tickets. Leaving us a with glaring 20% "margin of risk." Better put on my button-up . . .

It was a pleasant ride. The ease of it all raised the philosophical question: If no one asks for a ticket, is there really a fare? Was this really a scam?!

In cheating others, we were of course only cheating ourselves. But the oceanside view was captivating, the seats plush, conversation with the fellow retirees in neighboring seats spirited, and the ticket-takers simply not doing a thorough job!

Libby kept her job, and I was feeling a little more excited about not having one. I knew I would soon be riding the Sightseers' Lounge on to great things. Standing in the Oakland terminal, I looked at my glossy new Amtrak map. The heart of July and the cusp of a plan—no place I'd rather be!

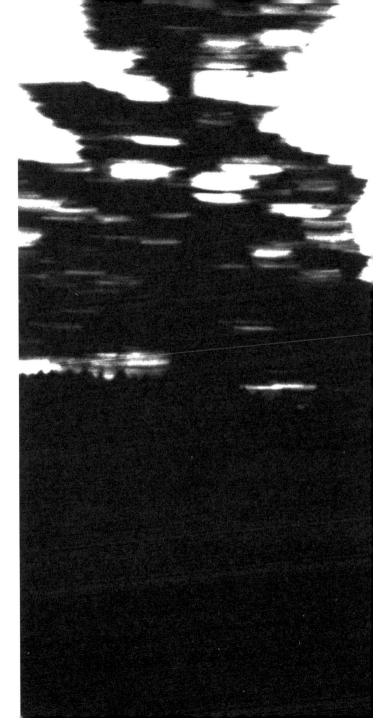

ONE

DEJA-GREYHOUND
GIT ON 'EM AND GO
CALIFORNIA SCHEMING

It was a winter rerun. I could clearly remember this Greyhound station, this movie theater popcorn, this recited story to the YMCA deskperson for access to the showers. I was here last July, like, *right here*, in this seat, hunched real low, paying $2 for a $5 ride, 20 miles past my stop and hoping the driver doesn't notice. The idea was a dose of danger one week before Christmas—Greyhound, adventure, home in two weeks. Problem with ideas is they are not direct orders—only suggestions. I was suggesting a chance meeting on the Greyhound, snowballing into freestyle hip-hop sessions on rooftops and Christmas dinner in her parents' boat. I was given a clean slate. If I wished for a chance meeting, I'd have to take a chance. But I'd forgotten how. Running from "spontaneity," I'd landed here——an uninspired repeat course of rooftops and record shops. Trapped in my own rerun—July in a copy machine—and somehow it was never as fun the second time . . .

My first impulse in San Francisco was to run to the furthest point from the bus. I made it as far as the bagel shop—fifty yards west. Finding no cups in the trash, I took my "free coffee" dreams to the street—like, *in* the street—pulling a sad cup from the gutter. More flat than round, and with a leak, but it soothed as all "hot" coffee does . . . and the temperature was perfect too! Ha ha ha! While I raced to put more coffee in my mouth than on the tile, I didn't stop to consider I was establishing a dangerous theme here—retracing last July's same path to the same bagel shop, the same table. Lifeless repetition: a symptom of a larger problem—mistaken for a cure. A cure for a broken heart. I drank cup after cup, trying to just forget my 200th shattered "Greyhound Romance." You know, with the girl in the next seat you spend twelve intimate hours with and build up elaborate plans around, whose eyes you're lost in, and to whom you've surrendered your future . . . peaking as your stop approaches and you burn to take the romance to a deeper level of commitment, but you sigh . . . talk to her? Yikes!

I wished to sit and think on my next move—and sulk a little—but this was San Francisco, a "fast paced" dot-com race to something. Seemed sitting still in San Francisco was to be the calm in the center of a suit-tornado. Where were they going?! At my table, I isolated two mistakes—wait—three . . . drinking from a tire-marked cup frisbee, sitting to *plan* spontaneity, and foolishly thinking I could get away with it in San Francisco—where sitting still in one place beyond five minutes you'll be elbowed, insulted, tagged, double-clicked on, bought, sold, then asked to leave. So I left. And it almost felt spontaneous.

Paying for the BART to Berkeley, failing to slip past the ID checker in the university library, fumbling the left-hand technique pitifully, and Whole Foods rejecting my very forged credit slip . . . If you then equate running this nearly identical course last July as "insult"—it equalled five very overt signs I should sell out, or touch up my credit-slip, or go to Monterey. My recipe wasn't flawed, no way. Unfocused plans and a Greyhound ticket? That one's solid. Well, "It's always darkest before the dawn," I'm told. It's what they say. Before the dawn—and rainstorms! It rained. A rewarding challenge on a better day, under, say, a Missouri cloud with an old friend, running for the cinema and having innocent fun prodding each other to pick up the cardboard Darth Vader and run. This wasn't like that. Just me, on the roof of the fitness place, enduring midnight wetness and unpleasantry. In the darker moments, some might reach for the assuring hand of their partner, lose themselves in a familiar film . . . I had "Christmas Rap"—Side B. That "Ghetto Santa" intro would bring whole funerals to a smile . . . "Mama—it's Santa Claus . . . an' eez *black!*" I see the sun now . . .

Two days off my bus, and I was revisiting my maps in public places, already longing for new towns with better graffiti. Though, that "T – O – F – U" piece on Ashby was awesome. Anyway, I could put away the maps now, it was the wrong approach. A lifetime of fun in a square mile, I say. I say it, then spend a lifetime running further from that square mile than anyone I know, looking for fun. What's wrong with me?! The whole of my trip's stimulation to this point came in the name of my coffee that morning—"Road Warrior Blend." Attempts to draw poignance from this failed pitifully. Just off the bus, already in wistful reflection . . . over days when *I* was a road warrior! Something of a nomadic mid-life crisis. Spontaneity was dead, and I thought of the pillows and warm meals I'd left behind. My last spontaneous act had been three weeks previous, celebrating Thanksgiving locked in a university library. Tofurkey in a stairwell—where did the creativity go . . .

Right there on Telegraph, through my downcast haze, cheer itself—bagels. A whole bag! Maybe life was trying to patch things up. I took my bagels to the record store. Then took five shiny CDs to the counter and sort of, um . . . "forgot" to pay for 4/5 my purchase! Whoops! I immediately recognized this act as simply awesome.

This was, however, tragically lost on the loss-prevention agent. Sir, I can explain . . . But the crudeness of it did all the talking—situation defused. It's not really shoplifting unless it looks like it. Face it—sometimes left hands "forget" that merchandise below the counter rim. Who can explain it? Demanding more urgent explanation was why a $2 CD was tagged. A disturbing trend, and when they begin tagging bulk-bin carob chips—we're all dead . . .

Margaret was in town from my hometown. Family vacation. She ditched her parents to meet me. I hoped she would reverse the tide. Coffee was a start—not enough to win my heart, but at least my attention. We stepped into the café, the one with the checkered floor, and I knew the "Winter Rerun" theme was going *too far*. Six months since July, picked up off the street and bought coffee, at the same café, again. I was nervous, but if she didn't hit on me, and try baiting me back to her apartment with vegan food, at least it wouldn't be an *exact* rerun . . .

Maybe coffee with a girl I *didn't* know, had never explored abandoned buildings with . . . A cure predicated on subduing my bashfulness. I tried that once in Santa Cruz—she broke my heart in eight seconds. Maybe I hadn't sat down at a stranger's table uninvited since. Let me say on behalf of all kids who will ever pick up a bag, run for it, and land in your town, alone—please talk to us. We're making eye contact longingly outside supermarkets, sitting wide-eyed on our bags in front of the laundromat, and I can't speak for all—but I spend a curious share of my hours on high-school bleachers after dark. We throw you bait—obscure band t-shirts, maybe an interest-specific zine placed prominently on a café table . . . though, I may be the only one to do this. Maybe I'm *crazy.* Anyway, we're still waiting. Forgive our silence—we're still getting over the Greyhound girl . . .

When is "action-and-romance-chasing-youth" just "bum"? Which library would I celebrate *Christmas* in? What novelty and scandal lay just feet away in *Chelsea Clinton's trash?* I thought on these things inside the Stanford University library. "July on Repeat"—beyond "resemblance," this was direct congruency. And yes, I'd sat in that chair before. Rain broke, and I sat up a little straighter. A mile short of genuine drama, of the Greyhound girl talking to *me,* but something. Sleepy eyes and falling rain: one of those rad circumstances where you have to *think*—struggling with unmarked doors, peering under stairs, sneaking behind counters . . . I settled face-down inside the 24-hour study lounge. The most cherished sort of moment—when the kid looks out at the storm to shake his fist at the world—"I win!"

This was a script I could mouth the words to. I tried an active role in writing the stupid thing, calling Chump in maybe this rerun's only asymmetric move. He wasn't home. I spiraled downward into a slumped position at the bagel shop. Six months since July, learning not all things acquire charm with age. Like tables. Maybe this *was* July! The paper at my table read "December," and I wasn't sure what to believe. Then I looked up and knew. The plump and jovial UPS man on a delivery. I'd chatted with him before . . . in July.

Perhaps my greatest contingency of support in this doomed time came from the town's population of *giant rats*, who, in my years of rooftop visits, had never bitten me once—not even a nibble! Though zig-zagging the church roof, numbering in the dozens, they always respected my space and, I felt, respected *me*. Rats and shoplifters are, really, respected by no one but each other. Then, that night, I returned to my place of rest—beside the skylight—and in that very spot lay *a huge snappy mousetrap!* It was the suburb's affront to me, and worse still—my friends the rats! With great rage I hurled loose objects and crude insults at the sinister thing, and made uncivilized swatting movements with photocopied zines. Maybe more than the trap snapped that night, maybe *I* did, and thought—drive me from your roofs . . . and I just might land on your strip malls with all new fury! This one's for the rats!

Flailing for pop music and bad rap magazines, I turned to a third coping mechanism: "Shoplifting"—which works better than you'd think. It was a misguided day of bus rides, chain-store CDs, and stolen baked goods. Reckless, uninspired, escapist hedonism with "peasant uprising" overtones. My self-defeating wave tore me through the suburbs—stealing books and scamming drug stores like a fiend, making money I didn't need or spend, and breaking the vow of moderation between man and scam. Calling "time out" at the health food store, I double-fisted free cider samples, wondering where this little storm was taking me. Prison? Coal in my stocking? And what *were* the limits of "Free Cider Sample"? I staggered through the suburbs in a daze . . .

At the point furthest from inspiration, I went further—finding myself collapsed outside a coffee shop—*feeding pigeons*. Ok, let me get my head through, and when I say "now"—yank the chair . . .

San Francisco to San Jose—I didn't need to think on my next move. I could read it in my own journal marked "July"—Santa Cruz. Continuing on the following page, I could plainly see I would exit the bus then visit the record store across the street, rescue a few, read lyric sheets in the coffee shop, visit the health food store and pull handfulls of vitamin receipts from the anomalous "All-Receipt Trash Can," etc. etc. . . . As an adventure-seeker, I was now past relevancy. Either old, or worse—out of ideas. Stealing several copy-keys from Kinko's as Christmas gifts for friends the day before had been my last one. From this point— only wistful novels and movie rights. But that copy-key idea was a sharp way to go out . . .

UC Santa Cruz: closed, my flashlight dying *inside* a dumpster, several forklift guys de-cloaking my secret place of rest and *laughing*, coastal coldness, bad records, expensive coffee . . . Clouds swirled and the air filled with a sense of doom, culminating in a rare moment of derelict despair, right there on the bus stop bench.

"Are you a vegetarian?"

Oh gosh. An Australian goddess. Justifying every dollar ever spent on "Vegan" patches, and, in one sentence—my entire trip. I told her the story my eyes already had. She cut me off, tossed me words like "intriguing," and could she take me out to dinner? Shucks, free food? With you sweet girl from down under, I might even pay . . .

There was no world beyond our table. The kid who stormed up, asking bluntly if he could *take* and *eat* our leftovers almost registered, but probably wouldn't inspire until tomorrow. Looking for free food and purpose, I'd found both. Five hours later and the "past" and "future" still lay obsolete— it was just her and me. A machine-gun exchange of "I know what you mean" moments, interspersed with those deeper— evoking only slow nods. A girl with a backpack, reminding us all of the ageless seduction of a one-way ticket and little or no regard for "the details." This was it, "Greyhound Girl." Just a day late or a dollar short. But all I'd built her up to be . . .

Me? Unemployed. You?

"Professional bum."

I felt the relationship was really blossoming.

She understood my uninspired condition—possibly a state only remedied through a coastal hitchhiking trip with a girl—but right now I wasn't sure why I'd left home.

"So let's go!" she said.

And then—I remembered . . .

The best advice I can give on hopping freights was given to me by a hobo in Missoula.

"What do you know about hopping trains?" I asked.

"*Git on 'em and go . . .*" he said.

"Which ones?" I asked.

"*The ones that move.*"

The words thundered like the voice of God.

And so it was with this hobo Zen philosophy that Penny and I hopped our first train. We were going to get on a train, and we were going to get on a train that *moved*.

I was the hobo that cried wolf. Always talking talking talking of that day, always in the very near future, when I would hop a train out of that town—and rarely making it further than the bagel dumpster. Something would always keep me in that town—a Hardcore show, or a book too big to carry on a long trip, but usually just the leisure of my routine and a life without struggle. And I liked to think that without me, my town would crumble. And without my town, well, I might start crying! The relationship was symbiotic. Maybe I *did* serve a purpose. I kept the change from piling up in the fountain outside the big hotel. And I can say, as humbly as possible, my friends and I justified the existence of dozens of security guards in my town and the surrounding suburbs. Although criminals, we stand in full support of economic growth. Shoplifting *means* jobs!

In the rare successful escape attempts, I would return to find my town fully intact, and in fact improved upon in my absence. After each short trip, my town surprised me with any number of upgrades—a new park, or piece of public art, or a new store. And the small changes only I noticed—a new bagel flavor, free copy machine in the bank, or new patio furniture at the deli on the main strip. I wondered if they waited until I was out of town to move things around and create a little "progress" to confuse me. So I could hitchhike around the country and explore new towns, then return to explore the new features of my old town.

. . . if I could ever make it to the on-ramp, which I did sometimes. But somehow I just never had made it to the train yard, though it was maybe two miles from home. I had gotten as far as the northern extremities, where Amtrak parks their trains for repair. It was so exciting running up and down the empty passenger cars, testing the beds and eating the train food, that I lost track of time. "Tomorrow . . ." I would say, but the train yard is nowhere near the thrift store, which is surely where I went instead.

Something in my life one day sparked more empty talk and hollow plans. Maybe I grumbled about another friend selling out, or that my life was growing stale, or how I had explored every street and alley, and that I would hop a train out of that town . . . *next* week. Really. When I did leave, no one ever noticed, and if they did, they never asked where I had been—though it might have been the most amazing trip of my life to an undiscovered paradise where I planned to die. They never asked and never listened. So that day Penny rocked my world when she asked me this—she said, "Can I come?"

Our friends drove us to the train yard to see us off. They waved, drove off, the dust settled, and I was left with a lot of talk to live up to. And Penny was left with someone she probably thought knew something about hopping trains. I had a short book full of useful advice. I had been street-corner schooled by true hoboes on the rules of the rails, many of which we had broken before stepping foot in the yard. Food? Water? Probably wasn't important. Penny had the foresight to steal a sleeping bag from Target. I had a blanket draped over my shoulders and a small bag filled with more cassettes than anything else. It was poor planning, naïveté, brazenness, illegality, directionlessness—all the ingredients of high adventure. Our drive for a good story would overcome the obstacles—ignorance, no clear destination, uncertainty as to where the train yard was or if we were in it. And where does one sit on a moving train anyway? It was d.i.y. hobo training.

And that day, they made it too easy. We had only been pacing the yard for 15 minutes waiting for one of the trains to start *moving*, when one of the trains started moving.

"Should we . . . ?" I asked hesitantly.

It was a nervous moment. We weren't committed. There were other things to do in the industrial district, we could dumpster dive at the comic book factory instead . . .

"I think we should," she said.

She meant the train.

They never tell you hopping trains is, like, the most inspiring activity *ever*. That hobo life opens up a world of infinite possibility and adventure. That every town of consequence has a train yard, and that any adventure seeker can wake up and wonder, "Where do I want to go today?" And rather than the coffee shop, or record store, or park, think Omaha, Miami, Boston, L.A. . . . and then *go there*.

Sitting in our first boxcar—legs hanging out the door—watching the ghetto scenery and all the towns we only passed through previously en route to the swap meet, well, it turned us into giggling children. We look back on those first moments of hobo life as the most stimulating of our lives. The ghetto turned into wilderness, the sun set, and we fell asleep in that boxcar on our way to . . . well, that wasn't the point.

We awoke with a crash in a train yard halfway across the state. A creepy small town, probably none we had ever heard of. Or maybe it was, but never knowing where we were or where we were going made the trip so exciting, and *dangerous* . . .

Our first successful illegal train ride was a monumental accomplishment in my life, and Penny was definitely glowing as well. Not very polite or appropriate, I thought, to mention the urgent sickness brewing in my stomach. It struck suddenly, just as we jumped off the train. As I stumbled out of the yard I swore that I would never again ingest that mysterious nutritional supplement I had dumpster-dived the night before. The vitamin mix so bad no one would take more than a sip of it at our going away party. The unidentified mix I thought I would impress everyone by drinking a whole glass of. Yes, whatever it was, I would never drink it again . . . guaranteed. There was the immediate concern of vomiting and where to do it. I was in intense pain, but it would have been rude to mention that to Penny, spoiling the moment of our glory. At a nearby truck stop Penny called our friends to boast, I stepped into the restroom to purge myself of that nutritional supplement. Nutritional supplement? Or rat poison? Cocaine? Careful what you throw away, I'll probably eat it.

Back at the yard we paced the perimeter, waiting to use the sum of our train hopping knowledge—when a train moves, you, like, jump on it. We watched the trains from the road. A couple pulled up in an old car and gave us eight dollars and sixty cents! Free money! You don't get *that* on Greyhound. Unless you "lose" your luggage, but anyway . . .

Another moving train to another small town in another state. A town where college friends of Penny's parents lived. They took us to lunch, and invited us to stay at their home. They wished they could show us the town, but, sigh, they had to baby-sit. Here are the keys, they said, take our car, show yourselves around. Free money, free food, free car, bragging rights . . . Oh yes! Turned loose in a resort town with the recklessly lacking inhibition of vacationers. It was our role, as models of delinquency, to make devilish trouble in that resort town. Now where is that resort . . .

We found the resort—all roads led to it. We found the pool, the hot tub, the sauna. We found the plush couches next to the fireplace in the lobby, and the lawn chair on the big patio outside with the humbling view. And in a remote corner, in a rarely used staircase, we found a ladder leading to a secluded perch where a crafty and stealthy person could live indefinitely—soaking in the spa, enjoying the view, and eating the leftover wedding food *forever*. I decided to definitely count that as a future plan . . .

We stole a basket of food from the supermarket and returned to our hosts' home where they told us we should stay through the week. Wow, thanks, we said. Maybe we can play Nintendo after dinner, and you can show us to our rooms and . . . wait a minute! We're hoboes! We had been tricked. Baited from the rails with showers and food into a sinister middle-class trap! Penny said we should definitely return to the trains. To our life, where the highs were euphoric and the lows desperate; but that at least stimulated our emotions, which makes this less stable life . . . well, what makes it really *living*. We did stay with our hosts that one night. We played Nintendo and took showers and told stories. But somehow a hot shower never satisfies like sneaking into the Best Western hot tub for a long bath. And before we left town, we did that too.

There were more train rides that trip, and we invented a bold, adventurous, and wildly daring approach to hopping trains, where any moving train was the right train. And if it was bound for Havre, Omaha, Denver or Ogden, then it would be exactly where we wanted to be, or rather, exactly how we wanted to get there. Never knowing where our train was bound or where we would wake up was our statement of defiance to a goal-oriented society. The hobo life emphasized the trip and not the destination. We lived in the craziness of the moment. So after ten-hour waits in those lonely yards, when the brakes hissed and the train lurched forward, we hopped on—not because it was headed where we wanted to be, but because it was headed anywhere at all. Bakersfield, Phoenix, Fargo . . . all issues of distance disappeared and the issue of time was irrelevant. Except for the Converge show. I definitely wanted to return for the Converge show . . .

It was an extreme explosion of options and possibility, difficult to grasp once I felt the weight of what we had tapped into. These train yards were like underground Greyhound stations without posted schedules. Chicago, Lincoln, Sioux City . . . Any morning, or night, or whenever, if I felt like reading in the University of North Dakota library, or roller skating in Oakland, or jumping in a boxcar just to have a story to tell, well then . . . And even if spontaneity never possessed me enough to inspire a cross-country train ride on a whim, it was enough to know that now, I could.

There was the anxious train ride home, noticeably less thrilling than the rest, being that on that ride we knew for where we were bound. I had the comfort of my dusty blanket, Penny had her big book, we had our freedom to do with as we pleased, we had a new story to tell, and between us we had our eight dollars and sixty cents!

Once home, I found my town as I had left it—perfection cannot be improved upon. From our travels and high adventure, my activities turned domestic—there was hobo history to research, and a new trip to plot. And with my cut of the trip's profits, to see Converge I still needed to steal 70¢ somewhere . . .

It was fall, or autumn, or that grey void between crazy and amazing trips; when the Mexican restaurant pulls in its patio furniture for the winter, and I wouldn't be traveling—or eating leftover chips and salsa—until spring. There was the massive swap meet in my town which I looked forward to all winter, a five-year tradition representing the gateway to spring and big plans for dramatic solo travels funded by misdemeanor theft. My summer travels that year had been maybe *too* inspiring, my transient skills had fully developed, and I wasn't sure why I hadn't considered vagrancy as a year-round pursuit. I was almost certain that that which I enjoyed most in life— long rides with sketchy truck drivers, petty crime, and sleeping on beaches—was as much or more fun in January as it was in July.

It was a theory I had developed during my studies in the "Travel" section at Barnes & Noble. I was a regular at my town's Barnes & Noble, a regular of one particular chair, within arm's reach of the maps on one side, and the "Travel—U.S." section on the other. So as winter rolled in, and the rain poured outside, I was left with my memories, and the slick, full color *Frommer's Travel Guides.* I would sit in that chair, staring longingly at pictures in travel books, plotting and scheming adventures for next summer . . . and in the meantime create small-scale local adventures, taking long bus rides to explore distant suburbs. But each night before returning home I would get off the bus at Barnes & Noble, eat bagels, and take notes on the wacky museums, factory tours, and crazy ghetto towns I would positively visit—*next* summer . . . It was a pattern repeated every few days—I would sit down with my books, it would happen to be the night of open mic poetry, or an author's book reading, I would become distracted from my very important studies, and just *steal* those books. My travel library was really coming along—I had *Road Trip USA - A Guide to America's Two-Lane Highways*, *Roadside America*, *Rock 'N' Roll Traveler USA*, an extensive collection of maps, and the soundtrack to my research—the *Truck Drivin' Man comp LP*. So while "18 Wheels A Rollin'" or "Ridin' Down Ole 99" played on my turntable, it always happened that I got a little dreamy and nostalgic, and thought of bigger adventures in warmer towns. It was a plan I had experimented with last winter, riding my bike around Florida in a post-trauma escape to "find myself." I knew I would never do *that* again. But there is an inspiration to migrate stimulated by shiny full-color pictures in yuppie travel guides, and made possible by a strong commitment to a life of unemployment. So in Barnes & Noble, on my chair, I would gaze dreamily at the photos of golf courses, vacation resorts, and dining out on the strip in those So-Cal yuppie travel guides; then finally resolve to chase big adventures that winter—to sleep on those golf courses, sneak into the swimming pools at those resorts, and eat leftover table scraps at those trendy cafés on the strip. The fluorescent lights in Barnes & Noble can induce wild fantasies . . .

Aiming south, I missed my mark and ended up north, in Eugene. It was a homecoming of sorts, returning to my rent-free apartment in the University of Oregon library—through the door marked "Fire Exit Only—Alarm Will Sound," to the door at the bottom of the staircase. It was great to find my second home untouched, and that in the past year no one had discovered that the door popped open with a forceful tug. It was a dusty little room, probably labeled as a storage closet on the library blueprints. But to me it was a second home, and without it I would probably visit Eugene just as often, and sleep on the roof of the pizza place across the street from campus—with the student apartments looking down on me from either side. A sketchy place to sleep, and if the police were called about a crazy Peeping Tom lurking on that rooftop, I wasn't sure I could explain my way out of it.

So at 12:45, when they flashed the lights in the library, I would take my book, sneak through the "Fire Exit" door, run down the staircase, fight with my door until it opened, crawl behind the boxes of dusty books, and read by flashlight amongst ancient debris from past visits until I fell asleep. It was certainly a craftier and more professional approach to vagrancy. A little musty, and without a record player, but perfect in every other way. A secret hideout with the important qualities I look for in a home—rent free and not legally recognized!

After stimulating study, I would lie in my sleeping bag and drift away into nostalgia for the early days of my Eugene squatting career . . . The upstairs porch of a now demolished apartment building—not really a squat, but it had a roof, and furniture, so I think it qualifies! The indecipherable map to an abandoned house passed to me by a gutter punk—the house I wandered endlessly through Northwest Eugene searching for, but never found. And the scary abandoned house on 11th Ave next to the hospital— with despondent and desperate homeless lying prostrate on every bench and bush in Eugene, we couldn't understand why they didn't do what we did immediately after spotting it: Take a bus to Springfield, steal a crowbar from Sears, and bust in! Wow, room to move, run in circles, and do whatever we please! We felt tough and empowered. Probably it was doomed from the first clunk of crowbar striking cedar, but one never fails in such adventures—each day of unemployment and no rent bill is a small victory!

From fighting with thuggish hospital security guards and the constant threat of eviction to a secure place in the library—I had come far. And the future only looked brighter when outside the Goodwill, a street corner lawyer provided me with exciting and functional *free legal advice*. He spoke of an obscure provision in Oregon state territorial law— which, when simplified, in effect meant that if a person was able to occupy a building for 7 years, they were legally entitled to the property! I had heard of such laws before, and thought it unlikely a law would exist which worked in such favor of the criminal underclass.

Though, if true, this legal loophole had profound applications. So, what does "occupy" entail? Would I have to receive *mail* at the library, or . . . ? It was all so confusing, and so exciting! When I pressed the street lawyer for the finer points of the law, he only shrugged. But he seemed to be saying if I lived in my storage room for 7 years, *I would own the U of O library*! First priority—rearrange the furniture!

Seven years . . . I thought about the day a judge would hand down my title of ownership, and that my life hadn't really begun until I graduated high school 4 years previous—so to me 7 years was more than a lifetime away! But it would be a rich and fulfilling life-and-a-half wait; and I had no doubt I could spend the next 7 years reading, walking, exploring, and eating free food. Which is what I did that week. Wait a minute . . . that's what I've been doing the last *4 years*! Well I was a better person for my habits, and in 7 years would be a well-read pro, and will have reached the apex of parasitic vagrancy! I couldn't wait!

Eugene's reputation of "sleepy college town," I had always felt, was a flagrant falsehood. Until recently, I had looked at Eugene as obnoxious and gritty—definitely overrated. And then I began traveling inside the U.S., away from the coast. "Stay to the sides, don't go in there," they warned. And after Omaha and Des Moines, I began to think they were right! I began to appreciate towns like Eugene more than ever before, even if the reputation of "progressive" only meant "intoxicated."

So to escape the inescapable smog and chain stores, I spent much of my leisure time in the U of O student center, which provided all the pacifying and mind-numbing conveniences of a middle-class home. A microwave, couches, push button hot water, and a piano! If all that I asked for in a vacation was comfort, there would be no reason to leave. Though, I would become restless and walk to the campus gym every other day—bypassing the ID checking brute at the entrance—and take a shower. But I always ran back to the student center and my favorite chair on the first floor—in the corner next to the piano. I would pretend to read, but it was an act, a front in the gaps between piano performances by passing students. Two or three times an hour a kid on their way to class would sit down for a few minutes, make use of childhood piano lessons, and play a little song. The piano put me in an euphoric trance. Each time someone sat down I would tell them "Play *Tubular Bells*!" Not one person knew the song, and I wondered why they learned to play piano at all.

Maybe I was in a contemplative state, or something, but that week I left campus only to steal food from IGA, and only then because stealing food from the student cafeteria every day for every meal just wasn't safe. It was during one of these shoplifting excursions that outside IGA a young woman who had been next in line ran up behind me as I left—"Hey! You got lucky!" she said, pointing to the fresh squeezed juice and bagels in my left hand. She had noticed the left-hand theft technique in action. She was young, seemingly a little drugged out, and clearly using her "heightened awareness" to learn a new shoplifting method. I had to rethink my commitment to straight-edge—just maybe drugs could "open my mind" to new techniques of theft! I explained to her the mechanics of the left-hand method, and she promised to try it. I hadn't gotten "lucky" as she had said. Luck is inconsistent—the left-hand technique is guaranteed every time!

Back on campus, in my chair by the piano, I reflected on past visits, and how all leisure and troublemaking centered on that building. The U of O student center represented late nights, random encounters, twelve-hour tea binges, and a gateway to great adventures. And stood as a monument to mischief . . . Attacking the long buffet-style tables of food during graduation ceremonies. Prowling around the cafeteria at midnight, finding the cooler unlocked, and making a dramatic escape with a bag of juice! And the two-part sneak attack on the espresso stand last year—once for a stack of unstamped "Buy 10—Get the 11th Free" cards, and a return visit for the stamp! My rebellion against commodified coffee! Well, on this visit there were no big receptions with free fruit, and the cooler was locked, but in my wallet I still carried 15 "free coffee" cards! Now, I didn't drink coffee for health reasons, but I don't pass up free *anything* for criminal reasons either. So between chapters in my book, if no one was playing me a song on the piano, I ran to the espresso stand for free coffee—the most flavorful kind!

Travel itineraries are way overrated, and after one week I left Eugene without one. Anyone is welcome to stay in my room while I'm away, and if you clean up after yourself and generally respect the place, come back to the library in 7 years and I'll let you skate my half-pipe—I'm building it in the map-room!

Somehow I ended up in Arcata, northwestern California. There was Arcata's reputation—eco-friendly, hotbed of environmental activism with brave and dramatic clashes between activists and the logging industry in the surrounding forest. Which was awesome, but after one day in Arcata and several nonsensical conversations with half-dead, drooling, and mumbling locals, I was reminded of *Night of the Living Dead.* Drug zombies—everywhere! It was scary. As I explored Arcata, I paced the streets with my "I don't smoke" response switched on rapid-fire. I grew tired of politely declining, and "I don't smoke" quickly became instead a cold contemptuous stare into their dilated pupils. Then I snapped, began choking those hippies to death, carving "Drug Free—I Win Again" into their foreheads with a boxcutter, and leaving their bodies outside the co-op.

Arcata seemed a condensed and exaggerated Eugene—the drug culture, the costumes . . . But unlike Eugene, instead of tripping over tied-up dogs outside the bookstore and falling on the *sidewalk*, I fell on *other dogs*!

Arcata did have spectacular bagels and an 80's arcade, both things definitely worth staying for. And I was filled with warm feelings when a big smiling kid noticed me reading *Thrasher* magazine on a bench and pulled a *Plan-B* skate video out of his bag—"I wanted you to have this." Shucks. "Thanks," I said. A video cassette, let's see, I'll just take this back to my bush, and, um . . .

Outside the co-op I ate many bagels and stroked my gift with wonder, just watching the misty drizzle. A kid with black hair and a black trenchcoat stood next to me, being obnoxious and talking to himself. Then he began talking to me. He asked me my "story," providing the perfect setup to launch into my *whole* story, from the beginning, like Chunk in *The Goonies*! What I really said was that I was traveling, with no plan, to a sunny paradise, looking for a place to live for the winter, somewhere . . . He too was from out of town, he said, and that his first day in Arcata, panhandling outside Safeway, a charitable girl brought him home—and he had lived there ever since. He asked if I needed a place to stay. I was happy on the roof of the insurance place on "G" street, but I did need a good story, so . . .

His name was "Tiger." He was insane, nervous, twitching, told a stream of lies and contradicted himself often. As a successful hacker engaging in "the electronic transfer of funds," he told me, he travels the country, *buys* houses, stays around for awhile, hosts extravagant parties, crashes a few cars, throws his money around, and hits the road! Insane . . . I decided I was definitely going to mess with him, use his stereo to put all the CDs I bought in Eugene on cassette, and eat his food!

He introduced me to his roommates (all insane), and within five minutes exclaimed that he needed drugs, like, right at that moment—that I was going to give him money, we were going to the square to buy pot, and then smoke it all night! I told him—"I'm straight." He asked how it was possible to be drug-free and cope with life on "the streets." Hahahaha! "The streets" . . . I hadn't ever thought of it like that. Yes, I fall asleep each night to the sound of my sobs, soaking the sleeping bag with my tears . . . Free food, high adventure, freedom to do whatever I want, no job . . . It's all part of life in da school of hard knocks!

On our way downtown he launched into more embarrassing boasting of girls and life in high society. All I could think was how excited I was—my first drug mission! We stood on the corner across from the liquor store with our hands in our pockets, waiting for our big score. "Excuse me," Tiger would mumble to each passerby—"Do you know if it's . . . 4:20?" Ha! It was every hippie joke ever shared with my straight-edge friends, the drug culture in all its absurdity, and I was *living it*. It was great!

Tiger found his man, bought his escape from the hard life, and ran around town assembling a small group of like-minded kids for that night's party. Outside the co-op Tiger preyed on two teenage runaways from Berkeley carrying their belongings in Hefty bags. With Tiger's promises of food and beer, they followed us back. As we walked, I was puzzled by the dominant themes of conversation in that small crowd of Arcata youth—transparent lies and obvious exaggeration were the standard. Girls, inherited wealth, celebrity acquaintances . . . It seemed with each puff of the pipe they blew a bit of reality right out of their heads.

I value these brief encounters with alien worlds. Huddled in the corner, I tried to make sense of it all. Five obnoxious hippies, two girls lured in with cigarettes, and me, dazed, drowning out the inebriated chatter with the sober sounds of XContemptX. It was my first party, and at 22, probably too late for socialization. Or maybe it's never too late to acquire a taste for malt liquor and teenage girls. I flipped the tape over—Day of Suffering. I was pretty sure they had a song about *killing* people with a taste for malt liquor. It was my own little party, crouched behind the bookshelf, deflecting occasional questions from the drunken mob with a scowl. "What's wrong?" "You're not drinking?" "Take a hit!" I was fighting for my right *not* to party. The Beastie Boys are 2/3 drug free now, they should rewrite that damn song.

When I awoke the next morning, I scanned the room to see five unconscious bodies clutching empty beer cans—it was an opportunity for straight-edge revenge clearly presenting itself. But they had rescued me from the rain, and fed me with their limited understanding of the word "vegan," so I rolled up my sleeping bag and left Arcata—maybe forever!

Visit Arcata, I really do recommend it. Play the nearly impossible to find *original* Pac Man at the café, explore the HSU campus, see a two-dollar movie, buy a tofu dog from the vendor in Town Square, sleep on the rooftops, and if they ask you what time it is, there's only one correct answer—"4:20"!

The man at the auto mechanic's place next to the 101 on-ramp has a great job—drinking coffee by the fence and talking with hitchhikers all day. "I never seen a hitchhiker dressed like you before!" It was true, I looked like the unthreatening fourth Beastie Boy. So I wasn't surprised when a late 20's female pulled over moments later. Before I got in, she had to clear a pile of gangsta rap tapes off my seat! Not Dr. Dre, but hardcore underground rap I hadn't heard of like Gangsta G and the C-Town Mob. She was one clean-cut professional, and I theorized gangster rap helped her keep in touch with youth culture and relate better to her clientele—she counseled "troubled adolescents." She assumed I was living a hard life, and at a mile-a-minute rattled off the addresses of every food bank and shelter in Northern California. "Write this down!" she barked. "No, no . . ." I tried to cut her off, to explain I represented the upper crust of transient youth—eating the most expensive food, occupying the most expensive real-estate without permission, and that I had only slept in a cardboard box once!

The stretch of 101 between Arcata and Ukiah was explained to me by a highway patrolman two years ago as being the most hitchhiked corridor in America. And Garberville, I had been told by everyone, was *the* convergence point for west coast travelers. After briefly strolling the strip, I confirmed that Garberville did host a crazy amount of kids with backpacks and dogs. After all the hype, it was sort of a let-down. The "travelers' town" . . . they must mean *paying* travellers. The Garberville supermarket was unusually resistant to being stolen from. Even in what was known as a great "counterculture oasis" of artists, activists, and progressive thinkers, I found the Garberville supermarket guilty of the commodification of foodstuffs. Everything costs money! That's not very "progressive." I'm staging a demonstration! At the door I was stripped of my backpack which they held at the customer service counter. They followed me around the store, and the counters were much too low to left-hand anything. They were simply not playing fair. I was nonetheless able to smuggle out bagels and juice, but they sure were jerks about it. It was a cold reception, no place for a criminal, and I decided to take my tourist dollars elsewhere!

From the 101 on-ramp in Garberville—possibly the most hitchhiked spot in America—I rode with two college girls from Arcata. They fed me, and were shocked and amazed I had never heard Paul Simon. "*Everyone* has a favorite Paul Simon song!" A British woman took me further south. She had left London two years ago for a change of lifestyle, settling in northern California where she read and played her Casio keyboard in a forest cabin for two years! Her complaints about the U.S. included the large number of crazy people, and the American concept of private property—our overprotectiveness of what's "ours." It was a biting truth, I told her. Americans just don't believe in sharing, and I was reminded of it every day being chased from the health food store for eating dates from the bulk food bins. Yes, yes, she said, Americans . . . One day she crossed the invisible line onto her neighbor's property for a picnic and was waved at with a shotgun. Americans want what's ours and will kill to protect it. It's all going downhill, and when the clerks at the health food store start carrying shotguns—I'm moving to London! In Healdsburg, a suit-and-tie yuppie picked me up in a stylish sports car. He makes his fortune selling accounting software to casinos. His job consists entirely of driving around the country, schmoozing and getting drunk with casino operators—who he said are the sleaziest breed on earth. He had recently attended a "gaming convention," where he met one of the most unethical of the scoundrels, his name was *Michael Jackson!* The "King of Pop" was paving over a jungle in Africa to build a big casino for white people!

My suburban eyes were better trained to appreciate the nicely groomed grass and shady tree-lined streets of Santa Rosa. Some trendy family had moved into the old vacant house by the mall since my last visit, which meant I probably couldn't sleep in the backyard anymore. I settled on the roof of a daycare on Humboldt Street, and recalled where I slept the first night of my *last* visit to Santa Rosa— when my ride checked me into the *Holiday Inn* and gave me twenty dollars! Take note: Never hesitate to make use of greatly exaggerated hard luck stories! The issue of free hotel rooms has always been a ponderous subject with me, and I definitely consider it a life's goal of sorts to find a consistent hotel room scam. Then I consider the weighty ethical issues of using a propensity for amateurish scams and petty theft beyond the basics of survival, the dark path of hedonism to which it could lead. A bouncy bed and HBO every night . . . I might get soft, and find every attractive element of uncertainty and danger in travel *gone*. There is a certain charm to sleeping on rooftops, a bittersweet attraction to fleeing a golf course at 4 a.m. with a sleeping bag over your shoulders to escape the timed sprinklers—I just might miss that! One permissive allowance made for convenience or material excess would lead to another, a downward spiral of inexcusable abuse of survival theft, and soon I might lose touch with the enchanting and rich experiences of poverty. And, slipping further, I just might start going to the department store, pulling expensive clothes off the racks, and taking them up to the return counter to "exchange" them for cologne and silk ties! For the sake of romantic struggle, maybe it's better to leave my hotel obsession where it stands—eat from the breakfast buffet in the lobby, jiggle all the closet doorknobs, and when I get sleepy—crawl into the bushes behind the parking lot. Nonetheless, there remains the lingering temptation to follow up on the one trick I do know of . . .

Often I'll corner strangers for useful information and criminal advice, and it was during one of these interrogations that someone, somewhere, confessed they might know of a free hotel room trick—learned late one night watching MTV! This stranger, when pressed, broke down and stammered through a hazy memory of an episode of MTV's *The Real World,* where the *"seven strangers picked to live in a house"* scam a hotel room! The details were fuzzy, but allegedly they asked to see a room at a ghetto motel minutes before 12 a.m.—when the front desk closed for the night. One of them hid inside the room while the others returned the key and explained the room was filthy and certainly *not* up to their standards. A half-hour after the counter-person had gone home, the person in hiding admitted everyone into their *free hotel room!* Such subversive and functional criminal instruction on MTV further blurs the lines between us and them. MTV . . . whose side are they on?!?

There was so much to do in Santa Rosa, I don't know how I missed it all the last time. The death star of downtown is the Santa Rosa mall, which actually had several sadly undervalued punk resources. They hide the really fun places where they think we won't look! It's not listed on the mall directory, but the double doors in the corner of the food court lead to the Santa Rosa mall's *extensive tunnel system*, which runs behind all the stores—and I couldn't be sure, but just may continue *forever.* I became very confused and scared when I couldn't find my way out, and retracing my steps sent me bumping into walls that weren't there before, and I almost cried. Every 100 feet or so were ladders to unlocked hatches for roof access, and one day I might *live* on the roof of that mall, subsisting on leftover french fries from the food court below. I see no flaw in that plan. But I couldn't settle down yet, there was so much left to do . . . The 99¢ bin at the Wherehouse chain record store is a puzzling source of classic Hardcore CDs, and I was two for two—Insted in '96, and this visit: Underdog, making it "America's Most Hardcore" Wherehouse! But it was the Fresh Choice restaurant which kept me anchored to the S.R. mall during my stay. Fresh Choice is a chain of "all you can eat" buffet-style restaurants, easily infiltrated and taken for free meals . . . and when you're finished eating—all that can be fit in a backpack! As the Fresh Choice chain expands and new franchises open in strip malls throughout the West, the future is looking brighter for America's homeless. Entire trips have been taken around the Bay Area sneaking into Fresh Choices—it's that much fun! Limitless salad, soup, fruit, tofu, coffee, raisins, pickles . . . A celebration of American gluttony. Bring Tupperware. Fresh Choice . . . where the cashier is so easily bypassed, the policy seems to be—"Well, you *could* pay, or . . ." Or grab a plate and eat!

One night in Barnes & Noble I was researching Santa Rosa and thought the "old railroad district" sounded fun, so I walked over there and found entire blocks of antique shops and *no trains!* I sat in the "Railroad Coffeehouse," or "Trainyard Coffeehouse," or whatever, and boldly asserted my right as a non-paying loiterer to sit and stare out the window as long as I pleased. I sat, looking for signs of authentic railroad culture—pinstriped overalls, a distant choo-choo, or something . . . I pressed my face against the glass, watching pedestrians, a soft wall of noise behind me— gossip, chess, role-playing games, etc. And through it all I heard . . . was it, yes it was—the bass line to my favorite old, *old* school rap song floating through the streets. I traced it to an old brick hotel across the road. The doors were locked, but I peered through a small space between the curtains and saw what was clearly a *hip hop wedding reception*, with tag-team breakdancing session in full effect! I was captivated, and for a few minutes I took a ride in the disco dream machine—Sugarhill Gang, a disco ball, breakin' . . .

At some point I felt that, for the sake of maintaining my middle-class cover deep in suburbia, I should clean myself and my clothing. Looking for a pool and laundromat, I drifted blindly through Santa Rosa and became so caught up in my music and the pleasant stroll through enchanting residential neighborhoods, that I walked several miles before coming to. But finally I did find a nice pool, a natural foods store, and a laundromat on one block. That morning I had stopped in Kinko's and cut out eight cardboard quarters, used for *free laundry*. Many old-fashioned coin-operated machines—like the superball machines at Safeway, washing machines, and the U.S. Postal Service stamp machine in the Portland Greyhound station lobby—use a primitive technology which measures only the diameter of a coin to determine its value. Sturdy non-corrugated cardboard—approximating the *thickness* of a quarter, and cut precisely in the *shape* of a quarter—can be used to fool machines into dispensing free product. This is very hit-or-miss, though oddly success is nearly 100% with the new fancy computerized washing machines replacing the rusty old ones everywhere I go. And the collected soap traces from fifteen detergent bottles scavenged from the trash cans inside rounded out a successful "free trip to the laundromat."

During the day I took long leisurely walks to explore Santa Rosa's back streets and supermarkets, and each night ate obscene amounts of salad and soup at Fresh Choice—on the table under the speaker. Each morning I awoke very excited, crawled off my roof, and ran to the alley behind the library where each morning they put out boxes and boxes of books! It was all very convenient, and very confusing. Like, were the books *free*, or . . . ? I couldn't be certain, but they put out great books anyway.

I found one day's amusement in very visibly digging through public trash cans, because . . . because *I love trash!* And for the same reason that wherever I live, whether I'm paying rent or living nowhere at all, I always tell strangers "I'm homeless." You know, to mainstream such things. I wanted to make trash-picking cool again! Santa Rosa had good trash. I found a Sonoma County Bus System map, which I spread out, examined, and pondered. Then I laid out my own maps and began plotting a zig-zag tour across the Bay Area on public transportation. Northern California drivers were sketching me out—those nice, polite, and sophisticated middle-aged people living out a youthful thirst for adventure through me. How depressing.

The Sonoma County buses were different than those where I come from—you had to pay. Standing in the Walgreens parking lot, wondering how I would pay for all these bus rides, a $40 receipt for a stop-smoking kit floated across the lot to my feet like a fateful tumbleweed. The subsequent "return" of that stop-smoking kit yielded money for bus rides from now until forever . . .

Sonoma . . . Lots and lots of antique shops. I slept on the roof of an antique shop; caught glares from elderly, antiquated shoppers; and dumpstered a loaf of very old, very antique bread.

Petaluma . . . I am almost running out of ways to say "homogenized suburb." Despite the chain stores and parking lots, there was the impression of Petaluma being on *my side*. Like Petaluma was stolen from the Man and was now the "*people's suburb*." Maybe it was the skate session at the Petaluma skate park: all female! Or then, prowling on the roof of the health food store, trying and failing to be surreptitious, I locked into a very cold eye contact with a man in his yard across the street. I was certain he would call the police—and in any other suburb he would have—but instead he just smiled and raised his hand in a friendly wave!

Thank you for understanding sir, goodnight! And earlier, in a failed attempt to crawl onto the roof of the library, I jumped onto the hood of an empty car to pull myself up, but, wait a minute . . . The car *wasn't* empty! I looked down through the windshield into the eyes of a *man!* He seemed more curious than angry, but I jumped off and ran like crazy anyway, and wondered: what does it take to get shot in Petaluma anyway?

Every visit to Safeway, in every town, before stealing juice, I go straight to the books and read a few pages of *Dr. Weil's 8 Weeks to Optimum Health!* It's an important piece of work. Only the suburbs inspire such amusements. Like that, all-night dumpster diving, going back in the cooler—like, *behind* the orange juice—just to see what it's like, etc. etc. With the suburban conveniences like food just lying around unmonitored, and people in line at the supermarket dropping money, all mental effort could be focused in a contemplative direction. So I pondered not survival, but the surrendering-of-autonomous-decision-making implications of the traffic signal. I crossed a lot of streets. And I ate so often, I almost finished that book.

San Francisco . . . After six hours in the Epicenter zine library, I had read every zine in the "Travel" section cover-to-cover—noticing an unjust "anti-suburb" sentiment. Philadelphia, Chicago, San Francisco . . . It all seemed very trendy. Campbell, Sunnyvale . . . Those towns got no respect. A tragic void in punk travel. Suburbs can be fun too, if you live *dangerously*.

I had completely lost track of time, and it was night-time before I finished all the zines I wanted to read. San Francisco was big and scary, and I thought maybe I would crawl on a roof somewhere. I was a good wall climber, but in S.F. I would need, like, *suction cups*. Let's see . . .

Palo Alto . . . It was all very scary and funny, sleeping on the roof of a big restaurant in Palo Alto, surrounded by rats. If they ate me, it would be a betrayal—I smashed every rat trap I found in alleys and behind stores. I had an admirable record of rodent-rights activism. Yes, eaten by rats, that would be funny . . .

University Way is where everyone is beautiful and poses on coffee shop patios. One sees lots of well-dressed highbrow posturing, seeing and being seen . . . and where, eating leftover bread outside the bakery, I learned it's not *hip* or *cool* to finish a meal! Hair seemed an important part of the Palo Alto hipster role—the "wet look." Walking down University Way was dangerous—the private-university elite haughtily strutted down the street in a fixed line, not diverting their path one degree for lesser creatures. College *library dwellers* are people too! I dodged, weaved, and suffered tense moments when nothing could save me from getting hit. So in the interest of self-preservation, I had to abandon the sidewalk altogether and walk in the alleys. Of course, alleys . . . I wasn't sure why I hadn't thought of it sooner. Being in foreign towns had disrupted all my habitual tendencies. Walking along the street was a silly idea. Shopping from the *street*, bagels cost 60¢; and in the alley—free! An often overlooked point of fact . . . But if you walk among society, beware the well-groomed and fragrant steamrollers of University Way—they yield to no one!

It was in Palo Alto that Whole Foods Market established itself as the new leader in free food—they've cornered the market! Whole Foods is a large chain of health food supermarkets cashing in on the growing interest in organic, surgar-free, vegan, etc. foods. *Evasion* stands in full support of economic development and expansion of this blossoming corner of the retail sector. Yes, it was during my stay in Palo Alto that I discovered Whole Foods, and the new shape of vagabond convenience. Limitless refills of (organic) coffee, countless bulk (free) food bins, and all the food I could fit in my (left) hand and walk out with. From then on, in each town, the first question was, "Where's the Whole Foods?" In the spirit of the health food craze, I used "recycled" theft techniques (not tested on animals), and believed strongly in shoplifting as a "natural alternative" to paying.

Somehow I started drinking coffee, like, every day. Coffee was trendy, I didn't like coffee. But I enjoyed the ritual. I enjoyed staring out the window at the crazy, happy, chirping birds. I enjoyed people's habit of leaving empty cups just lying around. I enjoyed complete disregard for the limited refill policy. And, I enjoyed having no place to be at any particular time, but having the option of going any place at any time. And with so many alleyways, bookstores, and big office buildings to run around in, drinking coffee was the only thing that kept me still.

A group of us met each morning at Noah's Bagels. We never actually met, but I think if one of us were to be absent, the others would be concerned. There was a suited man, who posed as a nervous and busy Palo Alto yuppie, but all he ever did was drink coffee. He was more hardcore than me—always there each morning when I arrived, and often drinking coffee and shuffling papers when I left hours later. There was a quiet, older Asian woman who *always* took the best seat by the window. We didn't like her. And the homeless man who mumbled and grumbled. I would watch his melancholy countenance and catch bitter scowls. Let's see . . . unemployed, drinking coffee all day . . . if he was unhappy, I just didn't get it.

He sat next to me one morning and asked if I was finished with the entertainment section. In a lifetime of reading the paper each morning, I swear no one has ever asked me for anything but the *"Sports"* section. He sat across the table, shaking the paper and sighing in exaggerated grumpiness. "You don't have to pay for that," I said, pointing to his cup. Criminal advice, I thought, was always a good conversation starter. "Usually I'll just pull a cup from the trash outside." Friendly advice, on the down-low, bum-to-bum. He was clearly poor, and it was sad to watch him count out a dollar and ten cents in panhandled change for coffee each morning. I had been responsible for life-changing homeless advice before. Once, at home, I met a sad and struggling panhandler while exploring downtown. It was nightfall, and his cup was nearly empty, so I gave him advice from the marketing perspective—"You need a gimmick, a funny line." I borrowed his cup and began asking passersby for "spare change to support my crack habit." A man gave me five dollars and said "Hey—good line!" It wasn't a good line, it wasn't even funny, but my new friend was dazzled and promised to use the crack line from now on. A month later I met him on the same corner, and he thanked me excessively—he had made more money with that dumb crack line than ever before in his sad and long panhandling career. I don't know, when I was really broke I used that line on my mom and it got me nowhere . . .

"Free coffee, it's guaranteed every time!" I told the man at Noah's. He growled and waved me off. "Bah . . . to each his own." A staunch *paying* customer. Well he was no friend of mine!

Organic coffee in the Whole Foods café was equally, or more, free than at Noah's, and the reading material on the magazine rack was better, but something about stealing food and then just waiting around in the café and eating in front of the employees seemed too brazen. I preferred the "four strangers from different worlds" plot each morning at Noah's. With the drama, the brief but meaningful moments of eye contact . . . We bonded, and if they didn't feel it, I no doubt did. The "one refill only" sign above the coffee dispenser was sort of a little joke between us. One daily mob-action assault on the Noah's coffee machine. The loiterers owned that bagel shop—four wired and dedicated coffee drinkers against two suspicious Noah's employees. And if the employees ever dared question us, well, the elderly Asian woman by the window packed heat. How could we lose? One refill . . . Ha ha ha ha ha ha ha . . .

A sleeping man jerking violently, a barefoot elderly woman with a distant and fixed gaze, a disfigured man with facial burns spilling a bag of jalepeños . . . Highly symbolic as scenes in a black and white German art film, but this was the #22 bus to San Jose . . . What did it all mean?!?!

The #22 runs through many of the finest suburbs in the Bay Area—Palo Alto, Santa Clara, Mountain View . . . With such a high-class route, I boarded with faith it would take me further into Silicon Valley suburban paradise. Which it did . . . *and kept going!* Stranded in East San Jose—gulp! I swear I had read an article on crime-ridden and lawless East San Jose, or heard rumors, or a gangsta rap song, or *something.* I was in "tha hood!" It was dark, and I sat listless on a bench, indifferent to my fate. A middle-aged man rolled by on a skateboard. We talked. His name was Bert. Bert was homeless, and just riding around the ghetto on his skateboard! Yeah—what the heck! Skate around, loiter on bus stop benches, snarl at drivers, live on mini-mart popcorn . . . awesome! Bert was a radiant model of reckless indifference and carefree troublemaking. And, although *drunk*, Bert displayed flawless form on his skateboard. "I don't know of a bigger drunk than me!" he boasted. Bert gave me good advice on getting *out* of the hood, and I gave him a banana. On the bus to Los Gatos, Bert playfully pulled the "stop" wire repeatedly—giggling and stomping his feet when the bus pulled over—and in a dramatic flashback to my hometown bus rides, the bus driver shouted, "Do that again and you'll be *skating* home!" Haha. If I had a dime . . .

Los Gatos . . . You have to be beautiful to live in Los Gatos. Santa Cruz Ave. was another suburban pedestrian strip of shops, cafés, trendy kids . . . like a big fashion show! But I felt my deep-cover disguise was undetectable—my backpack wasn't noticeably large, and my hair was very, um, *inoffensive.* Then "freak!" was shouted from a passing car! Moments later, a nice girl said "Hiiiiii!" So clearly I had friends *and* enemies in Los Gatos. More fun to think of them as *all* enemies.

It was a long way from East San Jose. I sat down to take in the crazy Saturday night scene. Someone stepped on my toes. Then I had a dramatic fall climbing on the roof of Walgreens. I was a bloody mess, but I wouldn't trade the rooftop views and occasional injuries for all the Holiday Inn rooms in the world! Certainly someone would notice me limping around, pity me as an injured stranger in a strange world, take me home and feed me a toasted bagel. But my limp only meant I was moving slow enough to be hit with requests for cigarettes and phone money. And I swear I will never give a quarter to anyone with a valley girl accent.

The Los Gatos Coffee Company was a good place to sit and bleed. I paid for coffee and listened to jazz.

Behind the coffee place and the little mall were lots of fun diversions. It really cheered me up. The shoe store left out piles of old shoes. The bagel place left me bagels, and the mysterious dumpster next to it brimmed with personal items, expired credit cards, and scandalous letters! So I just tried on shoes, ate bagels, and read strangers' mail for hours! Instead of following the voice of experience, I had thrown money at my problems—$1.35 on coffee. But it was street therapy that cheered me up. Dumpster diving—never fails!

I crawled onto the roof of a random building to sleep, and awoke to the sound of barking dogs coming from *inside* the building! This sort of freaked me out, and I was sure I was sleeping on the roof of a top-secret animal research laboratory. What would Earth Crisis do?!?!

Another suburb, another Whole Foods and Noah's Bagels—side by side! Big vegan cookies and lots of coffee over the morning paper. It was a life of leisure, but not without drama. One morning I sat at a table outside Noah's, enjoying the sun, when two cops—guns drawn and looking tough—ran towards me waving their pistols! This is it, I thought. They've been following me for 4 years, documenting over 12,000 counts of shoplifting, trespassing, forgery, and fraud. They know about the midnight raids on the thrift store donation bin, using the skate park after hours, the knife I took to the school administration building lock at 2 a.m., and the popcorn I cooked once inside. Born in suburbia, and now, here, with a gun in my face, I would die. They could never say that I sold out, that I betrayed my roots . . .

And the gun was within inches of my face, but they continued past. It was the man hiding under the truck they wanted. I had been sort of wondering what he was doing there. He was ordered out at gunpoint and taken away "without incident." Another fallen soldier, I lamented. "Part of the criminal underworld died today . . ."

I was nearest to the action, and all the pedestrians gathered around to ask what had happened. I didn't know, but I liked the attention. I had never been popular before. A styled-out young woman pointed an accusatory finger at me and said—"Did you know that man? Are you with him?!" *What?!?!* The suburban polarized world of good: white, well-dressed, and bad: minorities, kids with backpacks, *criminals . . . Hold me back!* I no longer wanted to educate these elitists, pleading to their inner-core of humanity, explaining that we're all just humans who deserve respect and dignity, no . . . I wanted to *scare* them! I swore to be more threatening—to spit on people, or get a mohawk, or something . . .

After a lifetime of rap music, I had always wondered where the action and danger was, you know, "on da streets." Finally—cops and guns and a brother in lockdown! I'm going to write a rap!

The entire Los Gatos police department diverted, I detected what is known as a "window of opportunity." So I walked across the street to the Long's Drugs grand opening celebration and left-handed a portable CD player! Possibly a detestable act of consumerism in defiance of ethical shoplifting standards. But, you see, music is very important to me, and in two weeks I had spent more money on music than food. Well, I hadn't spent *anything* on food, but by that point I did have twenty CDs. I lay in the park reading and listening to Wide Awake all day, daydreams taking me away to small towns in rusty boxcars . . .

Campbell . . . the recreational opportunities in Campbell —it was all too good to be true. Whole Foods, Fresh Choice, Noah's Bagels, Tower Records, UA Cinemas, Barnes and Noble, Trader Joe's . . . American retail, I don't know . . . it's all just so much fun! And all very post-apocalyptic—they had taken our communities, paved them over, put up nicely trimmed hedges, threw up huge stores, played nice soothing jazz music in the background . . . Clearly the only option was to laugh at the absurdity of such a mess—capitalist monuments to slavery and unregu-lated homogenization—view it as an amusement park, and play! So when I drank coffee and wrote for hours in the Whole Foods café, it was an act of defiance. Each bagel a pastry for the revolution. You know, subversive leisure. An unconfined outlaw eating mangos all day and never paying for them! Ever!

The best two blocks in suburbia—no doubt! Here, I could make my rounds in a convenient half-mile loop what would be an epic bus journey at home. Campbell, where everything was very, um, *accommodating*. Like how each morning one can scavenge a cup at Noah's Bagels, drink coffee, and read, for one hour or eight hours. And I never forgot to read my free copy of the *Noah News*. All timely and relevant issues concerning rounded baked goods are discussed—and don't miss the updated "Noah Celebrity Sightings," an often impressive compilation of hot stars, where they were seen, and what they ordered! Let's see, it says here that since Rage Against The Machine broke up, Zack de la Rocha visits the Noah's in San Diego and waits out back for the throwaways! Afterwards one can walk out of Whole Foods with very large amounts of free food and eat in the sun on the tables outside. Recommended: vegan cinnamon rolls, carob coconut haystacks, and big straw-berry bagels. In this setting, I understand it can be easy to forget all the suffering and moral depravity in the world. For a swift balancing of perspective, it's perhaps important to climb the ladder to the roof in back, and take a small pocketknife to the lock of the door *behind* the "Whole Foods" sign—exposing one to the shocking and unnatural *big secret room of porno!* Yuck! Climb down, dig for receipts, get money at Long's, and go half a block south to the huge record store with the huge $2 CD bins. One block south of that is Tower Records—often hissed at and ignored, but I know of no more generous chain store—where prices run on a sliding scale based on "ability and willingness to pay." Tower just might have that new punk CD you want, so be careful, and go well-dressed! Across the street, in the uniquely Californian "outdoor mall" is, among other fun places, the United Artists Cinemas. I put high-school lessons on this subject to use at that theater one night, and once inside realized that there was nothing I wanted to see. And, wait a minute . . . *I rarely even enjoyed movies!* OK, so I "got away with it," I can leave now! Barnes & Noble is around the corner and stands as an illustrious example of free-market success. Beyond CDs and spending money, *free knowledge* seems the most worthy of all criminal pursuits— and at Barnes & Noble, the books are *all* free. Sometimes in Barnes & Noble, like if you stand on a bench over by the magazines, and look over the entire store at all the books, one feels for a moment that maybe, in this one small way, we *have* progressed. Like we're paving over the planet, watering down the culture, killing billions of animals, and dehumanizing the populace with dull jobs; but we make lots and lots of books. Good, accessible, and effectively distributed books. Next to Barnes & Noble is Trader Joe's friendly grocery, the most abundant and consistent chain of dumpsters in the *world*. Coming full circle, Fresh Choice is across the street, next to Whole Foods. The all-you-can-eat free meal can seem too easy, and be cautious—Fresh Choice has been the site of occasional episodes of defeat, like the time of a round-table punk meal where we all looked up from our minestrone to see the manager standing over us demanding receipts! Then, at the end of the day, walk to the ladder behind Whole Foods and sleep on the roof! In Campbell I had possibly discovered a future retirement situation. If I didn't know better, I just might think this suburban chain store sprawl was created with my convenience in mind, that the obvious loopholes existed by design for the often overlooked 18-35 transient punk demographic. That would explain *everything* . . .

Everything except Barnes & Noble's new refund policy—photo ID? Wait a minute . . . ! It was a breach of what, over the years, I had come to believe was sort of an unspoken agreement between us. I of course promptly filled out a "customer grievance" card, and wondered—"What's next?" These unfair restrictions on free money return scams could only be viewed as a disturbing trend. Taken further, soon the stealing of books will be disallowed altogether! I just might revolt!

One night in Barnes & Noble I had lost track of time altogether reading a good book, and only when they announced the store was closing did I realize it was late. I needed to eat, *everything* had closed, and I walked over to the bagel dumpster . . . After twenty minutes I had found no bagels, and began grumbling to myself, yelling at the dumpster, and throwing trash everywhere. I find these brief moments of desperate hunger to be very charming. At the Whole Foods dumpster I found bags of bread and baked goods, and I wondered why people paid for food at all. I grabbed a small bag, crawled on the roof, sorted through everything, and found vegan cookies! But it was dark, and when I took a bite, the cookie was more mold than flour! This sparked a flashback to my *last* mouthful of mold . . .

It was in a book that I had read the theory of mold as a healthy nutrient, not to be avoided. That the American diet of washed, cooked, and completely sterile foods created weak immune systems where illness set in at the exposure to bacteria in small levels. Levels which would not affect, say, a dumpster diver—whose immune system had been strengthened by consistent exposure to small amounts of mold. One morning, many years ago—with this in mind—I thought it would be cool to *eat* mold! Maybe it was a cry for help, maybe I was *very* hungry . . . One morning I salvaged a bag of moldy pita bread. Surely, I thought, it would be an honorable thing to make a statement of defiance to a society obsessed with sterility—to prove all nonbelievers to be unhealthy snobs depriving their bodies of mold, which had been eaten since the origin of our species. I stole hummus, sat in the cafe of my favorite supermarket, laid out my plastic utensils, and made four hummus and pita bread sandwiches. They were tasty, and I felt tough, like I was challenging a deeply held "mold superstition." Then I spent the next three days rolling around on the floor of my friend's basement, the only time I had really been sick in four years. But that was a long time ago . . .

This time I lay on my back, high above the dumpsters on the roof of Whole Foods, just looking at the stars and waiting to get sick. It had been a large mouthful of mold, but somehow I never did become ill. I cursed that dumpster and the moldy food in its rusty belly. The next night I returned with a flashlight, feeling tricked, tougher but more bitter than before. The dumpster was *gone!* Certainly the dumpster was hiding somewhere, laughing at me. Well, after moldy cookies, I was more aware of my relationship with the dumpster than ever. It was all so clear now . . . Bloody heads from falling dumpster lids, near death dumpster experiences scrambling to climb out while the garbage truck approached, a poisoned cookie . . . On the path to dumpster knighthood one treads a trail of blood, tears, and coffee grounds. And the dumpster, I learned, has a vengeful side. . .

Gilroy . . . The last bus ride. 120 miles on public transportation. The road to Gilroy is bracketed with chicken farms. Not many people realize that in America, chickens outnumber people. No buses ran south of Gilroy. I was curious to see my next move—hitchhike? Hop a train? Sell-out and buy a plane ticket to L.A.?

Gilroy—"Garlic capital of the world." When you visit a thousand small towns, you begin to notice that each town has a gimmick—"Home of __," "World's Largest __," etc. Gilroy's claim to fame was the coolest ever! I once read an old hobo book where a tramp awakens in a boxcar, and determines through scent alone that he is rolling through Gilroy. But did he *get off* there? Should I? I hope the museum gives samples . . .

It was late. I roamed the streets looking for inspiration in sidewalk graffiti, tombstone epitaphs in the huge graveyard, or maybe just in reflecting on my situation: hundreds of miles from home, in a crazy ghetto garlic town, alone. I found inspiration, or something, in the alley behind the meat market. I was prowling in the shadows when I looked into the window of a ground floor apartment. On the walls, the ceiling, everything—*Madonna!* A Madonna *shrine!* Posters, records, *Teen Beat* pin-ups . . . It told the story of a lonely girl trapped in a small town, practicing her moves after school, crying herself to sleep at night, waiting for her big break. Worshipping Madonna, eating garlic . . .

All I wanted before sleeping in the graveyard was *one bagel*. Slumped on a bench outside Safeway, I wondered if shoplifting at 2 a.m. was funny-and-respectably-bold-stupid, or just stupid. Hungry and alone, but life was exciting and full of possibility—Gardena, Chula Vista, San Dimas . . . So maybe I was a little homesick. Like being hungry at 2 a.m., and how at home the overnight cashiers are too old and indifferent to chase a kid over a bag of bagels, and how the cashier at that Safeway looked like a track star. Then I was shooed away by the Posh Bagel dumpster gatekeeper who took up residence *behind* the dumpster—"No bagels here!"

The next morning I went over my options at Greyhound: $46 to L.A., $36 to Santa Barbara, $26 to San Louis

Obispo. I bought a $7 ticket to Salinas. Sneaky me, my scam was to sleep through my stop in Salinas, and well, to *sleep* all the way to Santa Barbara!

Fifty miles past Salinas I was still, uh, *sleeping*. In King City the mean bus driver did a head count.

"We have one too many."

Heh.

"I need to see everyone's ticket."

Moments later he tapped me on the shoulder.

"Ticket."

I feigned grogginess—

"Wha . . . oh."

Rubbing my eyes and stretching, I handed the driver my ticket.

"You're well past Salinas my friend . . ."

It all seemed very poetic, or romantic, or cinematic, or something, standing in a cloud of dust as the bus pulled away, holding my bag. And when I set my bag down and sat on it—that seemed like an album cover.

King City graffiti artists had written—"If art is a crime, we are guilty" under a bridge—the struggling underground artist's poetic declaration of rebellion in defense of an illegal culture. I too was fighting to keep alive the fringe tramp culture, and defending the often illegal "free travel" pastime. "If sneaking a free ride from Greyhound is wrong, I don't want to be right." I wished I had a can of spraypaint.

"King City—salad bowl of the world!" I was told. "We grow celery and we grow spinach. We grow tomatoes and we grow turnips. We grow . . ." Right. Okay. So where is the Safeway? Oh, right up the street . . . I stole a bag of bagels and found a laundromat with Ms. Pac Man. So I just ate bagels and played Ms. Pac Man for three hours!

At dawn I was on the 101 on-ramp, utilizing every hitchhiker bait tactic to increase my odds—smiling, making eye contact, wearing my best button-up shirt . . . And after an hour, playing my favorite hitchhiking game—insulting passing drivers with lines from Hardcore songs! "This time I'm not going to let you slide!" "It won't happen again—you drew the *last straw*!" etc. etc. Finally, after mumbling at a passing driver to "reject the anthropocentric falsehood," he pulled over. It was one long ride, with a man, conservatively dressed, in a mini-van. He spoke of the "right wing freight train" destroying America and the "strip mall onslaught" destroying L.A. The radical rightwing movement, I told him, needed to be challenged. Definitely. But I had spent one of the best nights of my life in a strip mall the night before, and, well . . .

When I stepped out of the car onto Santa Barbara's State Street, I was—well, shucks—I was a little jealous. It all appeared as an image of paradise. Everywhere people were sipping drinks in the sun, chatting in the street barefoot, and smiling at the sky. Palm trees lined each sunny street, and everything seemed to exist for pleasure of the senses and maximum leisure.

Everything in California is beautiful. A strip mall, say, anywhere else, is a strip mall. An ugly thing, exploiting the workers and polluting the scenery. A strip mall in California will be a building with the same chain stores. And vines growing up the walls. And well-groomed shrubbery. Maybe a big beautiful fountain in front. Probably a little courtyard with benches. And classical music playing softly in the background. And the building across the parking lot is still McDonald's, but it looks less like a murderer of billions of animals when ornamented with earthy tones and a cascading waterfall. Maybe it was the newness of the West Coast, not having had time for decay. Maybe every town earlier in its history was as shiny and aesthetically pleasing as Santa Barbara . . . Not Rapid City. Rapid City was never beautiful.

Everything fell into place—a new town, a new routine, and *two* new laundromats with Ms. Pac Man! I was definitely on to something . . . I immediately settled into a new leisure pattern in which I enjoyed long sessions of contemplation, and contributed *nothing* to the economy! Each morning I crawled off the roof of Winchell's Donuts—definitely underappreciated vacation lodging. Up the street was Wild Oats, the *other* mega-natural-foods chain, after Whole Foods. Not a business, a *service*! Across the parking lot, the Carl's Jr. patio was the center of social activity for Santa Barbara's vagrants and tramps. So I would lay out my food on a table and eat while pretending to read the newspaper, but mostly getting the down-low on Santa Barbara from a homeless perspective. The group of rough-n-tough middle-aged men would drink coffee and grumble about this and that. One morning they spoke to me—

"Hey kid, you passing through?"

I, uh . . .

"You lookin' for work?"

Well, n . . .

"You been down to the *wall* yet?"

The wall?

"You been here three days and you don't know the *wall?!*"

Let's see, I know the "return-Tylenol-at-Rite-Aid," the "demand-refund-at-movie-theater-for-stub-picked-up-from-ground," um . . . The wall, it was explained, was the slave-labor spot to be picked up for yardwork jobs. Each morning the men would grumble about their hard day's work, their hard life, and that pretty housewife over there on Palm Street . . . Mowing lawns all day, then wasting their earnings on fast food before 8 a.m. *Paying* for food . . . groan. Amateurs . . .

Santa Barbara's best pool was at the Radisson Hotel, right on the waterfront, and after breakfast I would spend hours lounging poolside in true Santa Barbara fashion. While I swam, I would wonder what exactly I was doing *right* here. Like how each morning I would march in through the huge wooden doors, through the posh lobby—hair in all directions—and past the counterperson with my bag. Then walk to the pool and shamelessly lay out my CD player and books alongside my lawn chair, catching suspicious glares from *paying* guests, and thinking—"What does it take to get kicked out of a place? Do I have to *insult people?!*"

I had sort of a little war going with a group of jovial Latino men at Winchell's Donuts. At night, after dinner, all I wanted to do was crawl on the roof and sleep. But each night it was a standoff with a group of crazy happy men who blocked my path to the ladder. They would sit in the bed of their truck, eating donuts, playing a little banjo, singing and laughing for *hours*. Santa Barbara seemed to be that kind of place, where friends would play music together and smile. My home was on the roof of Winchell's, and each night I would end up across the street on the sidewalk—for an hour or more—waiting for them to go home. I couldn't be upset with people playing music and drinking coffee while the rest of the world was playing Nintendo and drinking beer. But, I had gotten to know their songs—and one night waiting across the street, I fell asleep in an empty storefront! Certainly this was the first step down the path to a bright and liberated future of irreversible homelessness. Storefronts, then benches, the gutter . . . I was becoming a pro! Awakening in that storefront, dazed, I wondered who I was and how I had gotten there. Like, had I been *drinking* from those beer bottles? Were those men across the street singing about *me?!* It was all very confusing. I kicked a beer bottle, and went to find a spot on the beach somewhere . . . On the way, I found a ladder to the roof of a restaurant—right on the water!

Along the beach I would take my time passing through the waterfront park, sometimes stopping at the swing sets or watching the merry-go-round. A coffee place on State St. was the best place to sit and drink coffee. Or pretend to drink coffee, and read, or stare, or strategize my next Ms. Pac Man game. Then, when the counterperson wasn't looking, sneak one last refill and run across the street to *play* Ms. Pac Man.

On Saturday I went to the great haven for criminals—
the swap meet! But the Santa Barbara swap meet was an
amateurish display of business on the "up-and-up." Sort of
a let-down. There was none of the roguish dedication of
my hometown swap meet vendors, who would spare no
risk to their freedom or health to bring the public inex-
pensive stolen goods. At home, I would take the bus down
to the swap meet on Sundays and buy a big box of Frosted
Flakes for, like, one dollar, ride home, and eat Frosted Flakes
all day! One poor old woman at the Santa Barbara swap
meet sat on a tattered blanket in a lonely corner of the
lot—eyes lowered, looking sad and desperate—surrounded
by a cluttered mass of dusty old cassettes. I bought "Rock
of the 80's" and a blank tape labeled "Phat Homemade
Shit" for 20¢. The latter of which I hoped was, like, d.i.y.
rap, and I listened to right away. But it was d.i.y. *techno*, and
not even phat. After paying for the tapes, she offered me
the entire lot—like, 50 tapes—for 50¢! It was tearful, the
poor, humble woman spending her Saturday for what
could yield no more than a handful of change. You can
rise above poverty, sister! No one need go without, or
suffer, or work. You can reclaim what's yours. Shoplifting, sister, *shoplifting* . . .

I laughed out loud at the table I found across the lot:
a vendor selling what was plainly *all dumpstered merchandise!*
Dozens of videos, without covers, all treated to a crude
attempt at scratching off the "property of Blockbuster
Video" sticker. Looking at that table of tapes took me back
to a simpler time. . . Back in the day, *my* hometown
Blockbuster's dumpster brimmed with slightly damaged
and easily repaired videos. Expanding on this, I began plotting an all barter *dumpster swap meet*, where the divers of
each neighborhood meet to exchange dumpstered treasures. Coverless books swapped for bagels, bike parts
traded for discarded microwaves . . . My head swirled with
the potential for this new entrepreneurial approach . . .
Militant dumpster divers, under the cloak of darkness,

rounding up the richest dumpsters and *rolling* them to the swap meet! Awesome!

Wherever I went, I was always finding these great stickers in the Trader Joe's dumpster reading "I'm a Trader Joe's kid!" I would stick them up everywhere, my own "tag" of sorts. One morning I had run out and went inside Trader Joe's to ask for more. Going around, like, through the front, and visiting the *inside* of Trader Joe's was an entirely new approach. Let's see, a lot like their dumpster, a bit more organized, and, wait a minute . . . *everything costs money!* I stepped outside to catch my breath . . .

Things become blurry. My journal at this point becomes an indecipherable mess of overheard conversations and Ms. Pac Man scores. I remember trying to make a simple request of the Hot Spots Coffee cashier for a refill of coffee, but he didn't understand. He understood English, but I wasn't *speaking* English; only a nonsensical stream of nothing. The sun had melted my brain. If I couldn't solicit coffee, I probably couldn't solicit a ride. Then I'd just have to move in with the guys in the park on Cabrillo. But thirty feet from the beach sure was a smart place to go stupid . . .

It was a healthy lifestyle—the sun, the beach, Ms. Pac Man, swimming. Like one of those new-age health regimens. *Jail*, I decided, wouldn't mesh with my new naturopathic healing ritual. A week of twice-daily visits to the Wild Oats supermarket was a little reckless, and in fact beyond unsafe. Stealing too often from one store: a transgression of the laws of theft. Employees began eyeing me suspiciously. I wasn't pacing myself. It was a practice in direct conflict with what is known as "sustainable shoplifting."

It was time to leave Santa Barbara. On my last night, I spent several hours in Borders Books reading up on L.A., the new Abbie Hoffman biography, and of course Thrasher Magazine. The glossy pictures of sunny Southern California skate action had for years inspired dreams of living in an Orange County suburb—like maybe behind Safeway in a milk crate house, or in the dumpster—and just skating the parking lot all day for years and years. It would be the perfect life. . . . I finished reading, walked outside to the patio and found—a skateboard! In the interest of fairness, I waited for the return of its forgetful owner. But no one came. So that's it, I thought; I'm skating So-Cal forever . . .

I made L.A. in record time—one ride straight to Hollywood. The setting sun, huge cracks in the sidewalk, stray cats . . . I don't know what happened, I was *scared*. I bought a bus ticket to San Diego.

Downtown San Diego—it was like stepping off the bus into a big party! Laughter, patio dining, hi-fives, a couple slow dancing in the street . . . A festive scene. In my town it would be called a riot. But it was San Diego, on a Thursday night . . .

I walked three miles past a hundred palm trees . . . it was all very beautiful, and in this highly mobile society, I wondered why anyone lived anywhere except San Diego. Certainly if there were any flaws to San Diego, if anyone there *suffered*, it was far away from that place, from that moment . . .

I had been neglecting my finances. I was down to, like, 12¢! Which was OK, because my job is pretty fun. Back to the Rite-Aid trash cans . . . My job isn't what is typically thought of as "backbreaking labor," though after hunching over trash cans digging for receipts for an afternoon, my back did hurt. Sifting through the trash, peeling away coffee cups and plastic bags, flattening out a hundred crumpled receipts for that one gem—the $28 jumbo bottle of ginseng extract, or film, or *something* . . . Only lots and lots of cigarette and candy receipts. Very frustrating. A lot of people smoke, and a lot of people eat candy, and I've learned to *hate* those people. The best receipt I found—and it wasn't great—was for a $12 bottle of hair dye. I grabbed it off the shelf in Rite-Aid and went up to the return counter. Both managers seemed a little sketchy about the refund. Maybe it was my poor acting, maybe it was the tire-track on the receipt . . . They were uncooperative, rude, and asked too many questions. If they weren't giving me free money—I might be insulted!

Golly, twelve dollars . . . twelve dollars would buy me eight vegan cinnamon rolls, but I wouldn't ever actually pay. Twelve dollars would buy me 24 left-handed meals, a bus ticket to Tijuana, a shiny new paperback, twelve loads of laundry, 35 stamps, or 120 cassettes at my favorite record store back home.

Later, at the library, I examined my maps from all angles, studied *San Diego* magazine, the Frommer's Guide to San Diego, looked out the window, rubbed my eyes, and began formulating a plot unparalleled in hedonistic civil irresponsibility—I'll just skate around and listen to my walkman all day!

A skateboard tour through San Diego . . . My explorations, which at times felt like a series of destinations, had become, with my new skateboard, bummin' the hood for the sheer pleasure of the trip. Rolling through alleyways, parking garages, down hills, listening to music and gliding . . . I covered twice as much ground, and got twice as much done. The combined pleasure of sun, skateboarding, music, and beaches was bringing me closer to what Buddhists call "Enlightenment."

I skated to Old Town San Diego—a cartoonish monument to the Old West. A Mexican band played on the patio of a restaurant. I sat on my board against a lamppost outside and rocked out to Mexican music for hours! It may sound dull, uninspired, *pathetic* even. But you see, I am easily entertained, and it was a first-class performance.

Saturday night on Pacific Beach—alcohol flowing, men whistling, inebriated hollering, obnoxious chest-beating, cars screeching, people rolling on the sidewalk . . . I stole dinner and went to observe the madness. I took my frozen burrito into 7-11. Everything tastes better warmed up in a mini-mart microwave. Though, really, nearly every warm meal I'd had in the past four years had been heated in a mini-mart microwave, so there wasn't much to compare it to. On my way in, Mr. Growly Face threw himself between me and the microwave.

"No outside food!" he said.

"What?! Who am I hurting?!" I said.

"You're hurting our business, we could lose our insurance," he said.

He was a damned liar, and I told him so on the way out. Insurance, ugh . . . I swear they all read from the same script. The insurance line is universally given to justify the disallowing of anything fun—from skateboarding to dumpster diving. *Especially* dumpster diving. After digging through trash long enough and being thrown out of dumpsters countless times, it becomes easy to finish the sentences of the bad guys. A manager will bust out the back door, bright red, flailing his arms—

"Get *out* of the dumpster! If you eat that food, you will get sick, and you will die. Why, it's . . ."

"An insurance risk?"

There is really only one solution in that situation. I play nice, chat a little, and pretend to understand their position. Then I motion them a little closer as though I have something confidential to impart, and when they get real close, *I bash their head into the dumpster and eat their brains!* Yeah!

Outside 7-11 I sat on my board and cradled my burrito. The bustling Saturday night 7-11 parking lot scene had me feeling a little nostalgic and misty-eyed. Many of *my* Saturday nights in high school were spent in a 7-11 parking lot. Our suburban 7-11 dazzled and amazed us by regularly throwing out, like, *cases* of beer, which we sold in the parking lot. But that was years ago . . . Loitering in parking lots and malls became libraries and supermarkets, and something had happened in the last year—they quit asking me to leave. I hadn't been kicked out of anywhere, for, shucks, a long time. Maybe the collective retail community threw up their hands and surrendered. Maybe I was getting *soft*! Well it was still loitering, just more refined.

An hour later I was still waiting for someone to talk to me, still observing the 7-11 parking lot, and my burrito was still very frozen. Somewhere, beyond the drunken grunts and squeals, I heard *rock 'n' roll*. I skated off, tracing the music to its source, and found the Pacific Beach Sun-Fest in full effect. There was a neat beachfront boardwalk, a big stage with a band playing before a frantic crowd, and half-eaten servings of french fries—everywhere! Somehow I had been in Pacific Beach all day and missed the beach. I didn't even know it was there! Duh! The band played its final song, pointed to the sky, and a fireworks show began over the big beautiful Pacific! San Diego went all out. I like to think it was for me.

The next morning I awoke at a large beachfront resort, behind a dumpster. It was a ghetto spot, but, no sleeping on the beach! The San Diego lawmakers are clearly out of touch with their homeless constituents. Then, behind the grocery store, I found a shopping cart full of bread! What's up with this country?! After reading on the beach and swimming at a hotel, I skated off, northbound . . .

Not far beyond the "Welcome to La Jolla" sign I was quickly welcomed with a bag full of bagels behind the bagel shop. La Jolla won my heart immediately—bagels, beauty, and more visibly unemployed and shiftless people lying in the sun than anyplace I'd been! It was like a big, sunny, posh, upper class resort for bums!

Ironic, I thought, the accessibility of resources and free goods in these wealthy and exclusive communities— the easily infiltrated buffet restaurants, condo swimming pools, museums, huge natural foods markets, and unlocked dumpsters. The exclusive neighborhoods aren't so "exclusive." There are no gates or security checkpoints, no, you just walk right in! Really!

California was a land of extremes, and this trip had taken me through the side of the haves—pastel shopping malls, no graffiti, and every supermarket carrying soymilk. For two weeks I sponged off the luxuriance and took advantage of the loopholes in La Jolla's opulence. I felt tough and sneaky, like a well-dressed tramp in deep cover across enemy lines. My guise was indistinguishable from the real thing, so at hotels I was "kid on vacation with parents," in cafés I was "studying college student," and though it's difficult to look stately waist-deep in a dumpster, I was clean-shaven, and I always smiled . . .

My first morning in La Jolla there arose an uncomfortable confrontation at Whole Foods. Paying for a 50¢ bagel, I went to hand the cashier my two quarters. But instead of taking my money, she leans over the counter, looks at my left hand, and says "Oh, and are you going to pay for *that?*"—pointing to the granola and carrot juice I held at my side. Oops! Heh . . . Sloppy me, trying to left-hand food under the nose of the tallest cashier. She had an unfair vantage point. *Paying* for the food would, of course, be out of the question. My options were to either quickly *eat* the evidence, or cash in my very prized Whole Foods gift certificate—the one I'd almost forgotten I had. Several days prior, I had uncovered a tattered and faded slip for $100 in Whole Foods store credit, slipped to me the previous summer by the *Evasion* mole inside the Dallas Whole Foods. It had been floating around in my bag for months in my wallet, behind my I.D., which I never used anymore—the cops hadn't bothered me in a long time. Like I said, I'm getting soft . . . My plan was to save the gift certificate for the next time I was rolling-in-the-gutter broke. The hope was it could be converted into cash, like the Safeway gift certificates. I have a relative, who, once a year or so during a visit, will pull me aside and hand me a $100 Safeway gift certificate. She'll take my hand, close her eyes, and choking back tears will say something like—"I know life isn't always easy for you . . . maybe this will help." I, of course, am visibly moved. I look at her with sad eyes, and after a touching moment of silence, say—"I'll pull through this . . ." The next day I'll go to Safeway, buy a bagel, take the $99.50, and spend it all on records! It's a hard-knock life . . .

From this encounter I learned the Whole Foods policy is less generous than Safeway's, and in fact closer to the Barnes & Noble school—where they'll kick down money for the cause if the difference is less than $10. So, for the $6 meal I was trying to steal, I received a $90 credit slip and $4 cash. The obvious criminal-minded approach to this setback would be nine separate bagel purchases to yield $85.50 in cash. So, I got my food, and I got the four dollars. Getting caught stealing, and getting *paid* for it . . . There is a future in this, I thought.

During my stay in La Jolla, I occupied a bush behind Whole Foods. Sleeping in bushes is dangerously close to adventure-seeking youth/hopeless transient crossover behavior. But it was a nice bush, within two blocks of Trader Joe's, Tower Records, one thousand pools, and the University of California at San Diego campus. The surrounding college area was a dangerously addictive playground full of big hotels, apartment complexes, and office buildings to explore. Each morning I dropped my bag off at the Nordstrom's concierge desk and asked them to hold it while I, you know, "shopped," and picked it up each night before closing. The hours in between were endless dream-like periods of idle leisure, moral ambiguity, and skateboarding.

There was an Einstein's Bagels a short ride from Nordstrom's—past Robinson's May, over the skybridge, through the office building courtyard, past the suited guys eating lunch, left over the other skyway, down the ramp, past the Marriott and on the right. There were lots of cups in the trash outside for free refills, and after eating dumpstered bagels and getting all wired on French Roast, I grabbed my board and skated around La Jolla—all day!

Most nights I took my Whole Foods food across the street to the La Jolla Village Mall. It was fun to sit and watch people from the bench adjacent to the movie theater. One night—either through my exaggerated look of loneliness, or just the kindness of strangers—a young woman invited me to join her to a special preview screening of *The Rugrats!* Her pass was good for two, and it was very nice of her. Looking at the movie poster, *Rugrats* seemed completely worthless. But I never turn down anything free. We talked in line on the way in, leading up to an awkward moment in the theater where I wondered—does she, like, want me to *sit* with her, or . . . ? Well, I didn't, and when the movie began I split for the Robert DeNiro film across the hall.

Halloween . . For years I'd put off my plan of tearing a hole in the bottom of a Hefty bag and going as a *bag of trash*. Imagine all of your discarded secrets showing up on *your* front door! *You'd* be scared! La Jolla was totally unfestive for Halloween, the setup and atmosphere were all wrong. Trick-or-Treating would be impossible—most of the surrounding apartment buildings and luxury condos were secured with key-card access only, and the houses all lay behind huge gates and long driveways. All that inspired fear, fright, and horror among people was completely absent from La Jolla—poverty, minorities, shadows . . . I sat in the Whole Foods café to ponder my Halloween plans over dinner. While eating, I always read the newspaper to see what the other criminals are up to. When I opened the entertainment section, I became frantic upon seeing an ad for a special Halloween showing of *The Exorcist*, the scariest film *ever!* No doubt this was a Halloween dream come true. Looking at my maps, I pinpointed the Mission Valley Center Mall, grabbed my food and board, and ran to the bus.

On the bus, a kid commented on the Whole Foods carrot juice I was drinking. "That stuff is great," he said. "You know I used to work at Whole Foods and . . ." I grabbed him, shook him violently, and demanded he reveal every criminally relevant industry secret—cameras, security, all of it. The coast was clear, he said. Fill up a backpack, push a cart out the door, back your car up, anything—security was non-existent. We had sort of a criminal bond going, and he invited me to his Halloween party. I explained my plans to see *The Exorcist*, and that it was an important night for me. He promised lots of "hotties," and lots of beer. Girls? And beer? What? No way, I knew the score. Have fun at the meat market! Enjoy watching your friends vomit on each other, but I'm going to watch Linda Blair vomit-action on a thirty-foot screen in Surround Sound! Bye!

The Mission Valley Center Mall spared no expense in providing a first-class movie-going experience—plush carpeting, cushy chairs, arena seating, and side doors left wide open! "Horror Movie"—it wasn't creative, but it was fun!

University Town Center Mall was hours of fun—you could really get lost in the winding corridors looking at the fountains and palm trees. The best part was the Whale Fountain. A fantastic piece of pointless ornamentation with three metal whale sculptures timed—every thirty seconds—to shoot water from their spouts! It was neat, and hypnotizing. And it was the craziest thing, but the shoppers would just *throw away* their money, right in the fountain! Really! It almost seemed too easy, but I would scrape change from the Whale Fountain, and run around the corner to the food court arcade to play Ms. Pac Man. I would finish my game, stare longingly at the screen, scratch my head, run back to the fountain for more quarters, and do it again! America—they make everything so convenient!

In the evenings, exhausted, I would skate up to the UCSD library and lose myself in the big, dusty history books. My favorite was titled "Frontier Justice," with anecdotal tales of Old West militance. Like the story of a Sioux Indian uprising in 1862—government agencies were denying promised rations to the starving natives. "If they are hungry, let them eat grass," taunted government agent

Andrew Myrick. Look out . . . The Sioux stormed the agency, delivering *frontier justice* and repossessing badly-needed food. When the smoke cleared, the slain body of agent Myrick was found—his mouth stuffed with grass!

The UCSD library was open until 1 a.m., and each night they had to kick me out. University libraries were sort of a new passion of mine. The real gem of the UCSD collection was the long sought-after *Rand McNally Railroad Atlas*—extensive state-by-state maps of every train route. It was very exciting, and I spent hours getting caught up in hopeful daydreams and fantasy. I looked at the spider-web of tracks, smiling, and thinking that now, with that book, there was no end to the possibilities. The world opened up to me with those maps. It all seemed so easy now, I'll just hop trains to all the states that get no respect—South Dakota, Iowa, Montana . . . Just when I thought I had it all figured out, when I felt I'd reached the apex of unemployed prosperity and freedom, just when I thought I couldn't get any more excited about life . . . the railroad atlas would usher me to an ascended state of vagabondage. I never knew there were so many tracks! With those maps, the potential arose for trainhopping to evolve from a fumbling amateurish avocation to a full-time job! Why not?! It was almost 1 a.m. when I had photocopied the last page. I reshelved the book, and thought I probably wouldn't be home for a while . . .

Life in La Jolla was like living in a big punk resort—pools, free fine dining, good books, sleeping in bushes . . . um, wait . . . There seemed no reason to ever leave, barring defoliation of my bush. But even then, there were other bushes, *bigger* bushes . . . There were no flaws to this life, I would make a few friends and stay forever. I sat down back at the Whole Foods café to work out the finer points and financial details of my new plan. Let's see, OK . . . after breaking it down with precise calculations, adjusting for inflation and taxes, the punk cost of living in La Jolla for current fiscal year would be . . . $1.20 a day!

After two weeks, I knew it was time to leave La Jolla. But I wanted to make my rounds one last time—drink one more cup of coffee, skate down the big hill once more, finish a book at the UCSD library, and visit my favorite pool one last time . . .

Poolside, I thought about adventure, youth, other towns with bigger palm trees, seizing the day, life, love, regret . . . I reclined in the cushy lawn chair, staring into the sky, drinking fruit juice . . .

Well, it all just seemed like I had won, you know?

I checked my maps. No, this was just the beginning . . .

ABOUT THE READERS

Marley quit his job and never went back. He walks out of Wal-Mart with objects larger than himself. Takes objects smaller than his head to return counter at REI for climbing gear and bicycles. Says, "Nothing in this apartment is paid for." Pays rent through a sympathetic Walgreens cashier saving receipts. Reverse engineered ink-in-the-eye clothing security tags. Invented the preventive "Duct Tape Technique" for their safe removal. Keeps the stacks of Jamba Juice and Whole Foods coffee bar "frequent buyer" cards above the stereo. Keeps heart-shaped punch six inches away. Keeps lock-pick set in the front pouch of backpack and says no doors are closed to him. Proves it to me at the rear door to the University of Idaho library at 2 a.m. Pulls cases of Raisin Bran and pasta sauce from the dumpster of a regional natural foods distribution center, but mostly just steals a lot. Hitchhikes to small midwestern towns. Hangs out all night with high school girls there.

Bonnie quit her job and never went back. She pushes carts of food out the door at Whole Foods. Short of this, utilizes baby stroller props with inconspicuous pouches. Hides notes in my bag to discover on the train home. Exploits blind trust of concert promoters by requesting press-passes for non-existant publications. Interviews Tori Amos backstage.

Edge quit his job and never went back. He leaves me the key to his apartment under the pot when he leaves town. Doesn't pay for that apartment. Celebrated 3rd anniversary of no real job with me in the Home Depot parking lot. Sells dumpstered joysticks for $70. Has "free" connections in-side: movie theater up the street, major internet retailer warehouse, largest thrift store in the world, and a high-se-curity military equipment depot. Dumpsters me a red insulated pizza carrier as a crucial component in disguise for infiltration of concerts and exclusive events. Uses "the scam" for frivolities including televisions and video games. Understands the distractionary effects of such things, used by governments for generations to dumb the populace. Feels guilty. Blasphemously dismisses the left-hand technique as ineffective. Understands I bear no responsibility for the flam-ing wreck his life will become without it.

Sally never worked a day in her life. She plays role of diversion in felonious retail-crime operations. Trash-scores discarded wristbands for pleasant day of free amusement park rides. Rolls up sleeves and pulls change from mall fountain, though, really, has spent less than $50 in past year. Bypasses ticket taker for 6th row center at Ani DiFranco. Smugly passes cashiers with books, art supplies, clothing, Odwallas and Tofutti without pause, pretense, or concealment; explointing little-understood "obvious to the point of unbelievable" factor. Throws rocks at police cars. Is three years old.

Sammy quit his job and never went back. He navigates retail environments with the inconspicuousness of pink elephants and people carrying out large boxes they didn't pay for. Carries out large boxes he didn't pay for. Chased from department store with pants. Chased from drug store with shoes. Chased from natural foods store with natural food. Chased from grocery store with batteries. Is caught with those batteries, directs loss prevention agent to cashier next door from whom he swore the batteries were purchased, and the cashier then *confirms his made up story*. Is hypnotized by $400 stereo offering captivating LED light display correlating to the beat. Picks up stereo and moves for the door. Steers others into uncomfortable, often felonious circumstances. Enjoys confrontation at small town mini-mart for shoplifting the "No Shoplifting" sign. Lies, charms, and socially-engineers his way through three security checkpoints to reach celebrity-studded after-show party backstage at concert of a larger-than-life 80's rock group. Is found an hour later on a friendly first-name basis with the head of band security. Utilizes a cane and adopts role of pitiful teenage cripple as suspicion deterrent in supermarkets. Hobbles out with baskets of food.

Erica quit her job and never went back. She makes $40,000 in little practiced union of "road trip" and "travellers check fraud." Invented 1990's legendary and lucrative saltwater vending machine scam. Bites lip and rubs chin as Coke responds with nationwide installation of saltwater shields in dollar slots. Lightbulb over head, loads Coke machine onto back of truck. Dedicates months to basement surgical experiments on live vending machine. Reinvents technique using updated method used to induce vending machine quater-purging to this day. Carries phone/alligator clip combo for emergency phone calls behind butcher shops and vivisector's homes. Fills car with thousands of cans in nighttime recycling center raids. Makes $120 daily selling them back. With remarkable cleverness, names new Whole Foods coupon scam "Veggie Burglar." Suffers year-long streak of bad luck involving payphones eating change during $6 calls to Argentina. Pays rent with refund checks. Scams free vacation and sizeable food voucher from nationwide syndicated talk show. Understands and applies usefulness of foam balls jammed in change funnels at toll roads during rush hour. Carries cordless drill voiding obstacle of the problematic "vending machine lock." Social engineers local supermarket manager into installing natural foods department. As informal consultant in deparments layout, design, and placement; notices camera postitioning and insists on construction in known blind spot, while stressing the importance of high shelves and a generally secluded atmostphere. Eats very, very well. Rips from wall and brings home film vending machine in wealthy shopping district. Paid for copies once "in like 1992 or something." Makes free calls manipulating recordable Hallmark greeting cards. Goes big with retail office suppply store return scams, accumulating $35,000 credit. Stores in canvas wallet. Loses wallet. Hasn't really worked in 10 years. Takes scams further and bigger than anyone I know, enjoying sizeable gap between "income" and "expenses." Buys house.

We are the kids, and we're never going back . . .

ABOUT THE AUTHOR

The anonymous author quit his job and never went back.
Spends whole of post-high school life in evasion of adulthood and the monontony of nine-to-five life. Writes book
about it.

adventure

Bruns, Roger A., *Knights of the Road: A Hobo History*, Methuen, New York. 1980.

Allsop, Kenneth, *Hard Travelin': The Hobo and His History*, New American Library, New York, 1967.

Lee, Daniel, *The Freighthoppers Manual for North America: Hoboing in the 21st Century,* Ecodesigns Northwest Pub.

Littlejohn, Duffy, *Hopping Freighttrains in America*, Zephyr Rhoades Press, 1993

Crew Change Points in the U.S. and Canada (aka "Crew Change Guide"), Self-published annually.

United States Railroads (railroad map—"available" at Barnes & Noble) Map Link / 30 South La Patera Lane #5 / Santa Barbara, CA 93117—Good people. I knocked on the door of their factory after hours, and rather than be nervous and upset, they offered me a tour!

trash

Hoffman, John, *The Art and Science of Dumpster Diving,* Loompanics, 1993

housing

Corr, Anders, *No Tresspassing—Squatting, Rent-Strikes, and Land Struggles Worldwide,.* South End Press, 1999

gate crashing

Huthmaker, Ken, *The Gate Crashers,* self-published, 1992 {$15 post-paid to 15118 S. Budlong Ave., Gardena, CA 90247. khuthmaker@hotmail.com}

Abagnale, Frank, *Catch Me If You Can,* Broadway Books, 1980

Kerman, Scott, *No Ticket? No Problem!,* Summit Publishing Group, 1996

un(directly)related

Robbins, John, *Diet for a New America,* H.J. Kramer, 1987

Why Vegan? Vegan Outreach, contact: 211 Indian Dr. Pittsburgh, PA 15238, or write the Evasion address

I met this guy at the truck stop, and he seemed really nice. I was against drinking, I felt as if I could tell him so that I was drunk.

(Amanda
6-12-99

author's last words

Stories beginning on 1, 12, 64, 74, 79, 84, 88, 222, and 227 bled through a pen 11/98 to 5/99. Originally published in zine format. 5000+ copies printed, none paid for. CrimethInc.—we win again.

Stories beginning on 48, 90, 116, 157, 188, 201, 206 and 216, carved into stone with a crowbar 11/00 to 6/01. Day: Library with pen. Night: Abandoned broom closet. It was a golden time . . .

Guilty still at large: Catharsis, Zegota, and all who crossed state lines with *Evasion* and intent to riot; the *Evasion* copy cells and those who wrote; Paul F. Maul; all vegans; my Mixmaster (first, only, and forever); all "terrorists," "criminals," prisoners, and fugitives; and the unemployed vegan straight-edge.

To the rest I feel nothing, just as you have for so long xxx

Send letters; scams; books; zines; maps to abandoned buildings; Greyhound/plane tickets; backstage/press passes; vending machine keys; records; gift certificates; invitations; alarm deactivators; the cool little key that removes CD security shells; steam tunnel maps; authentic ID blanks, delivery guy uniforms; and all correspondence with the author to:

Evasion
c/o CrimethInc.
PO Box 13998
Salem OR 97309
U$A

or contact the author directly via email:
evasion@crimethinc.com

Dedicated to every animal tortured, mutilated, and murdered today in every slaughterhouse, laboratory, fur and factory farm. Our tears are not enough—consider veganism. Write the Evasion address for more info.

PUBLISHED BY

CrimethInc. Workers' Collective
PO Box 13998
Salem OR 97309
USA

WWW.CRIMETHINC.COM

GET IN TOUCH FOR MORE FUEL

manifestos or class struggle analyses. And as the old man says: in this system, if you're not revolting against work, then—like it or not—you're working against revolt.

Again, this is not to say that *Evasion* should or could be a blueprint for mass resistance—on the contrary, it is a personal testimony of unique, unrepeatable experiences, and should be read only as a documentation of what has been possible for one person . . . with earth-shaking implications as to what else might be possible for other individuals. There is an adventure waiting ahead for you, too, in some possible future, whether it be as a train-hopping poet or an anarchist parent or a hardworking union activist who finds a way to make labor organizing *dangerous* again. It is up to you, not the historical forces of dialectical materialism or anything else, to fight your way to this adventure, and liberate others on your way.

Today revolution is a song without words. Those words will be the individual, unique acts of resistance in each of our lives that, together in concert, change the world—that is, if we're ready to live them.

—Holden Caulfield Commando
for Crimethinc. People's Liberation Front

These solutions are *temporary*, because it is absurd to seek a sustainable life in an *unsustainable* world—better do whatever it takes to create new options, and go from there. They are *partial* solutions, for each of us is a fragment of the world that makes us, and can only act back on it as such. And they are *individual*, so other individuals can take them, revise them, apply them in their own ways in their own lives, without needing to wait for a mass movement to come along to save the day. That mass movement will proceed from the solutions hit upon by individuals, or else it will never come at all.

For the fact is, *all* solutions are individual solutions, or else this revolution business is just another way to force the masses into lockstep. Every moment of freedom, before, during, or after the revolution some speak of, proceeds directly from an act of personal courage and creativity. It is this initiative, this courage and creativity that make it possible for us to *participate* in life, to shape the circumstances that shape us rather than just reacting to them. This is as crucial in a consensus-based, ecologically sustainable utopia as it is in industrial, hierarchical hell . . . or else it isn't freedom we're after, after all, but simply more comfortable chains, more sustainable routines. If you ask me, revolution is not a far-off, singular event to be worked towards, but a question of how we act and interact in every situation—whether that means shoplifting food rather than buying it, organizing a peoples' army to face down the Mexican government, or challenging gender roles in your own family. The revolution I am looking for is a constant process of finding and exercising that courage and creativity within myself and with my companions, and it is for this reason that *Evasion* has been so inspiring for me.

To revolt against work—and thus boredom, routine, wage slavery, the exchange economy—*with your body* as well as your mind, to recognize and legitimize your heart's longing to escape by *trying* to, is to declare openly that we are not crazy for wanting more than the scraps of self capitalism leaves us. Such a decision can be more compelling, more infectious than ten thousand

I didn't take the email address scrawled on the corner of the last page of the zine very seriously—it seemed certain to me that whoever had put this zine together was too busy, too wise, and probably too headstrong to keep up an email address at all, let alone answer strangers who wrote him. But a more optimistic friend of mine tried writing, and several weeks later informed me that he'd received a little message in return! I sent off an email myself, and got my own little response months later. It turned out that the author had only made about ten copies of the original, and from one of these, all the thousands of copies that eventually covered the globe were photocopied. It made me wonder if I should bypass professional printing for the next issue of my own zine, and just leave a few dozen xeroxed copies in random outhouses!

I didn't think much more about being in touch with him until another fellow Crimethinc. ex-worker decided that a book version of *Evasion*, updated and revised, would be a good sequel to some of our earlier projects. Even as close to completion as the book is right now, I still have shaky faith that it will ever see the light of day, since such projects are necessarily as unpredictable and risky as the transient riffraff who undertake them. I hope it does, because *Evasion* offers an excellent example of practice as a follow-up to our earlier articulations of theory. This is not the only model for practice—it's one of thousands, maybe millions, and has little in common with many of the others—nor is it the only one we intend to put forward. Still, it is an example of an individual who found solutions of his own for the problems posed by capitalism, and put them to the test in his life.

Mere temporary, partial, individual solutions! will cry the radical old guard, always suspicious of anyone whose resistance to capitalism begins with their own life and for her own sake—and they're right, of course. But that is exactly what is called for right now, or else those long-suffering bastions of capital-R Revolution wouldn't be so short of company: millions of us *need* such solutions today, since without them we are simply paralyzed, hopeless, unable to find even a starting place.

How much can you get away with?

I first came across *Evasion* two years ago in rural Arkansas, at a house where we spent one night of a hot summer cross-country trip—it was just a ragged bundle of xeroxed pages at the bottom of a stack of zines in the bathroom. When I asked our host where it had come from, he told me that he had gotten it a few weeks ago on a visit to a local organic food store; a young man with a backpack had approached him and simply given it to him, offering no explanation except that he looked like he might enjoy it.

Of course I stole it. We passed it around and around during the remaining weeks of our trip, until it was barely recognizable, and as soon as the journey was over I mailed it to a friend who worked at a copy shop. The next time our paths crossed, she brought me a box of about thirty copies—it was pretty huge for a zine, and not easy to rip off, even for an employee. At first, I just gave these out randomly to friends and strangers, but after the rave reviews and testimonials of changed lives started coming back, I got my act together and mailed out the last half dozen copies to the handful of people I knew who both could be counted on and had mailing addresses. Within a few weeks, over a thousand copies of the zine had been ripped off and distributed across the world by the underground do-it-yourself network that thrives on material like this, and at least one kid had been fired for overindulgence in employee copy theft.